CHRIST IN OUR MIDST

The Fruits the Gifts and the Charisms
of the Holy Spirit

9/11/18
406 5283
To Rod, May God Bless your
Journey. to Jesus.
Love ya Clairann

Clairann Nicklin

ISBN 978-1-64003-334-4 (Paperback)
ISBN 978-1-64003-335-1 (Digital)

Covenant Books, Inc.
11661 Hwy 707
Murrells Inlet, SC 29576
www.covenantbooks.com

DEDICATION

This book is dedicated to my three grandsons: David Jr., Landen, and Owen Hidden, their parents Megan and David Hidden Sr., my Husband Nick, and to all who will choose to follow Jesus more closely after reading this book.

Clairann Nicklin OCDS (Order of Carmelites Descalced Secular)

FOREWORD

"There is an appointed time for everything, and a time for every affair under the heavens…" Ecclesiastes 3 (NAB)

I believe that now is the appointed time for this book.

In August 2012 the author of this book and I met in a Chapel in Henry, IL, early in the morning while on a WATCH (We Are the Church) retreat. I was praying, and Clairann was writing this book you hold in your hands when she had only just begun to exercise her Charism of writing. The Holy Spirit inspired us to begin a conversation which led to her sharing her writings. I was very taken with her words as I read because they were written with authority and knowledge. It was obvious to me reading her insights that she was being inspired by the Holy Spirit.

This book comes into the world at a time when people need to be reminded of their true identities as sons and daughters of God. When we know our identity in relation to God, it brings knowledge and understanding of the gifts, fruits, and charisms of the Holy Spirit. In turn, this knowledge helps us to grow closer to Jesus Christ and grow in holiness, so that our charisms can be shared with ALL for the good of the world.

My hope for you as you read this book is that you will be open to the movement of the Holy Spirit. Whether you open up in a deeper way, or open up for the first time, so that the truth may enter in and change you and those around you for the better.

"Seek first the Kingdom of God and His righteousness and all things will be given to you besides" (Matthew 6:33) (NAB)

Mary A. Billington
Spiritual Director/friend

"This is God—trying to help you get to heaven"
drawn by Landen Hidden 8yrs old.

The power of the Holy Spirit helps us through the "Fruits and Gifts" of the Holy Spirit. They come alive in us when we Give our hearts to Jesus, and become the 'Clay in the potter's hand.'

A CHARISM IS DIVINE LOVE SHARED

ACKNOWLEDGEMENTS

This book would not have been possible if it were not for the workings of the Holy Spirit within me, through the guidance of Fr. Terry Cassidy in 2012. He was my Shepherd chosen by God to awaken the Trinity in my Life. No matter how long I live, I will not be able to thank him enough for beginning this journey with me, and the *'Challenges'* from him that helped me search, study and learn how to *'Be with God.'*

My continued journey to God, was enhanced by my Spiritual Director Fr Bachara Awada, who helped me discern what was happening to me in my Interior prayer life. With his help, I was able to use those messages to continue to grow towards God, which is my ultimate goal. Life, in, through and with Christ.

My Pastor Fr. Stephen Willard, has been instrumental in my 'Action' in my parish, which is what the Charisms are all about. He guided me through his homilies, teaching me how to adore the Holy Eucharist more, asking Jesus, when He is elevated, what I need Him to do for me like blind Bartimaeus, Mark 10: 46-52. Also after receiving Jesus in Holy Communion, that I should ask Jesus what He wants *me, to do for Him.* Fr Steve has allowed me to share my newfound knowledge with others in our parish through the bulletin and our monthly Messenger, Holy Cards, and the prayer Chaplets that you will find out about later. All of which is my charism of writing in action. Many of his teachings are within the pages of this book.

Many others including Fr Don Roszkowski and Fr. David Whiteside, Mary Billington, Kathy Reliford OCDS, Deacon Kevin Zeeb, who took precious time out of their lives to read this manuscript to guide me. And other people and priests who have been instrumental in my spiritual growth to God. Some of them are mentioned in this book. I thank God for each one who has enhanced my growth towards God.

Thanks to my husband Nick and my sister Bonnie who have listened to the stories, and helped me discern. I Praise you God for choosing me as an instrument of your Peace and your messages.

Thank you.
Clairann Nicklin OCDS

PREFACE

When I began this journey into the fruits and gifts and charisms of the Holy Spirit, I had no idea that it would lead me to the Jesus within me and within other people.

Discovery of the charisms is the discovery of divine love within our world.

"He has won you for Himself…And you must proclaim what He has done for you! He has called you out of darkness into His own wonderful light" (1 Peter 2:9, liturgy of the hours, Monday of the fourth week).

INTRODUCTION

What makes this writing important is knowing where the writer came from and where the power of God led her.

God uses our weaknesses and with our cooperation turns them into strengths. In (2 Corinthians 12: 30), Paul says, "If I must boast, I will boast of things that show my weakness." Each one of us has our own particular weakness, and as we turn our lives over to God, we can turn them into strengths.

A big weakness of mine is dyslexia. There is a huge handicap that affects your whole life when you are dyslexic. For some unknown reason for me, certain letters—mostly small *b*'s, *p*'s, *d*'s, *g*'s—go the opposite direction when received in the brain, leading to writing it that way on the paper. We don't know it happens! We don't even know it is wrong until someone corrects it. And then it is difficult to understand what is wrong.

The challenge of a spelling bee devastates a child. Reading is slower because it's hard to figure out some words. I had no real prayer in my life other than the Our Father, because we said it at daily Mass when I was in Catholic grade school, and the Glory Be, because it was short. Even the Hail Mary was difficult for me, so I never said the rosary alone—just in a group—and then only the second half of the prayer.

Until the last few years I was not able to read along with the lector during Mass or in any group-reading setting. My mind's eye could not go fast enough across the lines to keep up, and if my eyes went over the words, I did not understand them, so I just listened. My comprehension and memory were not good, so learning was difficult for me. I never had the courage to read in front of people because of my shyness and fear of making mistakes. This inability to read well had an effect on my self-esteem.

I went through my life feeling that I was less than everyone else. What I took with me from grade school were the prayer of St. Francis, the Beatitudes, and the Ten Commandments and a very special connection to the Holy Eucharist. I tried to follow these beautiful examples of how to live my life for God. School was difficult, but my compassion for others pushed me to work hard, and I became a licensed practical nurse and worked forty years in that field. I was blessed at being a very good nurse, but until the end of my career, I was embarrassed by my spelling. I tried to overcome the mind-set of being less than everyone else, but I, Clairann, couldn't do that on my own—or with anyone else's help.

Around the age of sixty I went to a healing Mass with my sister. It was beautiful. I didn't understand much of what was happening with the "tongues" during the Mass, but it seemed it was a deeper way to praise God. It did not frighten me, and I was curious, and I kept coming back.

Gradually I began coming to the charismatic prayer group there (all this with my sister Bonnie's encouragement and promptings). Over about four years I participated in the charismatic prayer group at my church. I was part of a healing-prayer team with my sister. It was a gradual process, but I learned how to surrender to the power of the Holy Spirit. What an awesome gift.

I experienced a deep conversion (a life-changing event) in the confessional in March of 2012. Recognition of my sins brought a deep sorrow that brought me to deep repentance. That moment touched my life deeply, and I saw Christ, Persona Christi, in the person of my confessor. At the moment, the priest took the list of my sins from my fingers (I had written them out for fear of forgetting any of them), and he drew them up to his heart and began shredding them into tiny pieces, saying, "Give them to me, they are yours no longer, they are mine now." I watched as he shredded them into tiny pieces (what that did to my heart is inexpressible).

I looked up at his face. His countenance changed from that of a big man, with light hair and eyes, to a small man, with dark hair and eyes that were looking at me with great compassion and love. At the moment that I looked into his eyes, I felt as though I were being showered with cold holy water from the holy water sprinkler. It was such a shock, and I took a huge deep breath as I gazed upon my Savior. It only was a flash, but I knew at that moment that I was forgiven and as clean as fresh snow. I have never been the same from that moment in the confessional. That was God's grace being showered upon me.

That priest became my spiritual director. We began a journey into my soul that led to a deep desire to discover what the elusive "fruits and gifts of the Holy Spirit" were supposed to mean and how I was supposed to "bring them forward in my life." We struggled to help me understand.

Two months after experiencing Jesus through my confessor in the confessional, I was at a special Pentecost Mass with the charismatic renewal, and just before I was being prayed over by a prayer team, I had asked for "the fruits and gifts of the Holy Spirit to come alive in me. I said, "I know that I have them already, but I want the Holy Spirit to make them come alive when God needs me to do something for Him!"

I experienced an "infilling of the Holy Spirit." And how awesome it was! It is also called "Baptism of the Holy Spirit." That experience led me to a closer relationship with Jesus. And then my discovery of Jesus in my daily life has helped me grow closer to the Trinity.

Three days after my baptism of the Holy Spirit, I had my regular meeting with my spiritual director, and he challenged me to "write a paper on each fruit and gift of the Holy Spirit." Of course I said, "Okay." It wasn't until the next day that I understood the magnitude of what I had said yes to. I had no idea of where to begin or where to find the information.

So I went to my knees in front of the altar at my church and said to God, "I don't have any idea of how to do this! If you want me to do it, you will have to help me."

I was quiet for a while, then I surrendered myself to the power of the Holy Spirit and began to pray in my tongue prayer language. Some of us are given the spiritual gift of a prayer language, to be able to give praise and honor to God our Father. Since we lowly creatures don't have any idea of what to say to God, the creator of all things, God the Father gives us His very Spirit to help us learn how to pray.

About a year before this, I had been given the gift of prayer tongues. It was given to me slowly, to build up my own belief and trust in being God's instrument. Over a period of a year that I had been part of a healing prayer team, I only had one tongue prayer word: *shanaya*. The Holy Spirit used that word in me to build up my ability to surrender to God, and He used it through me to bring others to the "peace that only Christ can give" (John 4:27).

Shanaya in God's language is almost indescribable. I felt that it meant "I love you," and my friend Karen, who has the gift of interpretation of tongues, told me after I prayed with her for healing, "You have no idea what that means in God's language. He was saying to me, 'I love you! I love you, I love you, I love you because I love you!'"

She wept through the prayer and said to me, "I will take spiritual healing any day over physical healing."

The tongue words increased as I continually surrendered my heart to the power of the Holy Spirit (it was a very gradual process because my dyslexia created in me a lack of trust in myself first then in others).

As I knelt there at the foot of the altar, I held my hands out in supplication, and I put myself into God's presence in trustful surrender, and with spiritual humility, I allowed the Holy Spirit to pray to the Father of my great need for help (Romans 8:26): "Likewise the Spirit helps us in our weakness; for we do not know how to pray as we ought, but the Spirit itself intercedes for us with sighs too deep for words. And he who searches the hearts of men knows what is in the mind of the Spirit, because the Spirit intercedes for the saints according to the will of God."

I did not know this Bible verse or where to find anything in particular in the Bible. You see, just nine months before this, I went to my Bible to find where the Beatitudes were written. I found that the zipper of my Bible case was corroded shut! What an awakening that was to me!

After allowing the Holy Spirit to use my lips to pray to God the Father in asking Him to show me the way to discover what and how the fruits and gifts were supposed to work in my life, I went back and sat in the first pew, right in front of the tabernacle. I sat quietly for a while. Then a Bible verse came to my mind. I remembered that there was a Bible in the sacristy, so I went and got it and looked up the verse. That verse contained the word joy, and that surrender to the Trinity began my journey into discovery. The Holy Spirit guided me through the Bible, taking me back and forth from the New and the Old Testaments to explain the meaning of the fruits and gifts of the Holy Spirit. It has been an incredible journey of awakening for me.

Please remember that I am dyslexic, which makes everything harder: spelling, writing, reading, dictionaries, etc. I did not type much (just what I had to with my job, and it was with one finger typing on each hand; God blessed me with my yes, (Philippians 4:13), "I can do all things in Him who strengthens me," and now I have discovered what the fruits and gifts are to mean in my life.

But it does not end there. This is just the beginning! As the fruits and gifts come forward in my life, I am expected to reach out to another and share what God has given me. Now my gift from the Holy Spirit becomes a charism, one of which is the spiritual gift of writing, a written form of exhortation, and there are many more listed in 1 Corinthians chapters 12–13.

My great desire to understand brought forward the fruits of the love of my God, patience with myself, and the gift of fortitude or strength to not give up. As the Holy Spirit guided me, with the gift of counsel through each paper, I began to have newfound knowledge and understanding and developed my charism of writing. All this was achieved through the power of the Holy Spirit when I opened my heart and gave myself to God.

Gifts given, gifts received: the first two words describe the action of the Trinity, and then the next two words deserve our Hoped for reaction. In our world, we hear a lot about freedom of choice. That is the free will that God gave us, in action. Gifts given, gifts received. The choice is ours. Pray to choose wisely.

Upon our baptism in Jesus as our Lord and Savior, the Holy Spirit gives us all the tools that we will ever need to remain in the divine love of the Trinity. The list of these gifts is found in (Isaiah 11:2-3), CCC 1831, "They belong in their fullness to Christ, Son of David. They complete and perfect the virtues of those who receive them. They make the faithful docile in readily obeying divine inspirations." These gifts remain in us throughout our lifetime but are just there—until God decides. We are not born with the know-how of how to use them. We must seek it. (Matthew 7:7–8) explains what we need to do: "Ask and it will be given to you; seek and you will find; knock and the door will be opened to you. For everyone who asks receives; he who seeks finds; and to him who knocks, the door will be opened." Nothing from God will ever be forced upon us— nothing. Not even what is good for us. We need to cooperate with God to bring the gifts forward in our lives. Cooperate means to work together with the Holy Spirit and welcome Him, and His gifts into our lives.

If the gifts listed in Isaiah are not enough to help us on our journey, God gives us more. These gifts given, gifts received are found listed in (Galatians 5:22–23): "In contrast, the fruit of the Spirit is love, joy, peace, patient endurance, kindness, generosity, faith, mildness and chastity. Against such as these there is no law!"

The advice on how to use these fruits of the Spirit of love follows in verses 24–26: "Those who belong to Christ Jesus have crucified their flesh with its passions and desires. Since we live by the Spirit, let us follow the Spirit's lead. Let us never become boastful, or challenging, or jealous toward one another" (St. Joseph, New American Bible). "The fruits of the Holy Spirit are perfections that the Holy Spirit forms in us as the first fruits of eternal glory." CCC 1832. More are found in (2 Corinthians 6:6): "Conducting ourselves with innocence, knowledge, and patience, in the Holy Spirit, in sincere love as men with the message of truth and the power of God"; in (Ephesians 4:2): "With perfect humility, meekness and patience"; in (Ephesians 5:9): "Light produces every kind of goodness and justice and truth"; and in (Colossians 3:12–15): "Because you are God's chosen ones, holy and beloved, clothe yourselves with heartfelt mercy, with kindness, humility, meekness, and patience … Over all these Virtues put on love which binds the rest together and makes them perfect."

"Virtue is a habitual and firm disposition to do good." CCC 1833. Christian character is produced by the Holy Spirit, not by the mere discipline of trying to live as a good person. Paul makes it clear that justification by faith does not lead us to a life of sin.

When we use our gifts (Isaiah 11:2–3), our fruits (Galatians 5:23–24) come forward in our lives, and we are helped by the power of the Holy Spirit to share our spiritual gifts (charisms) with another to build up the body of Christ. These spiritual gifts are found listed in (1 Corinthians 12:4–7). They pour forth from us as a grace from God, and this is not meant to be all there is. Our charisms are as limitless as God is and are given to us as a gift given and a gift to be shared.

Our spiritual gifts bring joy to us and to the people who receive them. Our Catholic catechism says, "We are called to know God, love Him, and serve Him." We serve Him by knowing, loving, and serving each other. Discovering the gifts God gave you in particular will help you serve God and His people in the best way possible.

A charism is a spiritual gift from God (CCC 799, 800, 801). A charismatic is a person who is enthusiastic about using the spiritual gifts for God and His people, and then encourages others to use their spiritual gifts.

CCC paragraph 798 states, "The Holy Spirit builds up the whole Body in charity … By the many special graces (called "charisms"), by which He makes the faithful "fit and ready to undertake various tasks and offices for the renewal and building up of the Church."

St. Paul wrote about the charisms in (1 Corinthians 12:4–7) (Ignatius Bible). We have all heard them several times throughout our lifetimes. I will remove the extra words to leave the important words: "To one is given…Expression of wisdom, another…Expression of knowledge according to the Spirit, to another faith…Another gifts of healing by the one Spirit, to another, the working of miracles, to another prophecy, to another the ability to distinguish between spirits, to another, various kinds of tongues, to another, interpretation of tongues. All of these inspired by the Spirit, who apportions to each one individually as He wills."

To make it simple: the Holy Spirit knows what we are capable of accomplishing, and He showers us with the tools (graces) to bring others to Christ. This is what the charismatic gifts are all about, to bring another soul to Christ. But we must cooperate with the Holy Spirit. We need to invite the Holy Spirit to use us as His Earthly Vessel.

Take a look again at the individual words from Scripture, the Word of God, which is Jesus Himself. These words were given to Paul through the power of the Holy Spirit: "an expression of wisdom, knowledge, faith, healing, miracles (mighty deeds), prophecy, discernment, variety of tongues and interpretation of tongues."

I haven't changed any of the words! This is what St. Paul taught the followers in Corinth. This is what happens in a charismatic prayer group meeting when it is led by the Holy Spirit. It is the very work of our Lord. There should be no fear and no doubt, if it does not go against scripture. Jesus came to earth to save the brokenhearted, heal the sick and blind, to expel evil spirits, and bring us all to the Father. He asked the apostles to continue doing what He did, and to pass it on to their followers. Jesus not only prayed for the apostles (John 17:9) but also said, "I pray not only for them, but for those who will believe in me through their word, so they may all be one" (John 17:20). That is us!

"Jesus, I trust in you" is the motto of those who surrender their will to the will of God. And it is God's will that we surrender to the power of the Holy Spirit. That is why God sent His Spirit to us: to help us understand. But please understand not everyone receives all the gifts that are on this list, just the ones that the Holy Spirit gives them. Don't worry, He has something special that He gave you.

The CCC calls charisms "a special grace" (paragraph 799), so our Catholic Church believes in the charismatic renewal. Remember, a charism is a gift. A charismatic is the person who uses the gift. The charismatic renewal is the office of the church that is bringing this action of the Holy Spirit back into the life of the church again.

A charism is given to us to be given away, to build up the church. It is given in hopes that we will open this gift of God and use it to help another come closer to Christ, the One who intercedes to the Father for us. It was promoted by Pope John XXIII, Pope John Paul II, Pope Benedict, and now Pope Francis. Can all these successors of the one whom Jesus chose to be the head of our church (Peter) be wrong? It may be foreign to you in the beginning—it was for me—but I have grown to trust that the Holy Spirit will lead me to Jesus, and that is exactly what I am looking for. The charisms are meant to open our eyes to the workings and power of the Holy Spirit through other people.

This is what was expected of the followers of Christ. We are given these spiritual gifts as a free gift from God Almighty. There should be no fear when we receive a gift from God, or when others do. The gifts that I listed above are from (1 Corinthians 12:4–7), but there are so many more. In this same chapter (1 Corinthians 12:27–31), Paul tells us how important each one of us is to the Body of Christ: "Some people God has designated in the church to be, first, apostles; second, prophets; third, teachers; then, miracles (mighty deeds); then, gifts of healing, assistance, administration, and varieties of tongues."

This is God's great plan, that we work together to save souls. One person alone cannot do this. We need each other and each other's spiritual gifts.

Our Almighty God can save us without our help. But He wants us to help each other. In this same chapter (1 Corinthians 12:31), Paul says, "Strive eagerly for the greatest spiritual gifts, But I shall show you a still more perfect way." And he begins in chapter 13 to speak of love.

With our finite minds, we humans have trouble understanding the ways and workings of our infinite God. God gave us Jesus to bring those who will listen to salvation. Jesus gave us each other to help bring each other to our salvation.

God put me into situations where I met people who shared Jesus with me. It has taken over sixty years for me to reach this place where I am today. Each day I am renewing my journey to God. You see, God has touched my heart and has begun peeling off the layers of wounds from around my spirit through other people. That is their special spiritual gift to me.

There are some features that are common to all charisms despite their diversity. All are spiritual gifts. All are a grace from outside ourselves. All are forms of service. All are given to us by the power of the Holy Spirit to be given away to help another and to build up the church. In (1 Corinthians 12:4–7), it states, "There are different kinds of spiritual gifts but the same <u>SPIRIT</u>, there are different forms of service but the same <u>LORD</u>, there are different workings but the same <u>GOD</u> who produces **ALL** OF THEM IN EVERYONE." Look at the underlined words in the last sentence: Spirit, Lord, God. All three persons of the Trinity take part in bestowing the spiritual gifts to all who are baptized Christians.

We all receive all the gifts. But some of the gifts are stronger in certain individuals than others, because that is what God wants. If we all received all the gifts in the same intensity, we would be clones, and we would not be able to help each other grow and ultimately help our church grow.(Jeremiah 29:11) states, "For I know the plans I have for you, says the Lord, plans for welfare and not for evil, to give you a future and a hope. Then you will call upon me and come to pray to me and find me, when you seek me with all your heart, I will be found by you, says the Lord, and I will restore your fortunes and gather you from all the nations and all the places where I have driven you, says the Lord, and I will bring you back to the place from which I sent you into exile."

That's what we are all here for. God is calling us to grow closer to Him. He has taken the first step and waits patiently for us to respond. What I have discovered through my search for meaning of the fruits and gifts and charisms of the Holy Spirit is my relationship with God has been changing.

This relationship did not happen overnight. It took baby steps of discovery for me to come to this place. And it was my great longing to know and understand my relationship with God that began my search into the fruits, gifts, and the charisms of the Holy Spirit

I began to understand that phrase from (Jeremiah 29:11) that I just shared with you.

God promised our Savior. Our Savior promised another paraclete, who is the Holy Spirit. The Holy Spirit is the giver of all things from God, or the presenter of divine love form the Father. The Trinity's love for us is in full bloom.

The charisms are an expression of the Trinity's divine love for each of us. They can begin as a natural gift that is enhanced by the power of the Holy Spirit to help another person through a roadblock in their life, or a sudden empowerment by the Holy Spirit to do something that is normally unlike you to do. The characteristic that makes "just doing something" a charism is the love of Jesus that you do it with. This love is empowered by the Holy Spirit and is known as a spiritual gift, also called a charism or a charismatic gift.

The charismatic gifts are listed in 1 Corinthians Chapters 12–14. St. Paul did not mean for these to be an exhaustive list of spiritual gifts. If we do something for another person and it leads them to God, it is a spiritual gift or charism. Using our spiritual gifts as a charism for another is meant to build up the church and bring another soul to God.

My personal roadblock was an inability to pray like others in eloquent words. I finally discovered and accepted that God doesn't need eloquent words; He only wants my heart to be turned over to Jesus in trustful surrender, which leads to spiritual humility.

Don't be afraid of the charisms. They are given to us to help us share the love of God that has been given to us with our brother or sister. It does not happen by osmosis. We need to take that one small step into our own growth toward God. We need to say yes to the power of the Holy Spirit. That is what each one of us is here for.

We can help build up the kingdom of God within ourselves by asking the Holy Spirit to come forward in a way that we can recognize, which will enable us to build up the kingdom of God within our world.

In our Roman Catholic liturgy, somewhere after the consecration I heard the priest say, "Go out and minister to Jesus." I asked myself, "How do I do that?" Later I heard in my heart, "By ministering to my people." That is the essence of what the charisms are: sharing who I am in Christ with another.

God only asks us to give what is ours to give. This book was written to help me discover what I could never understand throughout my whole life. My hope is that it will help you discover your walk with the Lord. It's not a hard road; it has been an adventure for me. The only way we can fail is by not trying. This is about each of our relationships with God.

We begin by calling upon Jesus and asking Him to help us find our way to Him. Ask Him to uncover our blindness and send His Holy Spirit to come to our aid. Ask to see the truth in our hearts, and then close your eyes and receive.

Truth: what is truth? Truth is actuality. Actuality is a description of something that really exists.

Jesus really exists. Not just two thousand years ago; He exists today in all who call Him Lord and Savior. I have witnessed this truth in the people who have helped me on my journey to Christ when my world fell apart forty years ago. I felt His loving presence in them as they symbolically held my broken heart in their hands and helped me discover that "God doesn't mean for you to bear this all alone." God orchestrated my life so that I was "in a place to be found!" (Fr. Mark Toups, "Oremus"). A Christian counselor encouraged discovery of my thoughts through journaling. I discovered who was inside of me. I found God and a person who loves beyond the pain, me, and God has been present to me since then.

After allowing emotional and spiritual pain to overtake my senses, I found that God's loving presence has always surrounded me, even when I kept Him at arm's length. God is steadfast in His love for me. He was with me when I had my near-death experience when He gave me this prophecy: "Your child will die, you shall live. You've been given a second chance—a chance at your Christianity. Remember, there is a reason."

He was with me when my baby died. He held my broken heart as no one else could. He was with me when my marriage died, and blessed me with people who encouraged me to get my annulment.

He was with me in my recovery. I would not have recovered without the help of many Christians who reached out to me in my great need.

These are examples of charisms in action. Someone helping someone else come to reconciliation with God. He was with me when I placed myself in a position to be found by my new husband. He was with me when our daughter was born and when He orchestrated the infant-loss-grief support group that I developed in our home.

Even with all these graces in my life, it took me until four years ago (age sixty-three) to come to my conversion experience where the power of the Holy Spirit comes to you in a special way and completely fills you with the "peace of Christ that surpasses all understanding" (Philippians 4:7). God opens our eyes to His presence, and I have never been the same since. Praise God!

In my weaknesses, I didn't know how to talk with God. While I was in the process of trying to discover what the fruits and gifts were supposed to mean in my life, this journey to Jesus began. I discovered a longing to pray in a deeper way than I was experiencing at the present time. My spiritual director suggested that I read a book called *Open Mind, Open Heart* by Thomas Keating, and the journey into the depths of my soul began.

It takes a trustful surrender to the power of the Holy Spirit to go to "that quiet place" where God dwells. Our soul is the place where we experience union with God.

The description of "union with God" is as endless as there are words in the Bible describing God. Our individual union with God is uniquely our own, created just for us to draw us to desire more of God.

Union with God can be "an experience of timelessness." It can be "a feeling of suspension from our senses." We stand in awe before the Lord and wonder what is happening, and we desire more. We feel the joy of the Lord, and peace fills our souls. That is an interblending of the fruits and gifts of the Holy Spirit. Interesting.

Our action is to "put ourselves in a place to be found" (from Fr. Mark Toups's study called "Oremus," or "Let us pray").

When we make the time for God by setting aside a few minutes of our day just for Him, He will come. Ask the Holy Spirit to help you to quiet yourself, and allow yourself to let the thoughts of your day float away so you can just be present to Him. He will be present to you. The greatest and first gift of the Holy Spirit that we are given is love. This place in our inner room, or prayer closet, is the place where love is exchanged.

Do not concern yourself with the distractions. Just let if float away. If the thought keeps returning, write it down, and let it go. When you are done with your quiet prayer, you can revisit the thoughts that came to you during your prayer. It may be something that our Lord wants you to work on.

As you fill yourself with God, healing happens, even of wounds you didn't know you had. The Holy Spirit pours forth from the divine love of the Father and the Son to create us in the image and likeness of God. He wants the world to see Him through us. That is the essence of what a charism is.

When we allow it, through the surrender of our weak selves to the power of the Holy Spirit, we become the clay in the Potter's hands.

By finding our quite place and then spending time with God, He comes to us in the most personal way that two spirits can meet. I believe that quiet prayer is being in union with God.

I find Jesus in places that I have never looked before. I began seeing a brilliant light on the Eucharist when elevated in the priest's hands. Sometimes I would see the Holy Spirit in the form of a dove on the Eucharist when the priest was lowering the Eucharist back to the patent. Then the face of Jesus as he lowered the host, and the Holy Spirit came down and overlaid the face of Jesus before the host was laid on the patent. I began seeing the shape of Our Resurrected Lord on the host when elevated. Sometimes it is filled with radiant beams of light coming down from the top, giving me a glimpse of what heavenly light is.

I witnessed this action three times in one weekend, at three different Masses in two different churches, with three different Priests. When each of the priests broke the host in half, rays of brilliant white light burst forth from the center of the host, upward and outward into the world. In (Luke 24:30), like to those disciples who were on the road to Emmaus, truth was shone to me in the breaking of the bread. My eyes were opened.

The Eucharist is Christ in our world, made available to all who will believe that He is the Son of God who came into the world as one of us to share God's nature and divine presence and mercy, with all who will allow the eyes of their hearts to be opened and then invite Jesus to enter in and dwell in their hearts.

With this image of the light of Christ bursting forth from within the Eucharist, Christ Himself was telling me, "Clairann, I am with you here in this Eucharist. I am with you in your daily life. Come to me, and receive me. Receive my peace, the peace that only I can give. And then take me with you into the world everywhere you go. Be my disciple."

And, "Do not be afraid. I am the great gift to the world. I am with you always. Be my witness of the truth. I am the light coming into the darkness of this world to bring freedom from sin."

When I shared this with my spiritual director, he told me, "It is said that the moment when the Host is broken, it is the moment that Christ died, and He came to bring light into the world."

On Sunday March 25, we were in South Dakota on our way to Washington State, on a hurry-up visit to see my husband's dying niece. After my morning interior prayer, I was inspired by the Holy Spirit to write this prayer card about Adoration. This is the guidance I received from the Holy Spirit: "From the cradle to the Cross…Jesus reaches out to us in His humanity…to unite us with His Divinity… to make us "One" with Him…so that we can learn how to unite ourselves with Him in the 'Offering' during Mass. We each need to make our personal Covenant with the Father, Son and Holy Spirit (Trinity). Jesus, in His Divinity, humbled Himself (becoming 'Flesh and Blood') to walk with us and show us how to live in the world—and Not be 'OF" the world. Jesus 'gives' us Himself in the Holy Eucharist… to heal our brokenness, and to walk with us on our journey. Come, let us Adore Him and give Him the Praise that is due. Let each one of us become the 'Guardian of the Eucharist.' Clairann Nicklin OCDS

Throughout the trip, my husband and I had been praying a 'Hail Mary' each time we would see a yellow vehicle. There were yellow cars, yellow train engines, yellow semi-trailer cabs, and yellow airplanes! We were very busy praying our spontaneous prayers throughout the whole trip.

My friend Mary, had told me that if we took route 90, to keep a look out and we might be able to see a large statue of Our Blessed Mother, Mary, when we were near Butte, Montana. It was dusk when we were entering Butte. I was so afraid that the darkness would conceal the statue. So, I was ready with my camera turned on. I saw a river out my side of the car, so I decided to take the picture. When I pressed the button, I saw lightening in my camera. It surprised me so much that I pressed again so that I could get the picture. Just down the road about 30 seconds, I saw the statue of Mary, and zoomed as much as possible to get a glimpse of the statue. Then I looked at the pictures I had just taken and much to my surprise, I saw the image below. I did not see the image, only the lightening. This picture was taken in the darkness and facing the East after sundown.

This image was in both pictures that I took of the mountain. These pictures were on my husband's camera only. As he always does, he downloaded them to his computer when we got home and then deleted them. Weeks later he asked me, "Do you want the pictures of the trip?" I said, "I thought you deleted them!" He said, "I did..." When I downloaded them to my computer, there was another image like this one on the top of another mountain in another state the next day. There were also 6 other similar images found during this trip. I did not see any of these images, just the lightening in the first two pictures. I feel and many others with me including my Spiritual Director, believe that this is the image of the Holy Eucharist radiating out to us in our world. What a beautiful Supernatural Gift was given to me to support my faith. This was given to me the same day that I wrote the Adoration prayer to the Holy Eucharist, Sunday March 25, 2017. Our Savior, Jesus Christ is alive in our world in all who recognize Him as Lord and Redeemer and He is alive in our Holy Eucharist.

How did we as a people of God become so complacent with this truth?

Truthfulness is about being honest with yourself, others, and God.

The truth is that God wants to spend eternity with each and every one of His created beings. And that boils down to you and me.

How are we to get to this place of truth with God when we don't know or can't see the truth or find the path?

First, we must recognize the truth that we have blinders over the eyes of our heart.

Then we must learn how to pray for the Holy Spirit to remove those blinders from our eyes.

We must admit that we have those blinders on, or they will not be removed and we will not grow spiritually (Romans 8:26). Ignatius says, "We don't know how to pray as we ought, but the Spirit itself will intercede." But we must ask for this intercession, or it will not happen. God gave us free will, and it is by an action of our will that God's intercession comes.

Trustful surrender into the hands of Jesus will help us go forward toward God the Father. If we are not going forward, then we are slipping backward.

"Take, Lord, receive all I have, and possess…"

USING THE FRUITS
AND GIFTS

Using the fruits and the gifts in our daily lives is a display of God's merciful love. The first and greatest gift from God our Father is love. God, who created man out of love, also calls him to love. It is the fundamental and innate vocation of every human being. For man is created in the image and likeness of God, who is Himself love. Since God created him, man and woman, their mutual love becomes an image of the absolute and unfailing love with which God loves man. It is good, very good in the Creator's eyes. And this love that God blesses is intended to be fruitful and to be realized in the common work of watching over creation. "Be fruitful and multiply, and fill the earth and subdue it" (Genesis 1:28).

What a loving responsibility our Father is giving to each one of us. He created us with love and to love one another. Not only to love one another but also with that love of God to help each other on the journey through Jesus back to our Father.

So what does *fruitful* mean? Being fruitful means to "yield or produce fruit, to be very productive, bringing results" (Webster's). Each one of us has a different role to play in this venture.

Adam and Eve were created with this ability, but sin entered in and weakness came. Mankind lost the natural ability to be all that God desired us to be, but He provides us with the spiritual gifts that can change not only our lives but also, when shared with another, their lives also.

It is important for us to be fruitful and multiply physically for life to carry on, but it is the spiritual fruitfulness that will change the world. We each have an intricate role to fill whether single, married, laity, religious, man or woman, child or adult. God created each of us for a specific purpose. And He gives us the tools to do our work. They are the gifts of the Holy Spirit.

The Holy Spirit gives us the fruits and gifts from God, but Jesus gives us the example with His very life.

"The Seven Gifts of the Holy Spirit are: Wisdom, Understanding, Knowledge, Counsel, Fortitude, Piety and Fear of the Lord (Isaiah 11:2). They belong in their fullness to Christ, Son of David. They complete and perfect the virtues of those who receive them. They make the faithful docile in readily obeying divine inspirations" (CCC 1831).

"Let your good spirit lead me on a level path" (Psalm 143:10).

When we reach out to another person with the love of Christ in our hearts, we will find that we are using the gifts of the Holy Spirit to their fullest. This is our opportunity to build up the kingdom of God.

The gift of wisdom is "an ability to receive inspired insights enabling a Christian to come up with creative solutions to certain problems and make good decisions." They are given to us to help us know how dependent we are upon our Lord and Savior and to the Word of God that He wrote through the prophets. It will also help us to understand that each person who is baptized in the name of the Father, the Son, and the Holy Spirit is given the presents of the fruits and the gifts of the Holy Spirit to build their life in Christ.

"I will inspire you with wisdom which your adversaries will be unable to resist" (Luke 21:15).

In the book of (Wisdom 9:1–6, 9–11), we find guidance and a reason to seek the gift of wisdom. Verses 9–10 say, "Now with you is wisdom…Send her forth from your holy heavens, and from the throne of your glory send her, that she may be with me and toil, and that I may learn what is pleasing to you. For she knows and understands all things, and will guide me wisely in my actions and guard me with her glory."

The gift of counsel of the Holy Spirit will enable us to guide ourselves and others through the one book that God wrote (the Bible) to the places that will lead us to the gifts of knowledge and understanding in becoming present to the Word of God in and for our lives (CCR).

The gift of understanding in (Proverbs 3:13–14): "Happy is the man who finds Wisdom, the man who gains understanding. For her profit is better than profit in silver, and better than gold is her revenue." (Luke 24:45) says "Then He opened their minds so they could understand the Scriptures" (St. Joseph). It is the Holy Spirit who does this work in us to enlighten our hearts and minds to the knowledge that Jesus is our Savior, and to the covenant between God and man.

The gift of knowledge is empowered study of God. (Hosea 6:3) says, "Let us strive to know the Lord" (St. Joseph's). The Gospels will teach us everything that we need to know. In (2 Peter 1:5–8), it says, "Make every effort to supplement your faith with virtue, and virtue with knowledge, and knowledge with self-control, and self-control with steadfastness, and steadfastness with godliness, and godliness with brotherly affection, and brotherly affection with love. For if these things are yours and are abound among you, they keep you from being ineffective and unfruitful in the Knowledge of Our Lord Jesus Christ" (Ignatius).

If you weave Jesus into your being, your fruits and gifts will shine out like a lighthouse beacon in the night for others to find their way to Jesus.

These four gifts—wisdom, knowledge, understanding, and counsel—will help us to help others with good listening skills. The counsel of the Holy Spirit will guide you in your own daily life and lead others to Jesus, and help all with the healing of your hearts.

It will take the gift of fortitude (strength) for each one of us to walk the path that Jesus walked. Our world belongs to satan. "Fortitude" is a moral virtue that ensures firmness in difficulties and constancy in the pursuit of the good. It strengthens the resolve to resists temptations and to overcome obstacles in the moral life. The virtue of fortitude enables one to conquer fear, even fear of death, and to face trials and persecutions. It disposes one even to renounce and sacrifice his life in defense of a just cause." CCC 1808. (John 16:33) says, "I tell you all this that in me you may find peace. You will suffer in the world. But take courage, I have overcome the world" (St. Joseph).

Have we truly understood what has been done for us to reach eternity with God? Jesus overcame the world, which is full of sin and lies and spiritual death. Ponder what He did, and ponder what little we have to do to "overcome our world." Simply surrender our hearts to Jesus. This is not our home. Heaven is our intended home.

Piety is an expression of the Christian life. Piety is an action by which we try to grow closer to God. Increasing prayer in our lives will increase our chance of an encounter with God. Piety is all about spending time with God. We can use sacramentals such as veneration of relics, visits to sanctuaries, pilgrimages, processions, the stations of the cross, religious dances, the rosary, medals, et cetera (St. Pope John Paul II, CCC).

There are many types of prayer. Ask a spiritual leader where to begin.

Fear of the Lord means looking at our God with our hearts full of wonder at His great love for us, and awe at what the Trinity has done for us for our salvation.

As you can already see, the gifts of the Holy Spirit are individual yet intricately woven into each other, which is exactly how God has it planned to make us "rounded Christians" who are intricately interwoven into each other.

"The Fruits of the Spirit are perfections that the Holy Spirit forms in each of us as the first fruits of Eternal Glory. The tradition of the church lists twelve of them: 'charity, joy, peace, patience, kindness, goodness, generosity, gentleness, faithfulness, modesty, self-control and chastity'" CCC 1832, (Galatians 5:22–23). Infusing these traits of Jesus into our own lives will help us stay on the path to Jesus and the Father.

This is the beatific way of life. They are the very life characteristics of Jesus our Savior. And it is the Trinity's desire that we become a part of the community of the Trinity. To do this, we will need to take on the life characteristics of Christ. Look at the Beatitudes in (Matthew 5:1), and study the prayer of St. Francis of Assisi. He followed Jesus completely. He followed Jesus to the point of receiving the wounds of Christ for his great love of Jesus.

Subtle seductions of satan keep us mentally, emotionally, spiritually, and physically in this world that belongs to satan. From the tree in the Garden of Eden, evil changed the face, heart, and soul of all humans (original sin), and it is also from a tree that Jesus conquered evil (from the Roman Catholic Mass). Learn how to become an active participant in the journey to Jesus and the Father through the Holy Spirit, our Trinity.

Triangle

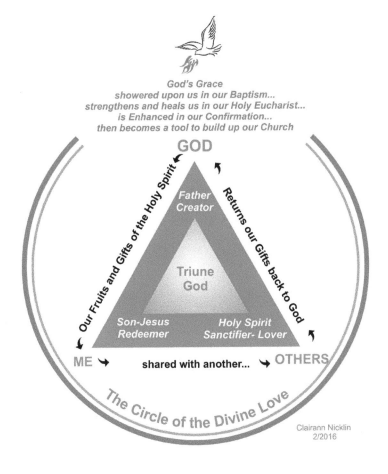

God's Grace
showered upon us in our Baptism...
strengthens and heals us in our Holy Eucharist...
is Enhanced in our Confirmation...
then becomes a tool to build up our Church

GOD

Father Creator

Triune God

Son-Jesus Redeemer   Holy Spirit Sanctifier- Lover

Our Fruits and Gifts of the Holy Spirit

Returns our Gifts back to God

ME   shared with another...   OTHERS

The Circle of the Divine Love

Clairann Nicklin
2/2016

Intro to Triangle

The fruits of the Holy Spirit our given to us by the Holy Spirit to help us see who Jesus was, who God is, and how God desires us to live our life in service to one another. They are given to us as a grace from God Himself to draw us into the Beatitude way of life that Jesus Himself lived here on earth.

God's grace is showered upon us in our baptism, with both the fruits and the gifts.

We are strengthened and healed each time we receive the Holy Eucharist.

We receive more grace when we are confirmed. This grace is given to each one of us to enhance our lives with the ability to love and care for one another as Jesus did.

These fruits and gifts become the tools that we need to build up our church.

This picture of the triangle depicts the workings of God in each of our lives. God gives the fruits and gifts to me. Through my growth in the love of God, my sinful nature gradually changes. God's grace transforms my heart. The love of God gives us His "Spirit in our hearts" (2 Corinthians 1:22) and forms Christ within us (Galatians 4:19), molds us and fashions us "into the image . . . and likeness of God" (Genesis 1:26). This is a gradual process.

As we give each little piece of our world to God, He fills that space with His abundant grace, and as God's love grows inside of me, it oozes out of me in the form of a gift to another. This is another gift from our loving God, known as a spiritual gift called a charism. The biggest list is found in (1 Corinthians 12:1–7) and then is sprinkled throughout the Bible.

This whole process is how God draws each one of His children into the circle of His divine love.

This is the Beatific way of life (indicative of great joy or bliss, which is complete happiness).

What are the fruits of the Holy Spirit

In (Galatians 5:22–23), St. Paul tells us that Jesus taught that: love, joy, peace, patient endurance, kindness, generosity, goodness, faith, mildness, self-control, and chastity (St. Joseph's) are the fruits of the Holy Spirit. The Catholic Catechism of the Catholic Church (CCC), lists them a little differently. This list was taken from the Vulgate version of the Bible, which is a translation from the original Hebrew and Greek texts into Latin, which was becoming the most common language at that time. This translation was completed by St. Jerome around 405 AD, he was a secretary to Pope Damasus. This is where the 'Traditions of the church' (CCC) list 12 'Fruits.' Knowing this has made it easier to accept the different lists in different bible translations. In my opinion, the translations from the Vulgate Latin version into English should be the most accurate. This list has twelve of them: "charity, joy, peace, patience, kindness, goodness, generosity, gentleness, faithfulness, modesty, self-control and chastity, which is the list I will talk about.

The fruits of the Holy Spirit are the perfections, that the Holy Spirit forms in us, to help us to become like Jesus. They are what makes us come alive in Christ. When we can share the love or joy of the Lord with another, it means, that particular 'fruit' is within us, and is shining forth from us like a beacon for all to see.

Fruits
Joy
Peace
Patience
Charity
Kindness
Goodness
Generosity
Gentleness
Faithfulness
Self-Control
Modesty
Chastity   **Gal 5:22-23**

Joy

(Jeremiah 15:15–16) says, "When I found your words, I devoured them: they became my Joy and the Happiness of my heart, because I bore your name, O Lord, God of Host."

What is joy? Where does it come from? Joy comes from a good relationship with God and others. It is a relationship of genuine love for another. Joy is a deep and constant gladness in the Lord that life's circumstances cannot destroy. Joy is a feeling of happiness that comes from success, good fortune, or a sense of well-being. Our relationship with God is supposed to grow so deep that we can feel His great joy when we come to Jesus for the salvation of our souls.

The joy of the Lord is found when you have embraced the cross and united your pain, sorrow, and weaknesses with Jesus, our Lord and Savior. It is on the cross of our redemption that we give our wounds to Him. He takes our burdens and bears their weight and helps us to walk in the world again, but now with lighter steps and the love of Jesus radiating out from our very center.

When you can feel the joy of the Lord in your soul, know that you have become the monstrance through which Jesus shines into the world.

St. Stephen radiated the joy of the Lord as he was being stoned to death. What a powerful witness of faith that was to his perse-cutors! Jesus prayed from the cross while deeply impaled with the nails of human weakness and sin and mortal pain. "Father, forgive them, for they do not know what they are doing." It wasn't just the Roman centurions who drove the nails that Jesus is speaking of. He knows that we don't understand what our sins and weaknesses do to Him either. We don't understand the gift that He gave us with His life, death, and resurrection. His hope is that we come to know and understand it all when He sends His Holy Spirit upon us to turn our lives around in conversion.

The pain that we project outward to the world destroys the reputation of all Christianity. It is the joy of the Lord that we should project! That joy only comes from the other side of the cross by the forgiveness and healing from Jesus of our sins. Only then can we live in the fruits of the Holy Spirit that Jesus taught.

As baptized Christians, it is not only our duty but also our responsibility to share this joy with the world, one person at a time. The joy of the Lord is meant to be shared; that is why we receive it.

So (Hebrews 12:2) says, "Let us fix our eyes on Jesus, the author and perfecter of our faith, who for the 'JOY' set before Him. He endured the cross, scorning its shame, and sat down at the right hand of the Throne of God." "The joy set before Him"—what was that joy? It was the joy and hope of our Lord that we would respond to His sacrificial love and come to Him.

The joy of the Lord gives spiritual strength. The Holy Spirit touches our hearts and then leads us to Jesus, and the touch of His healing hands brings us to the Father. Inward joy is a characteristic of the fruit of joy, as mentioned in (1 Peter 1:8–9): "Although you have never seen Him you love Him, and without seeing Him you now believe in Him, and rejoice with an inexpressible joy touched with glory because you are achieving faiths goal, your salvation."

Jesus's joy came out of serving and pleasing the Heavenly Father. In (Hebrews 10:7), it says, "Behold I come … to do your will." Our joy comes from doing the will of God. His will is that we serve one another.

I asked a friend Kathy one day, "What does joy mean to you?" She answered, "My family brings me great joy." Family includes all those that we share our lives with. Family are those we care about and those who care about us. It can be our parents, siblings, grandparents, aunts, uncles, children, etc., or it can be our extended family of coworkers, people at church or at school, or our neighbors. Our family can be found anywhere we are.

In (Genesis 1:26), it says, "Let us make them in our image and likeness." Those few words tell us how important we are to God, who desires us to share in the joy that is unique to only God the Trinity. The Trinity's love is called agape. Agape is selfless, sacrificial, and unconditional love for another; agape is the highest of four types of love in the Bible. This Greek word is found throughout the New Testament, and *agape* perfectly describes the love Jesus had for

His Father and His followers. (John 14:21) says, "He who obeys the commandments he has from me is the man who loves me; and he who loves me will be loved by my Father, and I too will love him and reveal myself to him." (St. Josephs). Jesus lived out agape love by dying on the cross for OUR sins. (John 15:13) says, "Greater love has no one than this; to lay down one's life for his friends." Wow! With what great love are we loved! Therefore, our redemption brings great joy to the Trinity.

Because of God's great love for mankind, God made a covenant with man. God the Son, Jesus, chose to be the mediator, the actual covenant between God and man. By the power of the Holy Spirit, Jesus was incarnate of the Virgin Mary and became man. (Luke 1:35) says, "And the angel said to her, 'The Holy Spirit will come upon you, and the power of the most High will overshadow you; therefore, the child to be born shall be called holy, The Son of God.'"

Mary became His very first Tabernacle on earth. In her yes, she gave us Jesus, the Son of God, our Lord, our Savior, our Redeemer, our King. Our yes makes Him all this and more—our brother, our friend, making His Father our adopted Father. Hence, we are family. Agape love from and to the Trinity brings great joy to the Lord.

Ponder this. If Jesus is our brother and the King of the world and our Almighty God, we need to remember what God sees when He looks at us: He sees the gift that Jesus gave to His mother from the cross, us. John was our representative. With Jesus calling us His brothers and sisters, we are His family and therefore are the adopted children of God, which makes all heaven rejoice. We are the treasures of the Trinity. His sparkling jewels of the earth, His pearl of great price! The price was Jesus's own passion and death, the life-giving body and blood of the Lamb. Our yes to Jesus is pure joy to the Trinity and should bring great joy to our hearts. All heaven and earth rejoices with each person's conversion. The ultimate joy of our God comes with each person's resurrection.

(Ephesians 4:23–24) says, "And acquire a fresh, spiritual way of thinking, you must put on that new man created in God's image, whose justice and holiness are born of truth."

(Psalm 43:4) says, "Then will I go in to the altar of God, The God of my Gladness and Joy. Then I will give you thanks upon the harp."

Our God loves us with an everlasting love. That means that there is no end to His love for us. He desires each one of His human creations to be intimate with Him so that we may know and understand the joy that the Trinity embraces each one of us with. It is our baptism in the name of Jesus Christ that brings us to this holy place. The infilling of the Holy Spirit with the fruits and the gifts in our lives is the infusion of the characteristics of God into our own personality. God is joyous when He sees His children reaching out to His other children through their charisms, and as we use our charism to build up the body of Christ in our church, we too are filled with the joy of the Lord.

(Proverbs 17:22) says, "A Joyful Heart is the Health of the body. But a depressed spirit dries up the bones." So let us be joyful and rejoice in our Lord and Savior Jesus Christ. My joy has come from deep within my spirit since my conversion, which is simply turning my life around to follow Jesus.

My hope is that my simple words will help you believe deep in your heart that the shepherds whom Jesus has chosen as His own devote their own lives to saving our souls. Jesus's death and resurrection and the shepherds whom God has chosen to lead us to Jesus give their lives freely in sharing their charisms. You see, it is all about us.

(Romans 15:13) says, "So may God, the source of hope, fill you with all Joy and Peace in believing, so that through the power of the Holy Spirit you may have hope in abundance."

These words were revealed to my heart when I thought I was finished with prayer and writing for the day. I usually wrote in the church, and as I was packing up my things and stood up and took a deep breath like I was tired, I received these words from our God: "Come, breath in my peace. Hold it there as long as you are able. Bathe in the blood of my Son, the Lamb of God who takes away the sins of the world. He is your shepherd, Jesus. Listen when He calls your name. Follow Him to the foot of His cross. He did this for you. Thank you for having responded to my call and coming home to my loving heart. Repent, receive forgiveness, and feel the joy in your heart that surpasses all understanding."

(Isaiah 12:3) says, "With joy you will draw water at the fountain of salvation, and say on that day; Give thanks to the Lord, acclaim His name; among the nations make known His deeds, proclaim how exalted is His name." Let us join our hearts, minds, souls, and spirits together and know that the fountain of salvation is found at the foot of the cross of Jesus, when His sacred heart was pierced by our sins and His precious blood and water poured forth for our redemption. It is with His divine mercy that we are saved!

The fruit of joy is a relationship with our God. "Every Baptized person has the ability to experience 'Union with God' in mystical prayer" (Sr. Mary Gabriel, SV). It is with great joy that the Trinity comes to us in our prayer to reveal Himself to us as we set aside a few minutes of our day to spend time with God. This is what God desires for each soul He created, not just the saints. We are the saints of the future. Come, receive all God has for you.

The fruit of Joy is what helps us to become 'One' with the Lord. I remember after my conversion in the confessional, I simply could not get enough of Jesus! Daily Mass filled my being with His presence and Love. I soon discovered that they were praying the Rosary before mass and the Daily office before that. I couldn't hardly stand to not receive Him daily in Communion and the sacred word. Jesus's presence in my life brought me great Joy that oozed out of me in a way that people would say, "I want what you've got!" At the time that I discovered all of this ... I knew so little about my catholic faith. But I am still learning every day, and I thank God for the Gifts of love that He touches me with.

The "Joy of the Lord" for Jesus, is when He can see beyond the Cross, to see us in heaven with Him.

Peace: The Fruit of the Holy Spirit

Peace is an internal calm or state of tranquility. We each are given the great fruit of peace that only the Trinity can give. The fruit of peace is given to us as a grace at our baptism, and the Holy Eucharist strengthens and heals us throughout our life by bestowing peace within us. The fruit of peace is brought forward in our confirmation with all the other Fruits and Gifts, and is given to us to help us become one of God's saints. We are each a saint in progress if we accept Christ's invitation to come to Him for healing of our wounds and sins.

Jesus became the bridge between God and man, and is the peacemaker. He taught the apostles and the people the Beatitudes in (Matthew 5) and focused on peace in verse 9: "Blessed are the Peacemakers: for they shall be called the children of God." Wow! What better job could there possibly be than to be a peacemaker? Jesus was giving all who would hear the directions on how to become a peacemaker just like He was.

Jesus was teaching the teachers (the disciples) how to carry on His work here on earth. We are being called by Jesus in (John 20:21): "Peace be with you! As the Father has sent me, so I send you." We need to become ministers of Christ's peace to all who surround us. Just like His disciples were. "Peace on Earth" is a phrase that echoes at Christmas time and needs to echo through the whole year. Let all who hear it take heart in Jesus's name.

The disciples lived with Jesus for three years while He walked and talked and shared His ministry with them, but they were not able to unlock the parables until Jesus left them, and sent them the Holy Spirit as their counselor and advocate: "Then their eyes were opened" (Luke 24:31). This happens to each one of us when we invite Jesus into our lives as Our Lord and Savior and are willing to turn our lives around from the ways of this world (sin and weakness) to follow Jesus.

The prayer of St. Francis is a powerful tool to follow:

> *"Make me a channel of your Peace; where there is hatred, let me sow your love. Where there is injury, your pardon, Lord. Where there is doubt, true faith in you. Where there is despair in life let me bring hope; and where there is darkness, only light. Where there is sadness, ever joy. O Divine Master, grant that I may never seek so much to be consoled as to console. To be understood as to understand.*

*To be loved as to loved as to love. For it is in giving that
we receive. It is in pardoning that we are pardoned, and
in dying that we are born into eternal life."*

These words are an "infusion of the Fruits and Gifts of the Holy Spirit." When we embrace them with our whole heart and soul, what we are sharing with others is our charisms in action. This is what God intended for us to do to bring others to Christ and build up the kingdom of God.

In (John 16:33), Jesus said, "I have overcome the world." His death and resurrection enable us to find peace. It's hard to understand the depth of that kind of love. We humans cannot understand that the peace Jesus gives us is a peace of the soul and spirit, not anything of the earth.

Our soul is made up of our intangible will, intellect, and emotions all held within our body, and it is the combination of our will, intellect, and emotions that ooze out of us as our personality. Our soul and spirit are two different entities. The Spirit of God is present within us when we are baptized in the name of Jesus Christ of Nazareth as our Lord and Savior. As we draw closer and closer to Jesus and learn how to live the Gospels as He taught the disciples, we begin to live the fruits and gifts of the Holy Spirit in our lives. The fruits of the Holy Spirit are the essence of God our Father, lived in the person of Jesus Christ here on earth. It should be our quest to take on the life qualities of Jesus, to be able to follow Him on the "narrow road to the Father" (Matthew 7:13).

Adam and Eve were created with these same fruits and gifts of the Holy Spirit and lived in union with the Trinity before their fall to sin. Jesus was born in a humble stable, into a humble family to show us the way to the Father is through spiritual humility. We need to surrender our spirit to Jesus in repentance and through conversion turn our lives around from sin and the world to a life filled with God's grace, to build up the kingdom of God.

In (Matthew 11:28), Jesus said, "Come to me, all who labor and are heavy laden and I will give you rest. Take my yoke upon you, and learn from me, for I am gentle and lowly of heart, and you will find rest for your souls. For my yoke is easy and my burden is light." Rest is peace.

Wow! The yoke that Jesus was carrying was the sins of the whole world and from people of all time. All mankind! Yet He said that that His burden was light. How can that be? We humans, when burdened under the weight of our own sins, weaknesses, and desires can barely lift our heads, and yet Jesus carried the weight of all humanity upon His shoulders with the weight of His scourging and the weight of the cross. Willingly, Jesus came from glory, to lowliness in a manger to teach us how to become peacemakers.

(John 20:23) says, "On the evening of that day, the first day of the week (Sunday) the doors being locked the disciples were in fear of the Jews. Jesus came and stood among them and said to them, 'Peace be with you.' After He said this, He showed them His hands and side. The disciples were overjoyed when they saw the Lord."

Again Jesus said to them, "Peace be with you! As the Father has sent me, so I am sending you." And He breathed on them and said, "Receive the Holy Spirit. If you forgive anyone His sins, they are forgiven; if you do not forgive them, they are not forgiven."

Forgiveness is the source of all peace. Forgiveness brings peace, and that is the very reason that Jesus came to earth: to bring peace into the lives of all mankind. But the choice is ours whether to receive or the reject that gift.

(Job 22:21) says, "Agree with God, and be at peace; thereby good will come to you." The "good" that comes to you in becoming grounded in Jesus Christ will be knowing Him as your Lord, King, Redeemer, loving Brother, and Savior of the world. Jesus sanctified His own life, His own Blood and Body, on the cross of our salvation. And in the forgiveness of our sins He showers us with His own sacred blood to heal our wounds and to clean us white as snow (Isaiah 51:7), and releases us from our pain and sin that keep us bound to this world.

The peace of Christ, which we all should strive for, is found deep within each of our hearts. Peace will be flowing like a river from our hearts if we let Jesus pierce through the walls of our heart with His love. That peace comes to us only with the surrender of our hearts, minds, and soul to our Lord Jesus Christ at the foot of the cross. Let Jesus bathe you in His own sacrificial blood. This will bring you to the place where you will feel "the peace that passes all understanding and will guard your hearts and mind through Jesus Christ" (Philippians 4:7).

(Proverbs 14:30) says, "A heart of (Peace) tranquility gives life to the Body". Jesus calls each one of us to find peace within our own hearts. If we do not have peace in our heart, we cannot give it away.

True peace is found in Your Eucharistic presence, sweet Jesus. Your body gives us strength and nourishment and healing. You come to us in the silence of our hearts and bathe us with your precious life-giving blood. Your blood is warm and soothing, and caresses our heart as it passes through to our soul and spirit, where it uplifts us to your divine love. We praise you, God, for your saving love for mankind. It is by Jesus's cross and resurrection that we have been made worthy of your promises.

I feel the peace of Christ every time that I receive Holy Communion, and whenever I am in His presence. Being in His presence can be the moments that I share with Him in Adoration, whether He is present in the Monstrance or protected in His Holy Tabernacle it makes no difference to me. I look at Him ... and He looks at me... I am so peaceful just staying in His presence. I'm in His presence in private Prayer or in communal prayer of Mass or special services. I feel His Peace especially when I am praying for others in healing prayer, or sitting in the woods listening to the rustling of the trees in the wind, or by a body of water, listening and watching the waves rhythmically come in and out on the shore, which is symbolic of how the fruits and gifts should flow into us, and out of us as a charism to others. The Peace of Christ has brought me to a place of reconciliation with God, and I love it. One morning during my prayer I heard, "You are My Minister of peace. Believe in yourself. I believe in you! [God]."

Patience Is the Fruit of the Holy Spirit

Patience is the fruit of the Holy Spirit that God gives us in our baptism to help us grow more like Christ. This is a fruit that we keep within ourselves so that we will be able to give it away to others when sharing our charisms.

(Romans 15:5), May God, the source of all patience and encouragement, enable you to live in perfect harmony with one another according to the spirit of Christ Jesus, so that with one heart and voice you may glorify God, the Father of our Lord Jesus Christ (St Joseph's).

What this passage of Paul's is saying to us is that God is very patient with each one of us, and He consoles and comforts each one of us as we walk through our life. We each have the fruit of patience within our spirit, and as we develop our relationship with God our Father through the example of His Son Jesus, we become like-minded with the Trinity, as this passage suggests.

This fruit comes forward in our personality to share with others. Paul is also telling us that "we, as a church, the Body of Christ, need to be of one mind and one mouth" as we glorify our Triune God. The hard part is learning how to become like-minded with the Trinity and with our community. In the word *community*, we see *unity* is the last four letters in that word that Jesus chose to build His church with. Together, everyone achieves more. This is the acronym for TEAM. It is with great patience that the Trinity waits upon each one of us to find our gifts and fruits of the Holy Spirit, and then we ask the Holy Spirit to bring them forward in our lives so that our works will become more effective in building up the Body of Christ within our world today through our charisms.

We each bring into every relationship that we are involved with a measure of pain and wounds. Wounds come from our past, our history. Some wounds are a mystery as to where they came from. Our great consular, the Holy Spirit, has been sent to us from God the Father and God the Son to help us to discern the path of our recovery. This is where the gift of counsel from the Holy Spirit takes action.

In (Psalm 73:24), it says of the Holy Spirit, "With your Counsel, you guide me, and at the end you receive me in glory." If we look at these words from the writer of Psalms, we see that the Holy Spirit is there for each of us. If we will choose to take the urgings in our heart as the beacons from the Trinity, we will find our hearts growing in the fruits and gifts of the Holy Spirit.

What does this really mean to us as individuals and as a community? As individuals, we each need to be as patient with ourselves and our brothers and sisters in Christ as the Trinity is with each one of us. The Trinity has given each of us a lifetime to come to this place in the realization part of our thought processes; it is the place that connects our souls to our hearts. Only when we can see the weakness within ourselves will we be able to accept the weaknesses within God's other children. The fruit of patience from the Holy Spirit will help us show self-control in our actions and be calm if we ask the Holy Spirit to help us to overcome our obstacles.

As an individual, we first look into our own hearts and search it for what is keeping us from true communion with the Trinity. I was sixty-three years old when I finally understood the need to look deep into my own heart. That moment led me to the confessional; a healing began, Two weeks of deep soul-searching, tears, and journaling brought me to another confession and deep cleansing of my pain. It was through the power of the Holy Spirit that Jesus healed my wounds and forgave my sins through the person of my shepherd.

I have absolutely no doubt that Jesus was in the person of my priest in that confessional with us. My repentance and Jesus's forgiveness actually took my breath away like a sudden cold spray of water on my face! I know in my heart that I was breathing in the very breath of God at that moment, like in (Genesis 2:7), when "the Lord formed man out of the clay (dust) of the ground, and blew into his nostrils the breath of life, and man became a living soul" (Ignatius).

I have been on my journey to Jesus since my childhood, and even though I had been to confession before, that experience in the confessional was my conversion experience. The fruit of patience was exercised by the Trinity as they allowed me sixty-three years to find my way to my healing and to my personal cleansing forgiveness.

If there is anything that is weighing upon your heart, it will put a barrier between your spirit and God's Spirit. What covers our God who dwells within us since our baptism is our human weaknesses or sin, or perceived hurt. It is through the searching of our souls that we find our weakness (and with the Trinity's help, we need to allow our self to have the patience that the Trinity has given us as a fruit of the Holy Spirit to come to this spiritual place of forgiveness within our own heart).

Through Jesus and the Holy Spirit, God will begin our healing, but we need to be an active participant in this healing process within our own selves. We need to come to Jesus at the foot of the cross, repent of our sins and weaknesses or anything that holds us in bondage to the world, ask Jesus to forgive us and the person who wounded us, and let Jesus have our wounds. That is why He came to earth: to teach us how to see Him as our Savior. With patience He endured the pain of being broken for each one of us. With His Holy Spirit He will lead us to our redemption, and He will free our spirit to grow in all the fruits and gifts of the Holy Spirit.

It says in (Hebrews 6:11–12)," "Our desire is that each of you show the same zeal to the end, fully assured of that which you hope. Do not grow lazy, but imitate those who, through faith and patience, are inheriting the promises" (St. Josephs). This is where we learn the importance of community that Paul was speaking of in Romans 15:5: "May God, the source of all patience and encouragement, enable you to live in perfect harmony with one another according to the Spirit of Christ Jesus, so that with one heart and one voice you may glorify God, the Father of Our Lord Jesus Christ" (St. Josephs).

Jesus's disciples did exactly what He asked. And because they did follow Jesus's instruction, we are part of the same church that Jesus instituted two thousand years ago. It is the same Holy Spirit that came upon them that comes upon us in our baptism, confirmation, and Holy Eucharist. It is those sacraments of initiation that establish and nourish each of our fruits and gifts of the Holy Spirit.

Baptism is where the fruits and gifts are given to us; confirmation is where they are brought forward (sometimes it is later in our lives that we understand that we need to become an active participant in bringing them forward); it is the Holy Eucharist that heals and strengthens us and enhances the presence of the Trinity in our lives. Then the Trinity's presence will shine forth like a lighthouse beacon.

Being patient is being steadfast or persevering, bearing trials without complaint and showing self-control. We all must share the love of Christ within ourselves first to the Trinity (depicted by the vertical beam of Jesus's cross). By accepting Jesus as our Savior and following His example completely, especially healing old wounds, we can each begin our journey to Jesus.

But a very important thing to remember is not one of us will be forgiven if we do not first forgive what we have perceived as wounds against ourselves from another. This is imperative. We cannot go to the altar of Jesus's forgiveness without first correcting the unforgiveness within our own hearts. My friend Mable told me, "Unforgiveness is like drinking poison ourselves and expecting someone else to die."

The horizontal beam of the cross is the representation of our relationship of the charisms of service and helps for others, by our being the hands, feet, and lips of Jesus within our community of church and the world.

In essence, when we look at the cross of Jesus, the covenant fulfilled for our redemption, we need to recognize that Jesus is the great intercessor between sin and redemption. It was with patient endurance that Jesus was broken for each one who will come to Him with the faith that surpasses all human understanding of what the Trinity has done for us to give us the choice of our salvation.

In (Luke 21:19), it says, "By your endurance you will gain your lives." (St. Ignatius). Once we have experienced our conversion, we will need to surround ourselves with other Christians who are trying to follow the path that Jesus left for us. But we as a community of believers need to understand and accept that not one of us is perfect! Only Jesus was perfect. Even after our conversion experience, we will make mistakes and hurt others. It is then that we will need to be patient with ourselves and go to Jesus for forgiveness—repeatedly.

I don't always learn things the easy way, but God is patient with me. He has been sending His Spirit to me since I was a teenager to help me discern questions, like when I wanted to join a Franciscan convent when I was twenty years old. After my prayer of thanksgiving about joining, I heard the word, 'Wait.' So, I waited. God had something else in mind for me.

Throughout my life I have made some good decisions and some poor decisions, like a marriage I entered for the wrong reasons. I fell in love with being needed. My first husband's wife had died, leaving him with four children, ages: six months to seven years old. We were married for three years, we had a miscarriage, and a baby that was twenty-three weeks' gestation that I had been praying for, and wanted very much. My appendix began leaking and I had surgery. Four days later I became critically ill, and nearly died with a 'paralytic illuis' that left my abdomen as hard as a table. My world kept tunneling in, like the pictures that you see of glaucoma. I was in excruciating pain, and I couldn't understand what was happening to me, my nurse aide was holding my hand... and yet, when I opened my eyes it looked like she was six feet away from me, I couldn't figure it out, so I just closed my eyes and prayed.

I heard my doctor's voice and opened my eyes. To my amazement, I was looking down upon my body there on the bed. I was about six feet above my head, no walls, no ceilings, no boundaries of any kind I had three-hundred-and-sixty-degree vision, and there was no pain. It seemed that I was looking through a gray veil. I could see a small white light behind me. When I opened my eyes, I could see my Dr. and three nurses at the end of the bed. My mind's eye came back to where I was and I 'heard' these words in my mind, "Your child will die. You shall live. You've been given a second chance. A chance at your Christianity. Remember... there is a reason." And I was back within my body... within the physical pain... and the heart pain of knowing that my baby was going to die. I didn't tell anyone about this. I kept it in my heart for months. Three days later I went into labor and my baby girl was born alive, ten and one-half inches and eleven and one-half ounces. Too small to survive, but she struggled to live for three hours. Her name is Heather Marie Reardon. I survived, but my world fell apart. My husband asked for a divorce. And I kept trying to remember . . ." There is a reason!" I kept finding reasons, and I found my faith again.

Praise God, I was urged to get my annulment soon after my divorce, which made me right with the church so that when I met my new husband, I was ready to marry again, and was married in the Catholic Church. God has given me a lifetime to discover the importance of my Spirituality, and the prominent role that God desires to take in my life. Now, that's patience on God's part.

God has a mission for me to complete. It is not only this book, *Christ In Our Midst*, it is about encouraging others to pray, and to help them to see miracles in our lives that we usually miss.

God is still patient with me every day of my life. While trying to get this book published and to get an Imprimatur, I began to worry that I was going to die before I got the book completed. Anxiety overrode my normal peaceful life. I had Open Heart Surgery with a double by-pass eight months ago. And two months ago, I got pneumonia. That is when I thought I was going to die. I was left with breathing issues, COPD and CHF. The evil one used my weakness to distract me from my work, and created doubt and anxiety in an otherwise peaceful heart. Maybe my work for Christ is a threat to him. Yeah!

Sometime about two months ago, while I was being *tempted* by the devil, my friend Dave from our prayer group, came to me after morning mass because he could see that I was troubled. We talked awhile and he said, "be patient." The next day, his wife came to talk to me, her comment was," be patient." She told me later that she did not know he had said that also. The next morning, we had a different priest, and in his homily, he said, "The two most important things are trust and patience!" Saturday morning Mass Fr. Steve talked about patience. Sunday morning Fr. Julius spoke about patience. Monday Fr. Don talked about patience, and in my Tuesday morning interior prayer, I heard patience. That was seven days that I was told to have patience by seven different sources. Do you suppose God was trying to tell me to *BE PATIENT!* Several weeks later, after speaking with my Pastor, and pondering our conversation for a while, I began to understand once again that this book is God's, not mine, and will be published in "His Time." And my heart became peaceful once again. The fruit of patience permeated my soul and is helping me to be patient with others.

Charity

Charity is the divine love of God and is a fruit of the Holy Spirit.

Charity is a special fruit of the Holy Spirit that is a description of the Trinity's great love for each other and all mankind. It is given to us for us to keep and to be able to grow more like Jesus. As we grow, this divine love (charity) is to be given to all of God's creation, and will enable us to share our charisms so that all might know the divine love of our God.

In (1 Corinthians 13:4–8, Ignatius), Paul says, "Love is patient love is kind; love is not jealous or boastful, it is not arrogant or rude. Love does not insist on its own way; it is not irritable or resentful; it does not rejoice in wrong, but rejoices in right. Love bears all things, believes all things, hopes all things, endures all things. Love never ends."

I think this is a description of divine love. It is what God the Father and the Son and the Holy Spirit feel about each other. It is what they desire for us to feel about each other and for our God. I also recognize this as a reading from our wedding vows to each other over thirty years ago, and is read in many weddings because of the great love and devotion that is verbalized.

It is God's desire that we humans care deeply enough about each other, that we desire only the best for each other. Divine love is self-sacrificing. Divine love of the Trinity is what brought Jesus to earth in such a humble example of self-giving love. Divine love is what God shared by making the covenant between Himself and humans. Divine Love is what Jesus was sharing with each one of us upon the cross. No one took His life from Him. He willingly laid down His life for us in hopes that we would see what He did and follow Him to the cross and then through the cross to the Father.

Divine love from the Holy Spirit is the tireless way He tries to fill our spirit with the Trinity's presence. In (Romans 5:5), Paul tells them, "And this love will not disappoint, because the love of God has been poured out in our hearts through the Holy Spirit who was given to us" (St. Joseph's). The Holy Spirit is the paraclete who was promised to "come after" to clarify the teachings that Jesus had taught.

In (Luke 24:44–49, Ignatius), then He said to them, "These are my words which I spoke to you, while I was still with you, that everything written about me in the law of Moses and the prophets and the psalms must be fulfilled." Then He opened their minds to understand the Scriptures, and said to them, "Thus it is written, that the Christ should suffer and on the third day rise from the dead, and that repentance and forgiveness of sins should be preached in His name to all the nations, beginning from Jerusalem. You are witnesses of these things. And behold, I send the promise of my Father upon you, but stay in the city, until you are clothed with the power from on high."

In (John 20:21–23), Jesus said, "Peace be with you. As the Father has sent me, even so I send you." And when He said this, He breathed on them and then said to them, "Receive the Holy Spirit. If you forgive the sins of any, they are forgiven: if you retain the sins of any, they are retained." Repentance and forgiveness are our keys to the kingdom of God. With what great sacrificial love they have loved us.

God has been trying throughout all time to help us understand this self-sacrificing divine love. Jesus came to earth to show us all about this special divine love that is also called charity. Charity is described in the dictionary as "goodwill or love of humanity, it is an act or a feeling of generosity, also lenience in judging others." The grand description of charity is mercy. God's divine love toward us is His mercy for us.

What Jesus is trying to teach us is found in (1 John 3:18): "Little children, Let us love in deed and truth and not merely talk about it" (St. Joseph's). Jesus says in (John 14:6), "I am the way, the truth, and the life. No one comes to the Father except through Me" (St. Joseph's). Jesus is the narrow door. Jesus is trying to lead us to the Father with these words by showing us the way through the

Beatitudes (Matthew 5:5) and by sharing His love with all who come to Him for healing.

God is asking us to come out of the darkness (world) and into the light of His divine Son's presence. Because Jesus is the light of the world. In (1 John 4:11–12, Ignatius), it says, "Beloved, since God loved us so, we must have the same love for one another. No one has ever seen God. Yet if we love one another, God dwells in us, and His love is brought to perfection in us." Wow! "His love is perfected in us." Those are powerful words that simply mean loving one another is divine love.

The sacrament of marriage is divine love. The sacrament of holy orders is divine love. The charism of celibacy is divine love. The virtue and charism of faith is divine love. The charism of healing is divine love. The charism of intercessory prayer is divine love. The charism of mercy is divine love. The gift of counsel is divine love. The charism of pastoring is divine love. The charism of prophecy is divine love. The charism of writing is divine love. The charism of tongues is divine love.

There are two kinds of this charism of tongues. "One is 'SPEAKING IN TONGUES' which is also called "PUBLIC TONGUES. It is a form of Prophetic utterance and is intended to communicate a specific message to others. That is why the Charism of Interpretation of Tongues and Public Tongues are used together" (Catherine of Siena Institute).

The charism of private prayer language of tongues and public tongues are different. Private prayer tongues is an expression of praise and worship toward God and is not intended to communicate a specific message to others. Public and private tongues are both divine love from God. The list is inexhaustible. If you have allowed the Holy Spirit to increase the fruits and gifts into your life, you probably already have been receiving and giving divine love to another.

In (1 John 4:13–16), it says, "By this we know that we abide (live) in Him and He in us, because He has given us of His own Spirit. And we have seen and testify that the Father has sent His Son as Savior of the world. Whoever confesses that Jesus is the Son of God, God abides in Him, and He in God. So we know and believe the love God has for us. God is love, and he who abides in love abides in God, and God in Him."

In (1 Corinthians 14:1, Ignatius), it says, "Make love your aim, and earnestly desire the spiritual gifts, especially that you may prophecy." The spiritual gifts are found in (1 Corinthians 12:4–11); they are the gifts the Holy Spirit gives to all to spread the kingdom of God throughout the nations. The gifts are many, but seek the greatest of all. Read all of (Corinthians 13), and find within it God's divine love. Verse 13 says, "In the end there are three things that last: faith hope and love, and the greatest of these is love."

Kindness

Kindness as a Fruit of the Holy Spirit

The fruits of the Holy Spirit are given to us to help us develop the personality of God. The fruit of kindness is one of the personality traits of Jesus that He lived as an example for us to follow Him to God, His Father.

Blessed Mother Teresa said," Let no one ever come to you without leaving better and happier. Be the living expression of God's Kindness: Kindness in your face, Kindness in your eyes, and Kindness in your smile." As a modern-day saint (who would herself deny it), we can look to her example for direction in how to reach beyond ourselves to another with compassion in today's world.

Compassion is an expression of sympathy, or an expression of mercy. Kindness is displayed in the touch of a hand that reaches out to another in their need. Kindness is caring for someone who is ill, or just is unable to care for themselves. Kindness is reaching beyond yourself to help another. God Himself showed His great mercy and kindness for all mankind when the evil one from a tree tempted Eve, creating original sin. And it was also from a tree that God showed His love for us when Jesus conquered sin. Praise God always for His great kindness, mercy, and deep love for His children: us.

Kindness comes in as many shapes and forms as there are people on this earth. There is no known limit to kindness. It is something that we do for each other that expresses compassion or mercy. Each person alive has the ability to display kindness. IQ or intelligence does not matter. Your station in life does not matter. The work that you do does not matter. Kindness comes from your soul and tugs at your heart until you reach out beyond your own self, too, that other child of God. Each soul that has ever been created has kindness at is center. We each have to look for it. Within our soul at the very center is the presence of God. Therefore, kindness is God Himself.

God our loving Father, has reached inside of Himself and given us a part of Himself. First was His great love for us as He created this world. Remember that old song, "He's got the whole world in His hands." If He has the whole world in His hands, trust that He is holding you in His loving hands.

Take a moment to quiet yourself and l-i-s-t-e-n. Do not be afraid! If you have experienced the transformation in your heart that has accepted Jesus as your personal savior, God is present w-i-t-h-i-n you. You are only alone on this journey of life if you do not choose Jesus over worldly pleasures and sensations. If you feel lonely, it is not because God has moved away from you. It is because you have allowed the desires of the flesh to cover the presence of God in your soul. It was the kindness and love of our God for His children that sacrificed His only Son for our redemption!

The fruit of kindness is a gift from God our Father to help us live the life of service Jesus did when He lived on earth. We each have the God given ability to be a servant or leader for God. None of us will serve in the same way as the next person. None of us will lead in the same way as the next person. None of us have the same personality as any other person on earth. We each were uniquely created by our Father, God. He made us with special capabilities that no one else possesses. He only asks us to love Him above all else, and our neighbor as ourselves, and that we share our gifts with each other. Sharing your distinct gifts from God, with each other is your special charism and your gift back to God, your Heavenly Father. It is out of kindness from God, our Father, that we have kindness in our hearts.

Let each one of us begin the search for kindness that is deep within our hearts. There is always more than currently shows. We each possess an unlimited ability to develop and express all the fruits and gifts of the Holy Spirit to everyone that we meet in our daily lives. It is given to us as a present from our loving Father. We are given them when we ask Jesus into our hearts as our personal Lord and Savior. It is at our baptism that this process begins. When we mature in our growth and development, we are presented with another opportunity to ask for more. We receive more when we decide that it is time for more of the Trinity in our lives.

We receive this infilling of the Holy Spirit at our confirmation. "The Holy Spirit FILLS us with the PRESENCE OF Jesus and His Sacred Humanity, of which the Holy Spirit is an intimate partner in. The Holy Spirit has been an indwelling presence within Jesus since His Conception" (a part from the book of *Gift of Gifts* by Bishop Edward O'Rourke).

All the fruits are brought forward in our lives, but we need to become an active participant in this process. Do not be embarrassed or ashamed if somehow this passed you by when you received your confirmation. Today is the day that we move forward in our life in Christ. Have you heard that saying "Yesterday is history, tomorrow is a mystery, and today is a PRESENT from God"? Remember, your present from God is your ability to make choices which is given to you as your free will from God.

Kindness from God is displayed in the covenant that He made and completed with us through His Son, Jesus—the Christ, the Anointed One, the Lamb of God who through His passion redeemed the world.

In (James 3:13), it says, "Who is wise and understanding among you? Let him show it by his good life, by deeds done in the Humility that comes from Wisdom." Humility is a virtue that helps us in acquiring the personality of Jesus. Humility means to be meek of character, patient with other people and yourself. Patience means being steadfast and persevering. Wisdom as a gift of the Holy Spirit means to have knowledge or insight. Someone who has humility that comes from wisdom is a person who has discovered the beauty of a life based on the principles of Jesus Christ, and he knows that the only way to the Father is though Jesus, beginning with repentance at the foot of the cross. It will take a steadfast heart to be able to walk with Jesus on the narrow road to the Father. All the fruits of the Spirit are at the very center of our personality and are all important in developing our Christ-like life of which kindness is very important.

Goodness

Goodness as Fruit

God's goodness is given to us as a fruit of the Holy Spirit. This fruit is given to us to keep and to help us to grow in the image and likeness of our God.

"One thing I ask, this alone I seek, to dwell in the house of the Lord all my days. For one day within your Temple, heals everyday alone, O Lord, bring me to your Dwelling." This is from a song, and would be a beautiful prayer for each soul that desires eternity with our Father. This is taken from (Psalm 27:4).

It is through the fruit of goodness from God that we are given the opportunity to choose to follow Jesus to the Father. We each will need to make the decision by our own free will to choose Jesus as our personal Lord and Savior. It is our baptism in the name of Jesus Christ that enables us to invite the presence of Jesus and the Holy Spirit to dwell inside of us. It is this infusion of the Holy Spirit and our renewed prayer that will transform our lives day by day and layer by layer into the "image and likeness of God" (Genesis 1:26).

Look to the book of (Matthew 5:1–11), and drink of the gifts of wisdom, understanding, and knowledge (the contemplative gifts of the Holy Spirit) that are found in the Beatitudes that Jesus tried to teach the people on that mountain that day. Some may have felt the passion and love that He projected. Some may have drawn wisdom from the phrases that He shared. Some noticed that Jesus was different. He cared about people. He cared about their pain. He cared about *them*. They noticed that unbelievable things happened when they were around Him. They felt the power that came from Him. They did not know that He was the Messiah. They did know that He could do amazing things. He healed the blind and the lepers, cast out demons. He healed all kinds of sickness—physical, mental, spiritual. He even brought people back from the dead.

One day, when the five thousand were gathered, in (Matthew 14:19–21) it says, "He ordered the crowds to sit down on the grass. He took the five loaves and two fish, looked up to heaven, blessed and broke them and gave them to the people. All those present ate their fill. The fragments remaining, when gathered up, filled twelve baskets. Those who ate were about five thousand, not counting women and children." And Jesus loved beyond human measure. Some embraced Him. Some rejected Him. It is still that way today.

There is a direct correlation between blessing the five loaves and two fishes and feeding the five thousand and when Jesus was at the Last Supper. In (Mark 14:22–26), it says, "During the meal he took bread, blessed and broke it, and gave it to them. 'Take this,' He said, 'this is my body.' He likewise took a cup, gave thanks and passed it to them, and they all drank from it. He said to them: This is my blood, the blood of the covenant, to be poured out on behalf of many. I solemnly assure you, I will never again drink of the fruit of the vine until the day when I drink it new in the reign of God. After singing songs of praise, they walked out to the Mount of Olives."

The bread broken and wine shared at that Last Supper became the body and blood of Jesus the Christ while He reigned in majesty upon the Tree of Salvation. That was the moment that Jesus was pierced for our transgressions and His blood and water flowed from His side, and He surrendered His soul to His Father. The covenant was completed—the covenant that now enables humans to choose God over the world.

Look at these two passages and see the words: "He took the bread in His hands and blessed and broke it, and gave it to them." This is what mystically happens during our Mass through the power of the Holy Spirit that was given to the priests at their ordination. It is only through the virtue of faith that we Catholic Christians believe that this transubstantiation happens. This power of the Holy Spirit is passed down from bishop to bishop at each priest's ordination. This blessing can be traced all the way back to the apostle Peter, when Jesus said to Him, in (Matthew 16:15–19), "'And you,' He said to them, 'who do you say that I am?' 'You are the Messiah,' Simon Peter answered, 'the Son of the living God!' Jesus replied, 'Blest are you, Simon son of Jonah! No mere man has revealed this to you, but my heavenly Father. I for my part declare to you, you are Rock, and on this Rock I will build my church, and the jaws of death shall not prevail against it! I will entrust to you the keys of the kingdom of heaven. Whatever you declare bound on earth shall be bound in heaven; whatever you declare loosed on earth shall be loosed in heaven.'"

Because of Jesus's resurrection, He lives even today. It is through the power of the Holy Spirit that He lives within each one of the Christians who have accepted Him as Lord and Savior. He abides within our spirit. To abide means to live within, to dwell, to endure, to remain with someone. It is only through the goodness of God that we are presented with the opportunity to choose to follow the narrow road with Jesus to the Father. It is through our repentance, which leads to the turning our life around to follow Jesus, that we have the ability to ask for forgiveness of our sins and receive redemption from them. It is through the goodness of God the Father and God the Son, Jesus, that they endured the Covenant with each of us.

In the book by Bishop Edward O'Rourke, Bishop of Peoria, called *Gift of Gifts*, he explains about the Indwelling Spirit. He states, "The sacraments of initiation, baptism, confirmation and the Eucharist, effect a marvelous transformation of the Christian. He is changed from a state of sin to a new creation." He receives a created but very real share in the divine nature and begins in a feeble way to live the God life.

At the same time, the Holy Spirit comes to dwell in such a baptized Christian. In the words of St. Peter, "You must reform and be baptized, each one of you, in the name of Jesus Christ, that your sins may be forgiven; then you will receive the Gift of the Holy Spirit" (Acts 2:38). At the Last Supper, Jesus promised, "If you love me and obey the command I give you, I will ask the Father and He will give you another Paraclete to be with you always: The Spirit of truth, whom the world cannot accept, since it neither sees Him nor recognizes Him; but you can recognize Him because He remains with you and will be within you" (John 14:15–17). Throughout the

Acts of the Apostles, there are repeated accounts of those who were received into the church being filled with the Holy Spirit or being overwhelmed by the Holy Spirit and who as a result lived revitalized, joyful, and apostolic lives.

The Holy Spirit abides in each repented soul. It is through the goodness of God the Father and God the Son that they gave us the Holy Spirit to empower each one of us to be able to live the fruit of the Holy Spirit of goodness in our lives, not only for our own spiritual growth and development but also to share with another through our charisms and to build up the church.

Our ultimate healing will come with our personal resurrection, and we can see the reflection of God's goodness in (Psalm 23): "The Lord is my shepherd, I shall not want. He makes me to lie down in green pastures, He leads me beside still waters, He restores my soul. He guides me in paths of righteousness for His name's sake. Even though I walk through the valley of death, I will fear no evil, for you are with me; your rod and your staff they comfort me. You prepare a table before me in the presence of my enemies. You anoint my head with oil; my cup overflows. Surely goodness and mercy will follow me all the days of my life, and I will dwell in the house of the Lord forever." (Ignatius).

This passage is one of encouragement, strength or fortitude, and counsel from the Holy Spirit, promises from our God to each who will declare Jesus as Lord and Savior. It directs our path to all the other gifts of the Holy Spirit; we receive knowledge and wisdom from our God who loves each of His children very much. We receive understanding of the way to follow and the great reward for following that road, even if it is a difficult one for us. This passage leads to a life of prayer as it is a prayer itself.

This passage also leads to the gift of fear of the Lord. Lord, which is usually misunderstood. What it truly means, if you search though the Bible, is to Look at our God with awe, wonder, and amazement. To know in your spirit that God created each one of us to spend our eternity with the Trinity. We each need to accept the gift of knowledge that our Father God loves us with an everlasting love and views each of us as His treasures. His Son, Jesus, paid the great price of our redemption. All the Trinity asks of us is that we accept this free gift of our salvation and invite others by using our charisms to build up the church.

Generosity

Generosity as a Fruit of the Holy Spirit

Generosity is one of the fruits of the Holy Spirit that is given to us to help us to grow in the image and likeness of our God. Generosity is a willingness to give even at a cost to yourself. It expresses a concern for others even if it means sacrificing something of your own.

God's great love and generosity for us was demonstrated in the creation of the world. Just look at the small details: the variations of thousands of creatures and vegetation, the hills and the valleys and massive oceans to tiny streams, the forests and the desert—all created with and by the great love of our Mighty God. He made each thing in the fullness of His glory. He provided for their every need.

It was with great love and a generous spirit that God created man from the dirt, clay, or dust of the earth. We came from very humble beginnings: soil, something that all vegetation draws its life from. God shaped and molded Adam with divine love. God said in (Genesis 1:26), "Let us make man in our image after our likeness. (Genesis 2:7) goes, "And the Lord God formed man out of clay of the ground and blew into his nostrils the breath of life, and so man became a living being." In (Genesis 2:8) it says, "Then God planted the Garden in Eden and placed there the man He had formed."

And it was with great love and compassion that He created Eve for Adam. It was with wisdom, understanding, and knowledge (Genesis 2:22) that God took one of Adam's ribs and closed up its place with flesh. The Lord God then built up into a woman the rib that He had taken from the man. God did this so that she would be a part of him. That is why a man leaves his father and mother and clings to his wife and "the two of them become one body." In (Genesis 1:31), it says, "God looked at everything that He had made, and He found that it was very good." Creation of the world and all that is upon it is a display of God's generosity and is an example of His divine love for each one of us, and His great desire that we humans share in His divine love. (All these quotes from St. Joseph's).

God, in His great generosity, had given humans everything that they could ever need, and when original sin blanketed the souls of humanity, our God still loved us with His unconditional love. He had only given them one requirement before original sin: not to eat of the fruit of the tree of knowledge of good and evil (Genesis 2:16, Ignatius). Now He would require more of us. So we must look to the one book that God wrote, the Bible, to find our way. (Matthew 6:23–34, Ignatius) speaks to us about conforming our lives with Jesus's, ending with this familiar phrase, "But seek first His Kingdom and His righteousness, and all these things will be yours as well." This truly is a generous God who will provide for our every need if we will only believe that Jesus is our Lord and Savior.

In (Exodus 25:4–10 St. Joseph's), it says, "This is what the Lord then said to Moses: Tell the Israelites to take up a collection for Me. From every man you shall accept the contribution that his heart prompts him to give me. These are the contributions you shall accept from them" gold, silver, and bronze; violet, purple and Scarlet yarn; fine linen and goat hair; rams' skins dyed red, and tahash skins; acacia wood; oil for the light; spices for the anointing oil and for the fragrant incense; onyx stones and other gems for mounting on the ephod and on the breastpiece. They shall make a sanctuary for me, That I may dwell in their midst This Dwelling and all its furnishings you shall make exactly according to the pattern that I will now show."

Read chapters 35–40 to understand that this was the temple to hold the ark of the covenant. It would hold the Ten Commandments and with it the second item, the rod of Aaron, signifying that he was to be the head priest over the Israelites, and a golden pot of manna. Manna was a starchy food that God miraculously provided (daily) for the Israelites for their forty years of desert wanderings (Exodus 16:4). The people, though they had sinned, came back to God and did everything God requested. Their fruit of generosity opened up their hearts to the charisms of craftsmanship and artistic creativity, faith, giving, leadership, and service, to name a few.

In John chapter 3, Jesus answers Nicodemus's questions about the kingdom of God and being born again. In (John 3:5, Ignatius), Jesus says, "Truly, truly, I say to you, unless one is born of Water and Spirit, he cannot enter the Kingdom of God. What is born of flesh is flesh and what is born of spirit is spirit. Do not marvel that I have said to you, 'You must be born anew.' The wind blows where it wills, and you can hear the sound that it makes; but you do not know where it comes from or where it goes; so it is with everyone that is born of the spirit."

The beginning of trust is found in the journey from our selfishness to our selflessness. Our need to find God in the mind, heart, soul, and spirit of our lives is of utmost importance. It will be there that our lives are transformed.

In (John 3:16), we read, "For God so loved the world that He gave His only Son, so that everyone who believes in Him might not perish but might have eternal life. For God did not send His Son into the world to condemn the world, but that the world might be saved through Him. Whoever believes in Him will not be condemned, but whoever does not believe has already been condemned, because he has not believed in the name of the only Son of God. And this is the judgment, that the light came into the world, but people preferred darkness to light, because their deeds were evil. For everyone who does evil hates the light and does not come toward the light, so that his deeds might not be exposed. But whoever lives the truth comes to the light, so that his deeds may be clearly seen as done for God."

Life has a very subtle way of pulling us into the world and away from God. In order for any one of us to be able to choose Jesus as our Savior, we need to be able to see Him. Jesus lives in the hearts of us and other people. It is through the generosity of our Father God that we can see Jesus in the lives of others when they are sharing their charisms with us. It is the fruits of the Holy Spirit (Galatians 5:22–23) that help us seek the Isaiah gifts of the Holy Spirit (Isaiah 11:2): "wisdom, knowledge, understanding, counsel, fortitude, piety, and fear of the Lord."

The gift of wisdom is the beginning of the realization that we need to diligently seek all of the gifts and fruits of the Holy Spirit and to ask the Holy Spirit to help us to bring them forward in our lives in order to 'grow into the image and likeness of the Trinity. "The Isaiah Gifts are part of our inner transformation as Christians and provide the inner 'Christlikeness' necessary for the effective use of our Charisms" (*Called and Gifted*, Catherine of Sienna Institute).

The most generous gift of all time is the gift that Jesus gave to us: His life. All of it! From His decision to leave His heavenly throne and then by the power of the Holy Spirit, He was incarnate (having human form) to be born of the Virgin Mary. Jesus humbled Himself and went from divinity to humanity (remaining divine). He surrendered Himself, His position upon the heavenly throne for us, for our salvation. I hope that you can accept and understand that it truly is all about us.

He spent His lifetime being a role model for the people of His time. He was already filled with the Holy Spirit from the moment that the Holy Spirit "overshadowed Mary." Then He, the Savior, humbled Himself again and was baptized in the Jordan River by John the Baptizer to give us the example of how to be baptized in the name of the Father, Son, and Holy Spirit and receive the gifts and fruits of the Holy Spirit. Then when His time came to teach us (beginning with the disciples), He surrendered to His Father's will. He put behind Him the simple life He had carved for Himself as a carpenter and became a "fisher of men."

Rejected in His hometown of Nazareth, He wandered, calling men, "Come, follow me!" Some did; some couldn't accept the requirements. Once again, He had no place to call home. No bed. He lived the Beatitudes and asked the disciples to live them also. Three years He traveled the region teaching, healing, and searching for those who would accept the news that the Promised Covenant, God's kingdom, was near. It was Jesus.

When the time came for the Promised Covenant to be fulfilled, once again Jesus went willingly. In the Trinity's eyes, Jesus's sacrifice was necessary for our salvation. Jesus paid the ultimate price for our sins: death upon the cross. Remember, it was from a tree that the evil one, through temptation, caused the original sin through human weakness. And it is from another tree that Jesus the Redeemer opened the gate of our salvation through His willing surrender of His life. No one took Jesus's life; He gave His life for everyone in the world, hoping we would recognize Him as Lord and Savior. Remember the generosity of Jesus: He died with our names upon His lips. That's divine love, and we cannot begin to understand this kind of love, but we need to reach for it with our arms opened wide, like Jesus did for us.

It is with great generosity that the Trinity has given us the covenant of our salvation, Jesus Body and Blood upon the cross and in the Eucharist. Most of us Catholic Christians do not fully comprehend the mystery and the miracle of the Eucharist. The communion of our souls with Jesus's soul helps us to grow into His image and likeness. Each Catholic has an opportunity to receive Jesus into themselves daily. Jesus is calling each one of us to holiness, and He generously gave Himself up in a gruesome death to heal our Brokenness. We need to look at our lives and see what we can do for Jesus to build up His church. Ask the Holy Spirit to lead you.

Gentleness

Gentleness or meekness is a fruit of the Holy Spirit. It is a very important part of the personality of God in the person of Jesus when He walked on earth two thousand years ago. He gave us an example of living the Beatitudes.

Gentleness and meekness are mistaken for weakness in our world today. Weakness means lacking strength or vigor. There is no comparison of meekness to weakness. Gentleness means to be kind (an essential quality of character). Meekness is characterized by being yielding, teachable, and responsive. Another word that is synonymous (nearly like) them is *humble*. To be humble is to be like Jesus.

The virtue of humility is hidden deep within the fruit of the Holy Spirit of meekness, also known as gentleness. In (Matthew 5:1–12), Jesus speaks to them (the disciples and the people) about how to "be" in the Beatitudes. The Beatitudes are a display of the attitudes of our God. This lifestyle is what God had in mind for each one of us on the day of creation. Be quiet in your soul, and listen to what Jesus lived and taught: "Blessed are the poor in spirit, for theirs is the kingdom of heaven. Blessed are those who mourn, for they will be comforted. BLESSED ARE THE MEEK, FOR THEY SHALL

INHERIT THE EARTH." The meek shall inherit the earth! What does that mean to us?

In (Genesis 1:1), it says, "In the Beginning, when God created the heavens and the earth," and it is described in detail, it says in (Genesis 2:9), "Then the Lord God planted a garden in Eden, in the east, and He placed there the man He had formed. Out of the ground the Lord God made various trees grow that were delightful to look at and good for food, with the tree of life in the middle of the garden and the tree of the knowledge of good and evil."

In (Genesis 2:15–17), it says, "The Lord God then took the man and settled him in the Garden of Eden, to cultivate it and care for it. The Lord gave man this order: "You are free to eat from any of the trees of the garden except the tree of knowledge of good and bad. From that tree you shall not eat; the moment you eat from it you are surely doomed to die." He created them as man and woman and gave them control over all things, including themselves with their free will. They were created to be the "the meek of the earth" (all quotes from St. Joseph's).

God gave to Adam and Eve the garden; it would provide for them everything they would need. Humans were the only creations that God gave the ability to reason out their thoughts to think about consequences. We are to think about what we desire to do and then think about the consequences. This is our ability to use our free will. It was God's desire to have us be able to choose Him over all else.

It was God's desire to be a part of this union of man and woman. God created them humans to walk in harmony with each other and with Him. God created them to be intimate with each other and to be able to share in the co-creation of human life that would inhabit the earth. God desired to be intimate with them, which means He desired to be a part of them and the lives that they shared together. That was the way it was; until first Eve then Adam desired more. Lust was planted in their mind and hearts. They surrendered to the desire to know more than the meek persons whom God created them to be. With their submission to the temptations of the evil one (Genesis 3:6), original sin blanketed their souls and every human to be born after them.

There was only one thing that was forbidden in their "heaven on earth" home: The Tree of Knowledge of Good and Bad. The tree was not bad. But God had forbidden them to eat of it. The desire that was created within Eve's mind by the evil one blinded her heart to what God had said, and she ate of the fruit, and deciding that it was good, she shared it with Adam. Their original sin (the first sin of humans) opened their eyes to their nakedness, the innocence and goodness, the joy—basically all the fruits of the Holy Spirit that God created them with were hidden from them. (Genesis 2) tells the rest of this story of the fall of man and how they recognized it and covered themselves and hid from God. That was the beginning of the end of meekness or gentleness that God had given them to enjoy as a part of the Trinity from the moment He created them in His image and likeness (Genesis 1:26, St. Joseph's).

For this disobedience, God exiled them from the garden, but He did not abandon them. He made His first promise to them (and us) that He had not given up on them or their descendants because of a moment of weakness that was led by the evil one. God demonstrated His great love and compassion for them in the promise of "one to come" in (Genesis 3:15 St. Joseph's).

Disobedience of the one rule from God changed all human life forever. The meek of the earth lost all the beauty that God had created for them, because of their weakness: their sin. The wrath of God came upon them. But the divine love of God and His tenderness for His beloved creations brought our God to a promise of a "covenant" (Genesis 3:15) that would allow their broken relationship of love to be healed.

Jesus, the Son of God, the second person of the Trinity, willingly became the covenant between God and man to give each person who would listen to the Holy Spirit's leading and then follow the path to Christ (the Anointed One). Jesus lived the fruits and the gifts of the Holy Spirit to give us an example to follow. Jesus lived each phrase of the Beatitudes. They were part of His being. Jesus's birth in a stable and being laid in a manger for His bed was meek, lowly, and certainly humble for Jesus, Mary, and Joseph. But it was meant to bring God's meekness back upon the earth as an example for us to follow. Little

Mary was the promised other woman in (Genesis 3:15). The fruits of the Holy Spirit were the personality of Jesus, who was the essence of God the Father. "The meek shall inherit the earth."

Humility is the state of being humble. To be humble is to be insignificant, unassuming, or not pretentious, not proud. I believe that being humble is to hold all things precious, that our God has created, including, but not limited to, ourselves.

Throughout the many pages of the Old Testament, there are gentle and meek people who listened to their God.(Isaiah 53) speaks beautifully of Jesus's coming and living a meek (lowly) life and going unnoticed until His ministry began. His gentle ways and meek personality were the very essence of His Father, God. Jesus was given to us for an example and ultimately for our salvation.

In (Isaiah 53:5 St. Joseph's), it says, "But He was pierced for our offences, crushed for our sins. Upon Him was the chastisement that makes us whole, by His stripes were we healed. We had all gone astray like sheep, each following his own way, but the Lord laid upon Him the guilt of all. Though He was harshly treated, He submitted and opened not His mouth; Like a Lamb led to the slaughter or a sheep before the shearers, He was silent and opened not His mouth. Oppressed and condemned, He was taken away, and who would have thought any more of His destiny? When He was cut off from the land of the Living, and smitten for the sin of His people, a grave was assigned Him among the wicked and a burial place with evildoers, though He had done no wrong nor spoken no falsehood. (But the Lord was pleased to crush Him in infirmity.) If He gives His life as an offering for sin, He shall see His descendants in a long life, and the will of the Lord shall be accomplished through Him… Through His suffering, my servant shall justify many, and their guilt He shall bear…Because He surrendered Himself to death and was counted among the wicked; He shall take away the sins of many, and win pardon for their offences."

Wow. It is hard for me to understand how Isaiah could trust himself enough to write this prophecy of things to come. The evangelist, who wrote the stories after Jesus lived, is understandable to me. But the faith of the prophets is inspiring. I am sure that he was filled with the virtue of humility in order to trust that His words were inspired by the Holy Spirit. "The meek shall inherit the Earth."

There is a wonderful power in the presence of deep humility within a human soul. Humility is a virtue that comes from the very personality of the Trinity. Having humility brings our souls into communion with our God, back to His desires for us in Genesis 1 when God created "man to fill the earth and subdue it" (Genesis 1:28, St Joseph's).

To live your life in humility toward our God and all that He created is to be "meek and to inherit the earth." It is through the gentle and humble way that Jesus treated all of God's creations that we learn how to be, humble, meek and gentle of heart and to live humbly with our God.

Read the rest of the Beatitudes (Matthew 5:1–12) to learn how to grow in the fruits and gifts from the Trinity.

By the life and death of Jesus, we were endowed with everything that we will need to surrender our souls to Jesus. All we need to do is to surrender our desires of worldly things (anything that our minds lust for, which means an intense longing) to Jesus at the foot of the cross. Jesus will send His Holy Spirit to fill us with the ability to be able to overcome the evil one's temptations by enhancing the "fruits, the gifts, and all the virtues" that God has given us as the way and the truth to a life in Christ. Christ means "anointed one, or the Messiah," the one who is sent to heal the contrite of heart. The contrite of heart is whoever surrenders their hearts to Jesus as Lord and Savior. Come study Jesus's life in the Beatitudes and pray for the virtue of humility, then Jesus's meekness will shine from your spirit.

The Beatitude "The meek shall inherit the earth" is telling each soul who will hear the call from God that if we choose to follow Jesus to His humble death upon a wooden cross, we shall become the meek who will inherit the earth, because it was from a tree that the evil one led us from God's divine love, and it is from a tree that Jesus will lead us through redemption to the Father. Jesus calls to us from the cross with His arms stretched wide.

Faithfulness

Faithfulness is a fruit of the Holy Spirit. It is a personality of the Trinity. As we try to infuse all the fruits into our lives, we display the persona of Jesus.

Our God is a faithful God. Faithfulness begins with God. He desired us from the beginning of time. He gave everything to us, for us to be able to live in peace, harmony, and justice. He gave to us the earth and all that was upon the land. He desired that we humans would rule over the vegetation and the animals. He had such great plans and dreams for us.

He also gave us a free will, to allow us to be able to choose. His hope was that we would choose wisely and choose God over all else. God created man. Then He created the woman out of the man's rib to make them part of each other. This was a sacred moment. God created the world and everything on it, including the humans, with His divine love. In this creation, He is sharing this divine love with all humans. Everything that God creates is sacred. Yes, that means that each human is sacred to God.

Satan was a fallen angel—the angel of darkness and evil, because he would not bow down and honor God. He desired to be the king. He wanted his own following, and through subtle seductions, he made the forbidden fruit of the tree of knowledge desirable to Eve, and being temped, she tasted the fruit and found it good and offered it to Adam, saying, "It is good." He also ate of it, "and their eyes were opened." Their sweet and divine innocence was gone, and they hid from each other and from God. The war for our souls began. Now original sin covers all human souls until we accept Jesus as Lord and Savior in our hearts and are baptized.

God did not give up on all mankind when the first humans made a mistake and gave in to temptation. In (Psalms 36:5, Ignatius) it says, "Your mercy, O Lord. Extends to the heavens, your faithfulness to the clouds." God's faithfulness to His plan for mankind in (Genesis 3:15) shines through (St. Joseph's) where He says to satan, "I will put enmity between you and the woman, and between your offspring and hers, he will strike at your head, while you strike at his heel." Mary is that other woman, and Jesus is her seed. Jesus is the Promised One who is sent to teach us and lead us to repentance, forgiveness, and redemption from our fallen human nature.

All throughout the Old Testament, there are stories of holy people, fallen people, and people of deep faith. Some believed in what God had said about His promise of salvation. God spent centuries building His holy nation, and through these chosen people, our Redeemer would come. The New Eve was born without "original sin" that has blanketed all souls since the fall of Adam and Eve. Little Mary grew in great faith taught by her parents' example. Her faithfulness and trust in God was total.

In (Luke 1:26–38, Ignatius) it says, "In the sixth month, the angel Gabriel was sent from God to a town of Galilee named Nazareth, to a virgin betrothed to a man named Joseph, of the house of David. The virgin's name was Mary. Upon arriving, the angel said to her: 'Rejoice, O highly favored daughter! The Lord is with you. Blessed are you among women.' She was deeply troubled by his words, and wondered what his greeting meant. The angel went on to say to her: 'Do not fear Mary. You have found favor with God. You shall conceive and bear a son and give Him the name Jesus. Great will be His dignity and He will be called the Son of the Most High. The Lord God will give Him the throne of David His father. He will rule over the house of Jacob forever and His reign will be without end.' Mary said to the angel, 'How can this be since I do not know man?' The angel answered her: 'The Holy Spirit will come upon you and the power of the Most High will overshadow you; hence, the holy offspring to be born will be called the Son of God. Know that Elizabeth your kinswoman has conceived a son in her old age is now in her sixth month with her who was called barren. For with God nothing is impossible.' Mary said: 'I am the servant of the Lord. Let it be done to me as you say.' With that the angel left her."

Mary went to help Elizabeth, and her greeting to Mary was, "Blessed are you among women, and blessed is the fruit of your womb." She could only have known this by the power of the Holy Spirit.

Mary's yes, gave us a Savior—our Redeemer, our Lord, our King, our Lamb of God who takes away the sins of the world. Her yes gave us the Promised One from God at the beginning of time in (Genesis 3:15). Remember, Mary, like all humans, had free will. What if her faith wasn't strong enough? But because of the grace of God, she had grown from childhood to a young woman with parents who were very faithful to their God. Her faithfulness and trust in God was complete and total. Mary's humility and great Love of her's and our God—and her knowledge of the biblical history gave her the virtue of courage to say yes.

Mary became the very first tabernacle to hold our Lord and Savior Jesus Christ. Jesus was the "fruit of her womb" and the "fruit of God the Father," and the "fruit of the Holy Spirit." Jesus gave us by example the ways we should live to be in union with God the Father. Jesus lived the fruits of the Holy Spirit. They became the very personality of God the Son, Jesus. When we weave these God-given fruits into our own personality, we become like Jesus in the way He was when He walked upon this earth, teaching us the way we are to be faithful to God our Father.

Because of our humanness, "know that we will make mistakes… but please know that we are not mistakes." That is a quote from my Shepherd. Understand and believe this deep in your heart, because God knew you before all time. He has great plans for each one of us. In (Jeremiah 29:11, St. Joseph's) it says, "I know the plans I have for you," declares the Lord, "Plans for your welfare not for woe, plans to give you a future full of hope."

I praise God for all He has done for me; He has forgiven my sins and weaknesses. And because I have been faithful to my Lord and God, He has showered me with the graces to listen to Him, to trust in Him, to display my faithfulness, and to use my charism of writing to help myself and others to understand the messages that have remained hidden to our minds for so long. Thank you, God, for loving and trusting me this much.

Our mission is to bring others to God. Join me in the doxology: "Glory be to the Father, to the Son, and to the Holy Spirit, as it was, is, now, and ever shall be, world without end. Amen."

Ponder those words, take them deep into your heart, and ask Jesus what, "whatever shall be, world without end" means. Let us thank Mary for her yes by the Hail Mary prayer. Say these words slowly, ponder them, and bring them deep into your heart and soul. This prayer is addressed to Mary, in thanksgiving for Her great role in our salvation, but it is all about Jesus. Listen with your heart: "Hail, Mary, full of grace, the Lord is with you, blessed are you among women, and blessed is the fruit of your womb, Jesus. Holy Mary Mother of God, pray for us sinners, now and at the hour of our death. Amen."

Yes, Mary was showered with graces. She was also showered with many sorrows—enough sorrow to pierce her motherly heart many times. It is still pierced today when we reject her son, Jesus, as our Lord and Savior. She was His very first tabernacle. She held the treasure of all time within Her womb. She is able, of all people, to show us the way to Her Son Jesus, our Savior and our Salvation. It is in this knowledge that we should call upon her help to show us how to be the very best tabernacle that we can be for the "Lamb of God who takes away the sins of the world." Please join me and say, "Lord, have mercy on us."

Self-Control

Self-control is a Fruit of the Holy Spirit

Self-control is a fruit of the Holy Spirit that is given to us to keep. It is one of the virtues of Jesus our Savior, that is given as an example to show us the way to the Father.

In the book *Praying God's Promises*, by Richards, it says, "God is the blessed controller of all things, but He also wants to teach us how to exercise a measure of self-control in our lives as well, through the power of the Holy Spirit. Self- Control entails: temperance" (which means: habitual moderation or abstinence of: indulgence of the appetites or passions or intoxicating drink),' Moderation and self- mastery" (possession of your own skills). Everything we are and have is God's in the first place, and this means that we are simply managers over everything God has given to us. As good stewards or managers, therefore, we need to be sure we exercise control over our finances, our possessions, our bodies, and our appetites. This kind of self-control is possible through the power of the Holy Spirit.

Self-control is "restraint exercised over one's own impulses, emotions, or desires." In (Galatians 5:19–21, Ignatius), St. Paul tells them again, "Now the works of the flesh are plain: fornication, impurity, licentiousness, idolatry, sorcery, enmity, strife, jealously, anger, selfishness, dissension, party spirit, envy, drunkenness, carousing, and the like. I warn you as I warned you before, that those who do such things shall not inherit the Kingdom of God."

I believe that most of us have heard these words before in the Mass readings, but quite honestly, when the reading is over, the words that I do not understand are out of my memory, so I do not think about them anymore. I myself need to study words and their meaning to discover what they are to mean in my life. So please join me on this journey to help us discover what self-control as the fruit of the Holy Spirit really means for our Christianity.

Here is what Webster's has to say: FORNICATION: willing, sexual relations between two (2) persons that are not married to each other. IMPURITY: not pure; thoughts that weaken us or pollutes our minds and heart. LICENTIOUSNESS: an unchaste (unmarried and/or lustful) use of your sexual drive, [such as masturbation]. IDOLATRY: the worship of a physical object as a god [car, house, clothing etc.]. SORCERY: the use of magic: witchcraft. ENMITY: mutual hatred. (Synonyms are; hostility, animosity, antagonism). STRIFE: conflict, fight or struggle. JEALOUSLY: distrustful of another person's faithfulness; envious; suspiciously watchful. ANGER: enraged, wrathful [violent anger or rage,] Irate, Indignant, or mad. SELFISHNESS: concerned with one's own welfare exclusively: or without regard for others. DISSENSION: disagreements in opinions. ENVY: painful or resentful awareness of another's advantages. DRUNKENESS: given to habitual or excessive use of alcohol. CAROUSING: "a drunken revel" [revel is to take great pleasure or satisfaction in doing something].

These are passages that show the consequence of the lack of self-control: In (Genesis 3:17–19), Eve and Adam ate the forbidden fruit, disobeying God (original sin covers our souls). In Genesis

4, Cain kills Abel and does not control his envy and jealousy. In (Genesis 19:15–26), Lot's wife turns to a pillar of salt, does not control longings. In Genesis 25:29–34, Esau trades birthright for porridge; does not control his hunger. In (Exodus 2:14), Moses kills an Egyptian, doesn't exercise restraint and seeks to extract justice that was not his to render. In (2 Samuel 11:1–27), David's adultery with Bathsheba and the murder of her husband; doesn't control his sexual appetites or his desire to go to any length to give in to them. In (Luke 22:49–51), Peter's impulsive blow to a servant's ear when Jesus is arrested in the Garden of Gethsemane.

More biblical support of this: in Paul's letter to the (Colossians 3:5–8, Ignatius), it says, "Put to death therefore, what is earthly in you: sexual immorality, impurity, passion, evil desires, covetousness, which is idolatry. On account of these the wrath of God is coming. In these you once walked, when you lived in them. But now put them all away: anger, wrath, malice (a desire to cause injury or distress to another), slander (to injure someone's reputation), and foul language from your mouth."

Any and all these human weaknesses are sins of the flesh, and will keep us from our life in grace and ultimately from the kingdom of God. Take a careful look inside your heart and ask Jesus to reveal any and all things that can keep your soul estranged or away from Him. Most of us (me in particular) have put blinders on the eyes of our hearts so that we cannot see our sins. Once you have truly assessed your heart and feel regret for those sins and the pain they have caused you or someone else and ultimately God, and if you desire to turn your life around, then repent of those sins that the Holy Spirit has revealed to your heart. Your confessor will help you to the place where "Jesus will wash you clean as snow."

Remember, Jesus came to earth to save us from our sins and heal us of our burdens and weaknesses. With our baptism, we become the holy temple of Jesus, and, as His temple (a holy place) or His tabernacle (a place to hold the Holy Eucharist), we need to treasure this gift of the Trinity in our lives. It is an unconditional gift we have been given (that means no strings attached). We can, with our free will, accept or refuse the gift of our redemption. We can change our earthly lives to try to follow Jesus, or we can stay within our world unchanged.

If we choose to follow Jesus, we are to let Jesus be seen radiating from within our soul. As His presence radiates out of us, we must know we are the beacon that is calling others to Jesus for their own salvation. A beacon is a signal fire or a guiding light or warning signal (like a lighthouse); it is something that gives out guidance.

The hard part for us to understand is this: being Jesus's tabernacle (which we have become with our baptism), we are also His Monstrance. Webster's says, "A Monstrance is a vessel in which the Consecrated Host is exposed for adoration of the faithful." As Jesus' monstrance, it is He who shines forth as a beacon in the night to lead God's children to their spiritual safety at the foot of the cross. The Consecrated Host is the body of Jesus, our Savior. So let us call upon the Holy Spirit to help us be blessed with the fruit of the Holy Spirit of self-control and through the gift of counsel from the Holy Spirit, let us pray that we become an active participant in transforming our lives. This is what conversion is.

In 1 Thessalonians 4:4 (Ignatius), it says, "That each of you should learn to control his own body in holiness and honor." In (Galatians 5:22–23, Ignatius), it says, "But the Fruit of the Spirit is Love, Joy, Peace, Patience, Kindness, Goodness, Faithfulness, Gentleness, and Self-Control: against such there is no law." Infusing these qualities or characteristics into our personalities will help us to grow into the "image and likeness of our God" (Genesis 1:26).

It is God Himself who gives us these qualities through the power of the Holy Spirit at the time of our baptism in the name of His Son, Jesus Christ. These are the very personality of Jesus as He lived and walked on this earth. These same fruits of the Spirit are enhanced when we ask that they are brought forward in our lives at our Confirmation or whenever we understand that they are ours for the asking.

What many Catholic Christians did not understand at the time of our confirmation was that it is necessary for us to become an active participant in this joining of our lives and spirits to the Trinity. It doesn't "just happen." God gave us free will so that we can make this decision for our lives. Original sin has made the effects of our decisions harder to see clearly. We will need to call upon Jesus to come forward and "awaken and release the power of the Holy Spirit" in our lives so that we can experience and feel the divine love of the Trinity.

Examples of self-control are found in (Matthew 4:11), when Jesus resisted temptations in the wilderness. And in John 11, Jesus waited for three days, not going to Lazarus before he died. Emotion did not dictate His actions. In (John 11:40), Jesus said, "Did I not tell you that if you believed you would see the glory of God displayed?" (Hebrews 4:15) speaks of Jesus being sinless. Jesus was divine first then human.

Each human after Adam and Eve was born with the stain of original sin upon their souls. But even in (Genesis 39), we find the story of a man named Joseph whom the "Lord was with." He did not succumb to the wishes of the Pharaoh's wife and was imprisoned, and the Lord remained with him. And in 1 Samuel 24 and 26, David did not kill Saul when he had the opportunity. We *can* overcome temptation if we ask for the Trinity's help.

Modesty

Modesty Is a Fruit of the Holy Spirit

Modesty is a fruit of the Holy Spirit that is given to us in our baptism to mold us into the image and likeness of Jesus.

Modesty begins in the home.

"What am I going to teach the world about womanhood? We each need to ask God to give us the grace that we need to change the face of the earth! Immodesty in a woman betrays manhood! Christ is in men and especially in our priests! Women, dress modestly so you do not lead them into temptation."

The Holy Spirit touched my heart with this message from an African priest during his homily when I was at a 'Mary' Retreat. Christ is also within women through the power of the Holy Spirit. As His holy temple, we need to radiate the love of God through our personalities. We do this in the display of our fruits and gifts of the Holy Spirit, not the display of our body.

As God's holy temple, and in our masculinity and femininity, we display not only the gift of the body—the one that God gave us to go through life with—but also, most of all, as Christians, the gift in our heart that is our belief in Jesus as our Redeemer, who is our Lord, our Savior, our King, our God, and He is "the Lamb of God, who takes away the sins of the world."

Jesus has given us the example to follow. We do this in sharing the love of our God with all we meet. We humans are designed to become His temple, His holy place of dwelling. We each are designed to be the monstrance, the vessel that the consecrated host, which is the Body of Christ, is exposed for adoration. We become the monstrance when Jesus who is within us, radiates out of us so that others may be able to see Jesus our Lord and Savior and follow Him. When our present from the Trinity which is Jesus, is given to us, and as Jesus grows more and more in our hearts, our hearts change into "the image and likeness of our God," our Creator.

We each are created to come to God. When we decide to bring Jesus into the center of our lives, we are given the tools to overcome the presence of sin. They are the baptismal fruits and gifts of the Holy Spirit. They are given to each one who invites Jesus into their hearts, and will be strengthened at our confirmation, and at each Eucharistic celebration of the Mass. He is the Lamb of God," who takes away the sins of the world. These are the sacraments of initiation in the Catholic Church.

The world that God created was changed in the Garden of Eden when the evil one "from a tree" (Roman Mass) conquered by placing doubt in Eve's mind about what she believed that God had asked of them. God had created, in their beings, all the fruits of His personality. It was a free gift to make their lives good. Humanity's free will makes us vulnerable to the subtle seductions of the evil one. Eve was seduced by the evil one, and she, in her weakness, led her man to follow her in disobedience to the Lord God, their Loving Father and their Creator.

With original sin, Adam and Eve could "see their nakedness and sewed loin cloths to cover themselves" (Genesis 3:7). They were trying to hide the pain that they felt in their hearts from God and themselves. But it could not be hidden. What Adam and Eve could not understand was that eating from the tree of knowledge (which God told Adam not to eat from) opened their minds, not just to the nakedness of their bodies but to their disobedience to their God.

The insight of their nakedness was a side effect of their sin. Shame was an emotion that they had never experienced before, and it covered their God that was present within them. God's trust in them had been betrayed by their free will. God had entrusted them with the world "to cultivate and care for it" (Genesis 2:15, St Joseph's). He only asked them one thing: not to eat from the tree in the center of the Garden, the tree of knowledge of good and bad (Genesis 1:16–17).

Their bodies were still just as God had created them—beautiful and holy, and made for co-creation with God—but their *souls* were changed. There was now emptiness and disappointment where the Trinity lived in their souls. God trusted them to follow only one instruction, and they failed! So God made them a promise—a promise of one to come who would be able to bring back all the fruits of the Holy Spirit into mankind. That is how much our God loves us.

"And it is from a TREE" (Roman Mass) that our salvation reigns, in the most precious Body of our Lord and Savior, Jesus, the Christ, the promised covenant from our God. Jesus is the Anointed One who comes in simple humility to anoint us with His Holy Blood that He poured out for the cleansing of our souls. Jesus came "not to condemn us," it says in Mark 10:45 (Ignatius). "For the Son of Man did not come to be served, He came to serve, and to give His life for many."

We need to remember it was little Mary who was asked to bring into the world the promised Messiah. It was she who said yes to God the Creator and allowed "the Power of the Holy Spirit, and the overshadowing of the Most High" (Luke 1:35) (Ignatius) to fulfill the covenant for mankind. As a faithful, humble servant of God, the Word (Jesus) was made flesh within her womb. (John 1:14, Ignatius).

Mary, His mother, was with Him throughout His whole life. Mary was at the cross, and His pain pierced her heart! Jesus was stripped of His garments and was nailed to a tree naked. He came into this world of ours like us, and naked He hung upon the tree for our salvation. Even while Jesus was hanging on the cross, the evil one still tried to tempt Him away from His Father by the embarrassment of His Nakedness. You see, it is only the modesty of the artist that puts a loincloth on Jesus our King, "who was enthroned upon the cross for our salvation! And never had His Father seen Him more beautiful" (a quote from Scott Hahn in a CD of *The Fourth Cup*). Know that His Father and His Spirit did not abandon Him there; the community of the Trinity was there with Jesus to the climax of the covenant that God made for mankind.

From the throne of the tree of our salvation, Jesus gave His mother to John, His beloved disciple, and He gave John to His mother. John's acceptance of this gift of Jesus's mother to be his own was also done in proxy for all those who will accept Jesus as their Messiah and brother. Mary's love for Jesus was shown when she accepted the role of our mother. She especially loves the disciples who have chosen the hard road of being His shepherds. It is a huge responsibility. Our Blessed Mother asks us to pray for her Son's chosen shepherds. They are being attacked terribly and need the community of the church to remain strong. Let us all pray earnestly for them as they try to lead us closer to Jesus.

In (1 Timothy 2:9–13), it says, "Similarly, (too) women should adorn themselves with proper conduct, with modesty and self-control, not with braided hair styles and Gold ornaments, or pearls, or expensive clothes, but rather, as befits women who profess reverence for God, with good deeds. A woman must receive instruction silently and under complete control, I do not permit a woman to teach or to have authority over a man. She must be quiet. For Adam was formed first, then Eve. Further, Adam was not deceived, but the woman was deceived and transgressed. But she will be saved through motherhood, provided women persevere in faith and love and holiness, with self-control."

How lovingly our Father reprimands us. His great love and compassion give us another chance at our eternity. But He is more explicit now. Women are to be modest in thoughts and actions. That means anyone who desires to be in unity with Christ needs to look in their heart and at the way that they dress and see what Jesus sees. We each need to let our beauty radiate out of us from within our spirit where God dwells. We, as women, are to lead our men to holiness by our example. We receive our example from Our Blessed Mother, Mary. She is the new Eve, the essence of what women were created by God to do and to be. A helpmate for her man so that both will be received into heaven with the Trinity.

The fruits of the Holy Spirit are listed in the New Testament (Galatians 5:22–23) to help us shape and mold our lives into the image of Jesus the Holy One. He was sent from His heavenly throne to redeem mankind from the original sin of Adam and Eve. Humanity's free will makes us vulnerable to the subtle seductions of the evil one. Eve was seduced by the evil one, and she in her weakness led her man to follow her in disobedience to the Lord God, their loving Father and their Creator.

The fruits and the gifts are the presents from Jesus to each and every one of God's human creations that God calls to Himself. We are each called to the Father by His Son, Jesus. We are called to see the sweet humanity of Jesus. There are many paths that we can follow as we walk through this life that has been given to us, and it keeps getting more complicated all the time. We are called to follow Jesus on this journey through our life. He came from His true place in the heavens with the community of the Trinity to the lowly stable, and was laid in a manger for His bed.

A stable is a shelter where the animals went for protection from the weather. The manger was a small trough that held food for the animals. Jesus comes to us in this lowly state to grow like us as humans so that He would show us how to serve each other. Being divine, He was not like us, but He became like us to show us by example that what God the Father asks of us is not impossible. We need to desire to be like Jesus and then turn our lives over to Him. He did not come to condemn us; He came to free us of the sin that holds us in bondage to this world that belongs to the evil one. Oh, how intricate is God the Father's plan. Jesus was laid in the manger that held the food for the animals. Later, Jesus in the Eucharist is the food for our salvation. What a paradox! We need to ask our Blessed Mother to help us reach this place of humility with her and Jesus.

The Trinity has given us the tools that we need to come to Jesus for the forgiveness of our sins and to help us get beyond our weaknesses and burdens. We all have them. We may have hidden them so well from ourselves that we cannot see them, but they are there, and they control our lives.

If you do not know what a conversion is, it is the moment when you feel the presence of God in your life. You know in your heart that this is real and that He came to walk this journey with you. It is just that personal! Take your pain to the throne of the cross so that Jesus can change your face into His own that is full of divine love.

Chastity

Chastity Is a Fruit of the Holy Spirit

The fruits of the Holy Spirit are given to us to help us to be created into the image and likeness of God, and the fruit of chastity was a quality of Jesus that he lived as an example for us.

Chastity is a quality of being chaste, which is sexual purity (Webster's). Chastity is a frame of mind. It goes beyond not having a sexual relationship outside of marriage. It is about the way that we look at and enter into life relationships. Chastity is about respect for one another, respect for ourselves, and respect for God. Chastity is all about learning to allow our thoughts to guide our actions.

We humans are born with original sin. It is our natural tendency to be selfish, and to sin. But we can overcome anything when we ask God to help us. Jesus will send His Holy Spirit to fill us with the grace that we will need to overcome the urge to sin. All we need to do is to seek the help we need, ask for the desire to be removed, and find that your spirit feels a little different. When you ask Jesus to heal your wounds, He fills you with His Holy Spirit, but this only happens when you actively ask for God's help and knock at the door of Jesus's Sacred Heart. Layer by layer the Trinity works to release us of our bondage to our particular sin. Come to Jesus to receive healing.

This is from the book by Thomas Keating, *Open Mind, Open Heart*, and has helped me to understand the roll of chastity in our lives:

> *"Chastity is distinct from Celibacy, which is the commitment to abstain from the genital expression of our sexuality. Chastity is the acceptance of our sexual energy, together with the masculine and feminine qualities that accompany it and the integration of this energy into our spirituality. It is the practice of moderation and self-control in the use of our sexual energy. Chastity enhances and expands the power to love. It perceives the sacredness of everything that is. As a consequence, one respects the dignity of the other persons, and cannot use them merely for one's own fulfillment."*

When we use our gifts of the Holy Spirit found in (Isaiah)—wisdom, understanding, knowledge, fortitude, counsel, piety, and fear of the Lord—our fruits of the Holy Spirit come alive in us. The fruits are charity, joy, peace, patience, kindness, gentleness, goodness, generosity, modesty, chastity, and self-control. It is with these fruits and gifts of the Holy Spirit in our lives that we are able to choose to share the spiritual gifts found in (1 Corinthians 12:4–7), also known as charisms, with another. Knowing this, for instance, the charism of celibacy comes alive when the gifts are used and the fruits of joy, charity, peace, patience, gentleness, goodness, generosity, kindness, self-control, chastity, and modesty are brought forward in our daily lives for the honor and the glory of God, and the building up of the church.

When we say that we desire to follow Jesus to the cross of our salvation, we need to take a look at what is in our heart. We must know where we are before we can change the direction that we are going to. We cannot do this on our own; we will need guidance.

Jesus commissioned His disciples to lead others to the kingdom of God and to what they formed into the church. The apostles and the disciples learned from Jesus, our First Shepherd, how to become a shepherd and then how to teach others to become shepherds. This was a special anointing from Jesus and His Holy Spirit to Peter, and His successors have been anointing the shepherds throughout these two thousand years.

I would like you to remember that Peter made mistakes (denying that he knew Jesus). Jesus loved Peter into being because Peter could see his mistake and repent. Know that our shepherds today are just like Peter: as humans, they can and will make mistakes, but as chosen by Jesus and plucked from our world of sin to help us find our way to Jesus, they will be qualified for this great work of our Lord spreading the kingdom of God.

All shepherds have the same fruits and gifts of the Holy Spirit that Jesus and the apostles had, and by the power of their anointing, they are able to lead us to the foot of Jesus's cross. If we will be still and listen with our hearts, we can receive forgiveness. Please remember they are human first, then priests, and it is our responsibility as Christians to help them remain chaste and not be any part of temptation for them. Their sacrifice has been great! Together we can make it to Jesus.

We each must discover what our sexuality is all about. Women draw their sexuality from the Blessed Virgin Mary, the New Eve. It is written in (Luke 1:26–38) that an angel "came to Mary and foretold the mystery that was to take place. The angel answered, "The Holy Spirit will come upon you, and the power of the Most High will overshadow you. So the Holy one to be born will be called the Son of God. Even Elizabeth your relative is going to have a child in her old age, and she who was thought to be barren is in her sixth month. For nothing is impossible with God." And Mary answered, "I am the Lord's servant, may it be to me as you have said." Then the angel left her. It was at that moment that Mary became the very first tabernacle of our Lord Jesus the Christ.

Mary, a young woman about fourteen or fifteen years old, was so grounded in her beliefs of faith, hope, love, and trust of her God that she said yes. Read Mary's prayer to God when she was greeted by Elizabeth in (Luke 1:46–56, Ignatius). She said, "My soul glorifies the LORD and my spirit rejoices in God my Savior. He has been mindful of the humble state of His servant. From now on all generations will call me blessed, for the Mighty One has done great things for me—holy is His name. His mercy extends to those who fear Him, from generation to generation. He has performed mighty deeds with His arm; He has scattered those who are proud in their inmost thoughts. He has brought down rulers from their thrones but has lifted up the humble. He has filled the hungry with good things but has sent the rich away empty. He has helped His servant Israel, remembering to be merciful to Abraham and his descendants forever, even as He said to our fathers."

Mary was betrothed to Joseph when the angel came to her. Her yes to God, changed both of their lives. Though pledged to each other in holy matrimony, they were first pledged to their God by faith. Joseph was devoted to his God, and when asked to be the earthly father of God's Son Jesus the Christ, he demonstrated his masculinity (having qualities appropriate to or generally associated with a man: resolute, steadfast, faithful, true, loyal) and transcended his own sexuality for the greater good of the salvation of mankind.

Yes, it was by special graces that they both lived a chaste life. We each can ask for that same grace to help us with our needs.

To transcend the genital expression of your masculinity and femininity means to rise above the limits of your human desires to the place that only God can reward your sexual drive: by turning it into spiritual drive. To live a chaste life, we need to ask for the Holy Spirit to help us to become like Christ in His thinking and His unconditional love. This was God's desire from the beginning of time: that we would become like Christ and allow the Trinity to permeate our being (penetrate: to understand or affect deeply).

While I was contemplating chastity, the Holy Spirit touched my heart with the words that follow:

"Throughout time some of my Holy ones have chosen to remain CHASTE. To be chaste, is to be innocent of unlawful sexual intercourse, virtuous, celibate. To be chaste is to be 'Pure in Thought or MODEST.' To be modest means to be observant of how you dress so that you do not tempt any one to sin in thought or deed! My Son Jesus was the example that you will need to follow to learn about Chastity."

"If you have a sexual drive that bothers you, or nags at you like gnats that fly around 'ripe fruits' and you have the desire to overcome this burden, ask Jesus to help you. I will send My Holy Spirit to touch your Mind and Heart in a way that the Holy Spirit will be able to help you turn your sexual drive into SPIRITUAL DRIVE. I could take away your 'Free Will' but then it would not be your Sacrifice! It is your attempts at Sacrifice that pleases me."

"The moments that you overcome your human desires, and direct them to My Son Jesus as Sacrifice—My Holy Spirit will Shower you with Graces. Then, the Graces that are needed to display all of the 'Fruits and Gifts of the Holy Spirit will come to you. You will discover them when you ask for them to come forward in your life. 'Yoke' your weakness to my Son's Strength. He will walk this Journey with you. That—'IS' WHY HE CAME—YOU SEE—IT IS ALL ABOUT YOU! My Grace is sufficient for you, but you must use your "free will'-and ask for it!"

Jesus was and remains our example of chastity. Chastity is more than abstaining from a genital sexual expression of what our world thinks that love is. It is about giving those genital desires that are natural and God given to express in the holy union of marriage, a mutual love for another and to be open to new life, to God, and allowing God to turn them into spiritual growth and development for the greater good of our soul. Chastity is important in our single lives and at times in our married lives.

In (Ecclesiastes 3:2), it says, "There is a time and a place for everything under heaven. A time to be born a time to die; a time to plant, a time to sow; ... A time to love and a time to be loved; ... A time to hate and a time to refrain from hating; ... Time to embrace, and a time to refrain from embracing."

To live a chaste life is to say to God, "I love you more than all else, even my human desires of gratification. Please help my weaknesses, Jesus. Help me to desire you more than what covers your presence within me." I praise you and thank you, Jesus, for your human example for us. Teach each one of us to understand what the fruits and gifts of the Holy Spirit mean for our own growth and development toward the Trinity. Understanding chastity and its implementation is just one of the tools that you have given us to "grow into your image and likeness."

The creed will help us to see that the Holy Spirit will help each one of us find the power to overcome the evil one and the subtle seductive way that we are lured into sin. We need to look to our Blessed Mother, the humble servant of her God, who sacrificed the life she and Joseph had planned, to choose to say yes to bring salvation to the world. There is only one way that we can show our fruit of gratitude for their sacrifice to the Trinity and the Holy Family of God here on earth. It is to receive the fruits and the gifts of the Holy Spirit and bring them into our daily lives, and then reach out to another person that our God has sent into your life to share this good news with. Doing this, you will be sharing your charisms with another to build up the Body of Christ.

Learning how to live a chaste life will help you on this journey to Jesus. There will be times in your life that you will need to be chaste, at times even in marriage.

Gifts

Wisdom

Understanding

Knowledge

Counsel

Fortitude

Piety

Fear of the Lord

Isaiah 11:2-3

Wisdom

Wisdom as Gift

Wisdom is a gift of the Holy Spirit that we are given in our baptism and is enhanced in our confirmation to help us grow in God's love.

My friend Vic told me, "I have heard that the beginning of wisdom is when we realize how much we don't know." My eyes were opened, and I began a diligent study of the fruits and gifts of the Holy Spirit. My hope is that something here touches your heart.

In (Sirach 1:1), it says, "All wisdom comes from the Lord." And in verse 12 it says "He who fears the Lord will have a happy end; even on the day of his death he will be blessed." And verse 14 says, "Fullness of wisdom is fear of the Lord; she inebriates men with her fruits" (St. Joseph's).

Fear of the Lord is looking at God with awe, or great reverence or wonder. And in (James 3:17, Ignatius), it says, "The wisdom from above is first pure, then peaceable, gentle, open to reason, full of mercy and good fruits, without uncertainty or insincerity. And the harvest of righteousness is won in peace by those who make peace." Ponder those words about wisdom. We each should pray for this gift to fill us. In (Proverbs 8:35, Ignatius), it says, "Whoever finds me [wisdom] finds life and draws forth and obtains favor from the Lord."

Seek wisdom; it is found within the pages of the one book our God wrote: The Bible. The Bible is full of information that we all need to learn to be able to come to our Lord and Savior for our redemption. The Bible contains many passages that speak to us of wisdom, but true wisdom is found when we take the time to be with our God.

Go to (Matthew 5:1–11, St. Joseph's) and read the Beatitudes: "Seeing the crowds, He went up the mountain and after He sat down, His disciples came to Him, and He began to teach them, saying:' Blessed are the poor in spirit, the reign of God is theirs. Blessed are the sorrowing, they shall be consoled. Blessed are the lowly; for they shall inherit the land. Blessed are they who hunger and thirst for holiness; for they shall have their fill. Blessed are those who show mercy; mercy shall be theirs. Blessed are the single hearted; for they shall see God. Blessed too are the Peacemakers, for they will be called sons of God. Blessed are they who are persecuted for holiness sake; the reign of God is theirs. Blessed are you when they insult you and persecute you and utter every kind of evil against you (falsely) because of me. Be glad and rejoice, for your reward is great in Heaven. They persecuted the prophets before you in the same way."

Wisdom is found in the simplicity of the divine love and compassion that Jesus showed and shared with His apostles and the people who came to Him to learn from Him, and to be healed.

Find wisdom in the passage from (Matthew 22:36 St. Joseph's), when the Pharisee tested Jesus by asking, "Teacher, which commandment in the law is the greatest?" Jesus answered "You shall love the Lord your God, with all your heart, with all your soul, and with all your mind. This is the greatest and first commandment. The second is like it. You shall love your neighbor as yourself. The whole law and the prophets depend on these two commandments."

Jesus is trying to teach all who will listen to Him, both then and now, that if we place God first in our hearts and treat others the way that we want to be treated, we will be fulfilling the commandments that Jesus feels is the most important for our salvation. True wisdom comes to us when we realize that there is an emptiness in our hearts that only God can fill. True wisdom comes when we understand satan is out to get our souls from God. Satan wants to lead us through subtle ways, to the ways of human pleasure, instead of God's joy and true happiness. God's joy and happiness come into our lives when we accept the power of the Holy Spirit working in our lives through the fruits and the gifts of the Holy Spirit. Wisdom comes to us when we intertwine Jesus's living example into our daily lives by using our fruits and gifts of the Holy Spirit to share this good news about our salvation with others. That is our charisms in action.

When each Christian uses their charisms for spreading the kingdom of God, we are all woven together, and will present the world with the one Body of Christ that our world needs so badly. We each have an intricate part to play in the grand scheme of things. In (Jeremiah 29:11 St. Joseph's) God said, "For I know well the plans I have in mind for you, says the Lord. Plans for your welfare, not for woe! Plans to give you a future of hope. When you call me, when you go to pray to me, I will listen to you. When you look for me with all your heart, you will find me with you, says the Lord, and I will change your lot; I will gather you together from all the nations, and all the places to which I have banished you, says the Lord, and bring you back to the place from which I have exiled you."

90

The sin of Adam and Eve has exiled us from a close relationship with God. Our baptism in Jesus as our Lord and Savior brings us to the place where we can choose to learn how to mend that broken relationship with God. This is personal, one on one with Jesus.

The fruits of the Holy Spirit that we receive in our baptism are the very personality of Jesus. They are joy, peace, charity, patience, kindness, goodness, generosity, gentleness, faithfulness, self-control, modesty, and chastity (Galatians 5:22–23 and CCC 1832). These were lived by Jesus and taught to us by His word and example, when He came to earth to mend our broken relationship with God. The gifts of the Holy Spirit are also given to us in our baptism to help us desire a close relationship with God. The gifts of the Holy Spirit are wisdom, understanding, knowledge, counsel, fortitude, piety, and fear of the Lord. These are listed in (Isaiah 11:2, St. Joseph's and CCC 1831), and are all present within us, waiting for us to feel the desire for more of God in our life.

This knowledge is a very important action of our free will that we need to activate. To manifest these fruits and gifts of the Holy Spirit, we need to become an active participant in this relationship that we desire to build with God, who is our Father. This comes through our acceptance of His Son Jesus as our Lord and Savior, and then the action of asking for the fruits and gifts to come forward in our lives is to help us develop our life in Christ and to share our life with others.

In (Matthew 6:33), it says, "Seek first His kingship over you, His way of holiness, and all these things will be given to you." We each are called to try to follow Jesus's example in what we think, say, and do. We are all called to holiness: "Be perfect as your Father is perfect." (Matthew 5:48 St. Josephs). Study the Beatitudes, and try to weave them into your life. St. Francis of Assisi chose to follow Jesus by living the example of His teachings. Look at the Prayer of St. Francis, and ponder those words. Wisdom comes, with knowledge and understanding. The words of St. Francis's prayer are truly a blending of the fruits and gifts of the Holy Spirit into our lives:

"Lord, make me an instrument of your peace, where there is hatred—let me sow love. Where there is injury—pardon. Doubt—

Faith, Despair—Hope, Darkness—Light, and Sadness—Joy. O Divine Master, grant that I may not so much seek to be consoled as to console. To be understood as to understand, to be loved as to love. For it is in giving that we receive. It is in pardoning that we are pardoned. And it is in dying that we are born into eternal life."

If we can shape our thoughts and actions around these words, we will be living the fruits and gifts of the Holy Spirit, and we will be walking in the very footsteps of Jesus.

Understanding

Understanding as Gift

Understanding is the gift of the Holy Spirit that we are given in our baptism and is enhanced at our confirmation to help us grow in God's love.

In (Ephesians 3:18–19, St. Joseph's), it says, "Thus you will be able to grasp fully, with the holy ones, the breadth and length and height and depth of Christ's love, and experience this love which surpasses all knowledge, so that you may attain to the fullness of God Himself."

Wow! God desires that we try to comprehend His great love for each one of us. Fullness means to be filled or completely occupied with a thought or a plan. God desires to be in complete union with each one of us. He will not force us.

Understand that the first move was from God when He created us in His image and likeness. The next move was from God. He placed us where we would be presented with an opportunity to hear the message that Jesus calls each one of us to repentance for our salvation. Then He waits for us to make the decision with our own free will. In our baptism, we are saying yes to the belief that Jesus Christ is our Lord and Savior. We are saying yes to understanding that if we follow the narrow road, we will find the way through Jesus to the Father. This message has been passed down by the power of the Holy Spirit through word of mouth (tradition) or through the written word through the prophets.

In (1 Corinthians 14:29, St. Joseph's), it says, "Brothers do not be childish in your outlook. Be Children as far as evil is concerned, but in mind be mature." In (Proverbs 2:6 ST. Joseph's), it says, "For the Lord gives wisdom, and from His mouth come knowledge and understanding, He has counsel in store for the upright, He is the shield of those who walk honestly, guarding the paths of justice, protecting the way of His pious ones." And in (Proverbs 9:10, St. Joseph's), it says," The beginning of Wisdom is Fear of the Lord [which means to look at Him with awe or wonder) and the knowledge of the Holy One is understanding."

We have so much to learn and we have so much to lose if we do not take the time to learn. We each need to aim for heaven by following the Commandments of God. If we should happen to fall into sin just before death, we might go to purgatory, where we have the chance of reaching heaven. At that point, we can no longer pray for ourselves or do anything to change our plight; we are totally dependent upon God's mercy and the prayers of the faithful here on earth. But if we would be aiming for purgatory and miss, we would have eternity without God. What a horrendous price to pay. Come with Jesus on this journey to the Father.

In (Ephesians 5:17, St. Joseph's), it says, "Do not continue in ignorance, but try to discern the will of the Lord." In (1 John 5:20, St. Joseph's), it says," We know that the Son of God has come and has given us discernment (understanding) so that we may know the One that is true. And we are in the true one—that is, in His Son Jesus Christ. He is the true God and eternal life." And in (Proverbs 3:13, St. Joseph's), it says, "Happy the man who finds wisdom, the man who gains understanding." And in (Job 32:8, St. Joseph's), it says, "But it is a spirit in man, the Breath of the Almighty, that gives him understanding."

This understanding is what I experienced in the confessional: complete sorrow for having offended my Father. When I surrendered my sins and burdens, I felt the presence of Jesus in the person of my priest and Jesus took my sins to Himself and freed me of my burdens. I felt clean and that I did not have to hide within or from myself any more. It was a beautiful cleansing and awakening of my own spirit within me! I praise God for loving me this much.

And it says further in (Luke 24:45, St. Joseph's), "Then He opened their minds to understand the Scriptures." This is God the Holy Spirit that the Father and the Son sends to us at our baptism and brings forward in our confirmation, to enlighten our hearts to the knowledge and understanding that Jesus is the covenant between God and man.

Since my repentance (which simply means that I took a deeper look at my life, and decided to ask if Jesus would show me my sins so that I could confess them to Him and ask His forgiveness), the Scriptures have been opened to my mind. They were not written for the people of Jesus's time only. They were written for all who will listen to their timeless message. It is amazing to me that the same passages that I read and heard several months ago that didn't make any sense as to how it pertained to my life today, now seems to have been written for me personally. Believe in your heart that if you know Jesus as your personal savior, He will help you find and stay on the path to our Father. That means you have accepted the knowledge that Jesus humbled Himself by leaving His rightful place at the right hand of His Father in heaven, to give us the opportunity to choose to walk with Him to the cross.

Let's talk about the cross. We each need to understand that it was an extremely painful torture and gruesome death that Jesus willingly accepted in order to fulfill the covenant that God had promised. Adam and Eve believed the temptations of satan. Their mistake was costly not only for them but also for all mankind and for the Trinity. Can you imagine God the Father watching His beloved son, His only son being beaten, and His flesh being ripped from His body during the scourging? Can you imagine the broken heart of the Father as Jesus walked the way of the cross? Can you imagine the agony of God the Father and the Holy Spirit as they watched and endured the pain God the Son experienced when He stretched out His arms willingly to receive the nails? And remember, He died with your name on His lips.

Through the author and Catholic theologian Scott Hahn and his book called *The Lambs Supper*, I have learned much about my

Catholicism and the Crucifixion. The Passover Meal of the Jewish tradition that Jesus shared with His apostles on that night before He died was just the beginning of the process of the covenant that would be completed upon the cross, where He shared the fourth cup—the cup of His blood that was poured out for all mankind, for the salvation of their souls.

Scott Hahn says, "Only a Jewish scholar would have noticed that Jesus had not completed the full Passover service before leaving the Upper Room that night. He KNEW the Service. Why would He DO that! He couldn't have just forgotten it! The service was not completed! Jesus DID NOT PASS AND SHARE THE CUP THE FOURTH TIME as it had always been done since that First Passover in Egypt, with Moses. Instead He folded His napkin (which symbolized He was finished), and He said, 'I shall not drink of the fruit of the vine again until My Kingdom comes.' Then He got up and went to the Garden to pray." It was from upon the Cross that, near THE END-Jesus said ", I THIRST!" And someone" gave Him sour wine on a Hyssop Branch", THAT was the moment that "HE RECEIVED—HE WHAT? HE RECEIVED THE FOURTH CUP of the FRUIT OF THE VINE of the Passover Meal that was started in the Upper Room and finished upon the Cross!" That was the completion of the covenant of our salvation! And then He surrendered His soul to the Father.

Surrender is a word that means to yield or relinquish or let go of. Sometimes we are frightened of that word. In regard to surrender to Jesus, we should not be afraid. Through the power of the Holy Spirit and the hands of the prophets, God has written in the Holy Bible 365 times, "Be not afraid."

The Bible is the one book that God wrote. It is a love story from God to us about His love for His children. In (John 6:35, Ignatius), Jesus says," I am the Bread of life. He who comes to me shall never hunger, and he who believes in me shall never thirst." Also in (John 8:12, Ignatius), it says, "I am the light of the world; he who follows me will not walk in darkness, but will have the light of the world."

Jesus is the light that shows us the way to God the Father. This light is shining all the time. To see this light, we need to look for it.

For the people who travel the seas, a lighthouse stands as a beacon in the darkness to guide travelers to safety. Jesus stands as that same beacon for each of us to lead us to the safety of His loving arms. Look for the light of Christ upon His cross of salvation. And do not be afraid.

Jesus is the light of the world. The Scriptures tell us that we are all part of the Body of Christ. Each one of us is important in bringing the light of the world, Christ, to other people. The gift of understanding from the Holy Spirit, helps each one of us to experience each gift and fruit of the Holy Spirit in our own special way—the way that is designed by God the Father and the Son, and breathed into each of us by the power of the Holy Spirit when we ask to be the instruments or vessels for the people whom the Trinity wants to draw to Jesus.

Here on earth, we are the vessels by which Jesus's message will be shared with others. We are the disciples whom Jesus has entrusted this great mission to. In our baptism, we become the temple that holds the Trinity within our bodies. Our soul becomes the holy tabernacle that holds Jesus as our treasure. JESUS is the pearl of great price that in (Matthew 13:46, St. Joseph's) the merchant, after finding the pearl, went and sold all that he had and bought it. In our Christianity, we each are that merchant searching for Jesus, the pearl of great price. The gift of understanding is realizing we don't have to search any further than our own hearts.

The gift of understanding comes to maturity in our life when we discover that "Jesus is the Way and the Truth and the Life, and that no one comes to the Father except through Him" (John 14:6, St. Joseph's). We are the hands and feet and lips of the Trinity! It is through us as Jesus's disciples, that the light of Christ will shine out to other travelers on this road we are on together. We will not do justice to the Trinity if we hold Jesus within the tabernacle of our soul. I just got comfortable with the knowledge that Jesus dwells within me all the time.

We need to find the way to share this light. We need to allow our body to become the monstrance, which is a holy vessel, that holds our bread of life, Jesus, our Savior, in full view for all to be able to see. We are to become the vessel that the light of Christ shines out of as a beacon to be able to draw others to Jesus. Let us begin this growth with thanksgiving and praise for God's great mercy for each of us. I thank you, God, that you have opened my eyes to this understanding.

The Spiritual gift of understanding is given by the Holy Spirit to help us to be able to help another. It intertwines with the gifts of wisdom, counsel and fortitude depending what is needed by the receiver, and will help the fruits come alive in you and *blossom* to show, and share the love of Jesus.

In the Fruit of Patience, I shared with you the story that changed my life the most. The death of my daughter, Heather Marie, on May 25, 1976. Already Crushed by the sorrow of her death, my husband asked for a divorce one week later. With him, went my four step children whom I loved as my own. I went into a deep depression. I simply *existed*... We were divorced at the end of July, I went back to work as an LPN in August. I was blessed with several good friends at my church in Manito, two of which invited me to 'make a Cursillo.' At that time, there was a two-year waiting list, but God orchestrated it so that there was a cancellation in November. Those three days left me with a warm feeling inside again, and I knew that God was out there waiting for me to call on Him for the help that I needed.

In depression, it's hard to know how to call out to God. But I found in my journaling that Jesus was right there walking beside me...waiting for me to call His name.

My help came in the form of Christianity. The love of Jesus flowing out of other people. First Ann, who sponsored me to Cursillo. Then the Priest, Fr. Tom who listened to my story of pain, and I could see his shoulders weighted down for me, and my deep pain. He told me, *"God did not mean for you to bear this all alone,"* and that I needed to share my pain with someone to be able to heal from it. He gave me the name of a family counselor named Joe, who helped me begin my journey back to a healthy life. Joe encouraged me to journal my thoughts, In the beginning I didn't even have thoughts...I was *empty...broken...and discarded*, but, there was a place deep inside of me that I could feel goodness and kindness, these fruits of the Holy Spirit came alive in the Christians who were sent by God to help me heal. By the power of the Holy Spirit, these Fruits, radiated out of them ... into me...even if for only a little while. The above story demonstrates how, when a Charism is needed for someone... the Holy Spirit sends someone with those gifts to be the hands, feet and lips of Jesus to the wounded person.

In my brokenness, I needed to be loved. God sent someone to me with the Charisms of Encouragement, Celibacy, Counsel, Helps, Discernment, Giving, Knowledge, Mercy, Pastoring, Healing and maybe more. The Priest probably had all these gifts...but the Team work of a Christian Community in action...'The Body of Christ,' came to my rescue...and I found the Jesus within me once more. The fruits of the Spirit radiated out of each person to help me find my way back to God. Those fruits were Peace, Love, Patience, Gentleness, Faithfulness, Generosity, Goodness, Kindness, Self-control, Modesty and Chastity. These are the very personality of Jesus, flowing out of each person.

As I look back at these events...I can clearly see the Charisms working in each person. Thank you, God. The beauty of a Charism is that it never stops. It is received, then the recipient will find some-one who will need the Charism that they can give. God's gift to us is returned to Him, through our love for each other.

I married again about six years later and about 2 weeks after our daughter Megan was born, a chaplain from Methodist Hospital called me to help a mother who had just experienced her third mis-carriage...and needed to talk to someone who could 'understand' her pain. I said 'Yes" and she came to my home to talk. Three weeks later the chaplain called again, and said, that he 'had a few more people who needed to talk to me. That week there were seven couples in my home. We shared our expectations and losses, our pain and sorrow, tears and laughter. Yes, *laughter!* Looking back, the Holy Spirit led us through the gamut of emotions. I had learned how to LIVE with my loss. It was simply by allowing others into my life, with all that it entailed. We never had a meeting that did not share laughter and tears and back to laughter. That is a necessary process in learning how to live with the loss, not die with it. The Spiritual Gift of Understanding coming full circle within 'The Circle of God's Divine Love."

Knowledge

Knowledge, a Gift of the Holy Spirit

"O Christ Our Lord and God. You chose Twelve apostles and seventy-two disciples and sent them into the world to preach the Good News of Life and Salvation. You chose four evangelists; Matthew, Mark, Luke and John, as children of your love, that they may announce your word by the Power of the Holy Spirit. Matthew proclaimed the mystery of your mission as the Messiah. Mark spoke of the mystery of your humanity. Luke announced the mystery of your plan of salvation. John reflected on the mystery of your Divinity."

"O Christ through the four Evangelist you gave us the "BOOK OF LIFE," the gospel of your life-giving Good News, which gives life to all the faithful. Now we implore you through your Holy Apostles to guide our lives according to your will." This is a prayer that the congregation prays during the Maronite Rite Mass, of the Catholic Church.

This was the beginning of evangelization of the new kingdom through Jesus Christ. When Jesus spoke to the apostles before He was crucified, He said in (John 14:12), "I solemnly assure you, The man who has faith in me will do the work that I do, and greater far than these. Why? Because I go to the Father, and whatever you ask in My name I will do so as to glorify the Father in the Son." (St. Joseph's).

Whoever believes in Jesus receives the commission to carry on the healing work. "The only reason it will be greater works, is because it would not be only Him, one person Healing it would be multiplied by the number of believers," from the book by Barbara Shlemon Ryan called *Healing Prayer*. And He sent them to all the nations of the earth.

Alone I can do little. All my life I have tried to follow Jesus. I did okay, but it was not until I surrendered my heart to Jesus in the confessional that I truly met Jesus. It is difficult to explain the life change that began taking place inside of me. I don't feel much different, but I *am* different! There is a longing for more of Jesus that calls me to Him. Four and one-half years later, and I still can't get enough of Jesus. The more that I give of myself to Jesus, the more He multiplies my fruits and gifts that have been lying dormant inside of me for my whole lifetime. I do not remember much of anything about the fruits and gifts of the Holy Spirit from when I was confirmed. So my quest has begun, and the Holy Spirit leads me through the Scriptures (the gift of knowledge being opened up for me), much like I believe that He led the apostles and the disciples.

God has placed me in places that were beyond my ability to have chosen, and He has surrounded me with people that could see my possibilities and have helped me to this place in my life. That is what a Charism in action is all about. I tell you now that it is never too late to begin this journey to your inner spirit where the Trinity dwells. I was sixty-three when this journey began for me.

If we believe that Jesus is our Lord and Savior, these words are speaking about each one of us. It is our lack of knowledge of the Word (the Bible) and our lack of faith or trust in ourselves that holds us back from being all that God desires us to be.

In (Colossians 2:2, St. Joseph's), it says, "I wish their hearts to be strengthened and themselves to be closely united in love, enriched with the full assurance by their knowledge of the mystery of God namely Christ in whom every treasure of wisdom and knowledge is hidden."

In (Proverbs 15:14), it says, "The mind of the intelligent seeks knowledge, but the mouth of a fool feeds on folly." Choose wisely what you do and say. In (Hosea 6:3), it says, "Let us know, let us strive to know the Lord." The gospels will teach us everything we need to know: to come to the well and drink the living water that only Jesus can give! Do not be afraid. Everything He asks us to do, He has done before us. He has left His footprints upon this earth for us to follow, and He has left His wisdom upon the pages of the Bible, the one book that God wrote. Jesus is the covenant between God and man.

When we encounter Jesus, our lives change. When others see this change coming forth in us, they want to know what happened. When we have encountered Jesus in our heart and have asked Him to come into our lives, it is just the beginning for us. To be able to have the love of the Trinity grow in our hearts, we must infuse Him into our lives. We infuse Him by becoming an active participant in our Christianity.

We need to ask the Holy Spirit to bless us by bringing our fruits and gifts forward in our lives so that we can try to follow Jesus.

As we try to live the Beatitudes and others see this beautiful change taking place in our life, they will want some of this joy! Sharing this joy of the Lord (a fruit of the Holy Spirit) and what He has done in your life becomes your gift; it is now transformed into a charism that you give away to "build up the kingdom of God." When the sharing of your charisms causes another person to realize they also have fruits and gifts that need to be brought forward in their own life, this is when your charism has now become a gift to God.

In (2 Peter 1:5–8), it says, "This is reason enough for you to make every effort to undergird your virtue with faith, your discernment with virtue, and your self-control with discernment; this self-control, in turn, should lead to perseverance, and perseverance to piety, and piety to care for your brother, and care for your brother, to love."

This is what Jesus taught by His life example. And when we have the beauty of Jesus oozing from within us, we must know in our hearts that it is by the power of the Holy Spirit that Jesus shines out through us. Let him shine. We need to be knowledgeable of Jesus to grow like Him and follow Him to the Father. Make the time to get to know Him in Scripture, and most importantly in the Eucharist.

(Luke 12:6) says, "I tell you, whoever acknowledges Me before men, the Son of Man will acknowledge him before the angels of God." Wow! What a promise to us from our Savior! All we need to do is to stand up with Jesus as one of His followers and be willing to do as He did.

In (2 Peter 1:3), it says, "His Divine Power has given us everything required for life and godliness, through the knowledge of Him who called us by His own glory and goodness." Jesus calls us to Himself through the power of the Holy Spirit. He has left His footprints behind for us to follow if we desire to spend eternity with the Trinity. Our free will lets us make the choice of our eternity. It is with the fruits and gifts of the Holy Spirit that we obtain this knowledge understanding, wisdom, and strength. It will be through prayer and fear of the Lord that we can make an informed decision about our eternity.

"It is God's great Mercy that heals and leads us to Jesus, and if we rejoice in God's Mercy, the way we believe in miracles we would lead others to Jesus." This is part of a homily on the feast day of St. Peter and St. Paul, sinners turned saints by the love of Jesus. There truly is hope for each one of us. Be patient with yourself; we cannot take it all in at one time. The apostles lived with Jesus for three years, and could not understand until the Holy Spirit came upon them "in a mighty way" at Pentecost. We have a patient and loving God whose desire is to spend eternity with each one of us. Place your trust in our Triune Godhead.

In (Proverbs 24:3–5), it says, "By wisdom is a house built, by understanding is it made firm; And by knowledge are its rooms filled with every precious and pleasing possession. A wise man is more powerful than a strong man, and a man of knowledge than a man of might." Knowledge does not mean being a scholar. It means knowing the Trinity in your mind, heart, soul, and, most of all, in the "inmost part of you"—your spirit! Each one of us has this capability. It does not matter how much you know; it only matters how much you feel the Love of Jesus in your being.

All Bible quotes are from St. Joseph's.

Alone I can do little. The Spiritual Gift of knowledge changed me from an, "I don't understand this," to, "I can't get enough of this information about God, and what He has done for me!" I began to wonder, "Why didn't I know this before? Where has my mind been throughout my life? How did I not hear this and understand?" The words that I was beginning to understand for the first time, were familiar, but the message was lost to me.

We are all given the Spiritual Gift of Knowledge at our baptism (found in Isaiah). I believe that it simply laid dormant until the moment in the confessional when I truly met Jesus for the first time. Through the power of the Holy Spirit, Jesus became ALIVE for me in the skin of the shepherd that Jesus chose for me.

After my deep examination of conscious while reading the book by Max Lucado called, "The true meaning of Christmas," my heart was split open…and the wounds of my lifetime poured out. In my fear of not being able to recall them in the confessional, I wrote them down as a backup for my poor memory and the emptiness that my mind feels when I am anxious. After I confessed my sins and pain, I reached for the 'list in my purse,' and as I did, my shepherd asked, "Is that, what we were talking about?" Timidly I said "Yes." He reached and took the list from my hand…he drew them up to his own heart, and began tearing the list of my sins into tiny pieces. (pause) As he was shredding them, he was saying to me, "Give them to me! They are yours no longer! They are mine now!" I felt a weight being lifted off me, and I looked up into his face, and my shepherd's countenance had changed from a large man with light hair and eyes, to a small man with dark hair and eyes. At that same moment, I felt an 'ice cold' 'spray of water' (almost like a shower) all over me like when we are sprinkled with holy water at church. That spray was so powerful that I was forced to take a HUGE deep breath into my whole being. At that same moment, I was looking, into the eyes of Jesus, my Savior, who has nothing but compassion and love for me. It was only a *moment*, but I feel Jesus knew that I needed the 'extra' sensory gifts of His presence in my life to help me experience conversion.

I know that through the power of the Holy Spirit, God's Merciful Grace was showered upon me for my own sanctification. What made this confession different than all the ones before was the deep, deep sorrow in my heart for having offended my God. I know I had never understood that, what I do and say, affects my relationship with God for eternity.

This *MISTICAL* experience in the confessional, was the beginning of my *New life in Christ* and my quest for more of God began. This quest for knowledge of God, is a drive to study in a way that I have never experienced before. I am driven by the Holy Spirit to understand and share what I am learning with others. The Spiritual Gift of knowledge is given…to be shared in some way. Therefore, the Holy Spirit endows me with an ability to sort out my thoughts on paper. As I gather them together, it becomes my story.

My Charism of writing comes alive in me, because the Holy Spirit has increased my desire to understand what God has done for me! What Jesus has done for me…and what the Holy Spirit has done for me and continues to do for me for the salvation of my soul and the souls of all those whom I can touch with my Gifts.

As I discover the passion which Jesus shared with all that He encountered in His life, the fruits of His life become my own. Peace… and love for myself as Jesus's adopted sister, and the love for those whom I encounter in my life that need to know and understand what Jesus did for them, becomes my gift back to God.

My deep sorrow for having offended God by my desire for sensual pleasure…brought me to *encounter* Jesus's great love for me in the confessional! The desire for those forgiven sins has left me since that confession. I praise you and thank you God that you have empowered me with your gifts of counsel and understanding of what sin is in my life, and have given me the strength to overcome them, and to continue to see the deep ones in my soul.

The gift of knowledge is intertwined with the other gifts, which enable us to come close to our creator and Loving Father. Do not be afraid of turning your life over to Jesus, it has made my life much fuller.

Counsel

Counsel as a Gift of the Holy Spirit

The gift of counsel is one of the active gifts of the Holy Spirit. It is designed to bring the gifts of the Holy Spirit from deep within our being to share with another when it is needed. It is ours to keep.

The gift of counsel is given to us in our baptism, to help each one of us to be sensitive to another's pain and sorrow, and enables us to support them with and through their burdens. In (Isaiah 49:13–16, St. Joseph's), it tells us, "Sing out, O heavens, and rejoice O earth, break forth into song, you mountains. For the Lord Comforts His people and shows mercy to His afflicted." But Zion said, "The Lord has forgotten me." Can a mother forget her infant, be without tenderness for the child of her womb? Even should she forget, I WILL NEVER FORGET YOU. SEE, UPON THE PALMS OF MY HANDS I HAVE WRITTEN YOUR NAME; your walls are ever before me."

Our names were written upon the palms of God our Father's hands (He said so) as He created each one of us. Our names are also written upon the palms of Jesus's hands within the nail holes when He willingly stretched out His arms and accepted the nails for our redemption. It is unbelievable to me yet quite comforting to know that when Jesus surrendered His soul to His Father, to complete the covenant, each one of our names was upon His lips as He went to the Father.

Knowing all this makes it a little easier to accept the responsibility of when we feel alone; it is not because God has moved away from us. It is we who allow the presence of temptation and pain to cover the presence of God within our soul so that we cannot see Him. Once we are blinded to the presence of God within us, it is easy for satan to draw us from the narrow road to Jesus, on to the "wider path of destruction" for our souls.

Jesus now reigns in majesty with His Father. Together they send their Holy Spirit down to help us through our burdens and sorrows. The Trinity knows what it means to be hurt, rejected, abandoned, and to have a broken heart. It is through our sin that they know this pain. That is why it was so important for them to give us the gift of counsel. The Trinity needs each one of us to use our hearts of compassion, and our body (the only one Jesus has here on earth, the church) to envelop the wounded into Jesus's loving arms and help them come to healing.

Each one of us is invited to come to the cross for healing. No one is left out of this covenant except by their own decision. Don't just accept that what you are going through is what God wants for you. God said in (Jeremiah 29:11, St. Joseph's), "For I know full well the plans that I have for you. Plans for your welfare, not for woe! Plans to give you a future full of hope. When you call on me, and when you pray to me, I will listen to you. When you look for me you will find me. Yes, when you seek me with all your heart, you will find me with you, says the Lord, and I will change your lot."

God says, "When you seek me with all your heart," those are the key words.

Jesus came to heal all wounds of all people who will call Him Lord and Savior. We need to learn to pray for healing for whatever our pain is. We each need to ask the Great Physician to heal our wounds and then present ourselves to the ones that God has given the charism of counseling and the charism of "intercessory prayer and healing." They will become the "hands, feet, lips, ears, heart, and soul of compassion that envelop you with the loving and forgiving arms of Jesus. Come receive consolation.

It says in (Psalm 73:21–24), "Since my heart was embittered and my soul deeply wounded, I was stupid and could not understand; I was like a brute beast in your presence. Yet I am always with you; you take hold of my right hand. With your counsel you guide me, and at the end you receive me in glory."

The Holy Spirit is our counsel. He is sent from the Father and the Son to lead us in the ways of Jesus. Through the power of the Holy Spirit, our gift of counsel will be manifested through our charisms of the Holy Spirit. Don't worry about what you will do or say. When you reach out in the love of Jesus to another person, the Holy Spirit will fill you with the gifts of wisdom, understanding, and knowledge. These are the contemplative gifts of the Holy Spirit. It's all about sharing the love, sacrifice, and salvation of Jesus our Savior.

You who are blessed with the gift of counsel need to thank God for that gift. It comes directly from God the Father and from Jesus. Reach out to the people who God sends to you. Do not be afraid. The Holy Spirit will direct your movements, your words, and your heart.

Fortitude

Fortitude as 'Gift of the Holy Spirit'

The 'gift of fortitude from the Holy Spirit', is given to us to keep. It is a quality of inner strength given to us by the Holy Spirit to face all fear with faith.

Fortitude is a word that is much more than the word Strength. It means: 'strength of mind that enables a person to meet danger or bear pain or adversity with courage. Courage is the ability to conquer fear or despair.'

Jesus, both human and divine HAD to be baptized by the Holy Spirit. At the Jordon River He received this Baptism, and began His Mission of giving all mankind the ability to follow in His footsteps. Through the POWER of the Holy Spirit, 2000 years later Jesus is still gathering His brothers and sisters to Himself. I THANK GOD for that. All that each person has to do is RECEIVE JESUS, as their Personal Savior, ask Jesus into your heart and BELIEVE that the Power of the Holy Spirit—will fill you with the Trinity's great love and desires for you. This power gives you all of the 'Gifts and Fruits' of the Holy Spirit, and fills you at your Baptism. The Holy Spirit waits, until YOU decide to put GOD FIRST in your life, and then will direct you on the path of righteousness. This decision will bring you to a place that will begin—your Journey to Jesus. Like the Samaritan Woman, who 'met Jesus at the Well', you too will need to 'Come to the Well'—and drink of the Wisdom that lies within.

'The Well', is the Bible. It is a love letter from God to us, His children. To mature as Christians It will take Fortitude, Courage, Piety, Trust, Faith, Joy, just to name a few for you. Drawing all of the Virtues into your life will bring you into a better relationship with Our Lord and Savior. They are: Faith, Hope, Charity, Humility, Patience, Perseverance, and Obedience. Pray for them. God DESIRES us to be HIS Children. We can only become God's Children when we ask Jesus into our heart as our Lord and Savior. Jesus truly—only asks of us two great things; to LOVE GOD WITH OUR WHOLE HEART, MIND AND SOUL—and our neighbor as ourselves.

If we follow these two great commands of Jesus, all the other commandments will fall into place for us. The Trinity gives us a lifetime to accomplish this. God the Father plants the seed of desire in our hearts. By YOUR WILL—YOU must choose to allow Jesus into your heart. He left a path for us to follow—He did not say that it would be easy—but He did promise that He would send us the help that we need to reach Him on this Journey of OURS, to the Foot of His Cross. Jesus and His Father—Our Father because of what Jesus has done for us; sent us the third person of the Trinity to BE WITH US, and guide us through life, to the "Way and the Truth, and the Life," which is Jesus, Our Lord and Savior.

Look to the Holy Family to find the example of Fortitude. Without Fortitude, Joseph on his own could not have protected Mary and this tiny, PRECIOUS infant—Jesus—that had been entrusted to him to love and care for—and protect—from the forces of evil that sought to destroy Him. Mary could not have said "YES," without Fortitude! Slowly read her Magnificat (Luke 1: 46-56), and listen, to her great devotion to God. In His humanity—even Jesus, fully human and fully Divine needed fortitude to overcome the evil one. JESUS HUMBLED HIMSELF—and came to earth as a tiny baby—-to give us the example of how to LIVE. The "Fruits and Gifts of the Holy Spirit', when brought forward by our 'free will', is GIVEN to us as a Gift—to lead each one of us to our personal Transfiguration!

The evil one seeks to destroy all that is good in our world. He seeks to destroy each one of us. The evil one reaches for our souls through the pleasures of the flesh. Subtle seduction's lure us away from the narrow road with Jesus. But, and there is always 'a but', Jesus sends us His Holy Spirit to direct and lead us to the VERY FOOTSTEPS OF JESUS!—We find THESE FOOTSTEPS— within the Words of the Gospels! We cannot do this alone! We NEED the Trinity! And we NEED our Christian Community of Church, to support us while we Journey to Jesus.

Wisdom, Knowledge, and Understanding, are the 'Contemplative Gifts of the Holy Spirit', and are necessary in our lives, for us to be able to utilize all of the other 'Gifts of the Holy Spirit', which are the 'ACTION GIFTS OF THE HOLY SPIRIT'. Fortitude is where we draw Courage from. I invite you to come to 'The Well' (Bible), and start, or re-start YOUR PERSONAL JOURNEY TO JESUS!

In (Ephesians 6; 10-12) it says, "Finally be strong in the Lord and in His mighty power. Put on the Full Armor of God so that you can take your stand against the devil's schemes. For our struggle is not against flesh and blood, but the rulers, against the powers of this dark world and against the spiritual forces of evil in the heavenly realms......Stand firm then, with the belt of Truth buckled around your waist, with the breastplate of righteousness in place, and with your feet fitted with the readiness that comes from the gospel of peace." Paul is telling us in this letter to the Ephesians, that we need to be TOTALLY dependent upon the Power, Mercy and Grace of our TRIUNE GOD.

How is it, my Sweet Jesus—that YOU—have entrusted this GREAT TASK to me—I, who in my weakness wore blinders to my own sins? It is true My Lord—-That I have ALWAYS LOVED YOU! AND Because of your GREAT Love for me, (and everyone else who will LISTEN to your call) YOU were never far from me. I have always felt the Trinity's presence in my life—-but, I—did—NOT—-UNDERSTAND—the importance of MAKING GOD—FIRST— IN MY LIFE! Or, with the demands of LIFE; HOW to make You more than a Sunday Obligation FULFILLED (now, I am ashamed of those words). I, like so many others, did not know how to bring forward the 'Fruits and Gifts of the Holy Spirit' into my daily life—and SHARE them with your other brothers and sisters through the other Gifts known as Charisms. I am SORRY JESUS—I did NOT know what I was doing, or what I was NOT DOING! Once again, I Beg— your forgiveness. And I Praise you and Thank you for giving me a Second Chance at my Christianity. For you said in (Jeremiah 29:11) "For I know the plans I have for you," declares the Lord. "Plans to prosper you and not harm you, plans to give you hope and a future."

In (Ephesians 6:10) it says, "We are strong in the Lord and… In the Power of His Might!" And in (2 Corinthians 12:9) it says, "His strength is made perfect in our weakness". What this means is, whatever our weakness is, when we ask for The Trinity's help to overcome it—it is then that we are made strong and able to resist that temptation (Isaiah 40:31) points out that true fortitude comes when "They that hope in the Lord shall renew their strength." (St. Joseph's). And, Fortitude is a quality of inner strength. The believer is strengthened by the MIGHT of the Indwelling Holy Spirit. This results in Fortitude that faces all fear with Faith."

Now I need to take you to another place where Fortitude Abounds! The MOST IMPORTANT PLACE OF ALL! Place yourself at the Table, with the Apostles, at the Last Supper—-The beginning of 'The Covenant' that Jesus came to fulfill! Throughout the meal, also called 'The Lamb's Supper', Jesus puzzled His twelve chosen Apostles with changing the Traditional words from where He

OFFERED and SHARED, the traditional Passover Meal with His Apostles… Think of the 'Strength of Mind' called FORTITUDE, that it took for Jesus to tell them this: found in (Luke 22:14-22, St. Joseph's), "When the hour arrived, He took His place at table, and the Apostles with Him. He said to them: "I have greatly desired to eat this Passover with you before I suffer. I tell you, I will not eat again until it is fulfilled in the Kingdom of God." Then taking the cup He offered thanks and said: "I tell you, from now on I will not drink of the fruit of the vine until the coming of the reign of God." Then taking the bread and giving thanks, He broke it and gave it to them, saying: "This is my body, to be given for you. Do this as a remembrance of me." He did the same with the cup after eating, saying as He did so: "This is the new covenant in my blood, which will be shed for you." And yet the hand of my betrayer is with me at this table. The Son of Man is following out His appointed course, but woe to that man by whom He is betrayed." Then they began to dispute among themselves as to which of them would do such a deed." Read the rest of the discussion with the Apostles in Luke 22. Before the Passover meal was completed, Jesus "Went out and made His way to the Garden…On reaching the Place He said to them, Pray that you may not be put to the test." He withdrew from them about a stone's throw, and then He went down on His knees and prayed in these words. "Father, if it is your will, take this CUP from me; yet not my will but yours be done." An angel then appeared to Him from Heaven to Strengthen Him. In anguish He prayed with all the greater intensity and His sweat became like drops of Blood falling to the ground. Then He rose from prayer and came to His disciples, only to find them asleep, exhausted with grief. He said to them, "Why are you sleeping? Wake up, and pray that you may not be subjected to the trial." While He was still speaking a crowd came, led by Judas, one of the twelve. Judas approached Jesus to embrace Him and Jesus said, "Judas, would you betray me with a kiss?" read the rest of this on your own to become familiar with it. Through prayer, Jesus had been fortified by the Love of His Father…. To ENDURE AND COMPLETE THE COVENANT that had been 'appointed by the Trinity, for MANKIND'S REDEMPTION.

Now… read about His OWN TWELVE, one who had… Betrayed Him…and the ones who were so afraid, they ran away and Deserted Him. Let's remember how Peter followed His Master… to see… but out of Fear…Denied Jesus three (3) Times. An Angel had Strengthened Jesus for what He would have to ENDURE… for us. His PASSION…INCLUDING: Condemnation, Scourging, The Crowning of Thorns, the Mockery He Endured while walking and carrying His own Cross…The DEEP SORROW THAT HE EXPERIENCED SEEING HIS MOTHER…Knowing her deep pain for Him…He did this WILLINGLY for each one who will, by their own free will CALL HIM LORD AND SAVIOR. Jesus…freely stretched out His arms and accepted the Nails…and Hung there with OUR SINS…Our names WERE WRITTEN IN THE HOLES OF HIS NAIL EMBEDED HANDS AND FEET and…THEY THRUST THE LANCE INTO HIS SIDE…and HE poured out Blood and Water for our Cleansing and Healing and REDEMPTION. This is what it means to be WASHED IN THE BLOOD OF THE LAMB… When we Repent of our sins and come to Jesus for our Forgiveness… The Kingdom of God is now able to set Humans free from Original Sin. This was the finish of the Passover Supper. The actual 'Fourth Cup' was shed and Shared from the Cross. With GREAT FORTITUDE JESUS ENDURED ALL OF THIS AND SO MUCH MORE… FOR…US! THIS COMPLETED THE COVENANT…and enables each one of us to be able to CHOOSE HIM…

In (Mark 16:14) it says, "Later Jesus appeared to the Eleven as they were eating; He rebuked them for their lack of Faith and their stubborn refusal to believe those who had seen Him after He had risen. He said to them, "Go into all the world and preach the good news to all creation. Whoever believes and is baptized will be saved, but whoever does not believe will be condemned. And these signs will accompany those who believe: In my name they will drive out demons, they will speak in new tongues; they will pick up snakes in their hands; and when they drink deadly poison, it will not harm them at all, they will place their hands on sick people, and they will get well." "After the Lord had spoken to them, He was taken up into heaven and He sat at the right hand of God."

What Jesus did for them, is also written in (John 20: 19-23) "On the evening of the first day of the week, when the disciples were together, with the doors locked for fear of the Jews, Jesus came and stood among them and said, "Peace be with you!" After He said this, He showed them His hands and side. The disciples were overjoyed when they saw the Lord. Again Jesus said, "Peace be with you! As the Father has sent me, I am sending you." And with that HE BREATHED ON THEM AND SAID, "RECEIVE THE HOLY SPIRIT. If you forgive anyone his sins, they are forgiven; if you do not forgive them, they are not forgiven." Jesus...GAVE TO THE Apostles the ability to be able to USE THE 'FRUITS AND GIFTS OF THE HOLY SPIRIT" THAT THEY HAD RECEIVED ALREADY... and in (LUKE 24:45) it says, "Then He opened their minds so that they could understand the Scriptures. He told them, "This is what is written; The Christ will suffer and rise from the dead on the third day, and repentance and forgiveness of sins will be preached in His name to all the nations, beginning in Jerusalem. You are witnesses of these things. "I am going to send you what my Father has promised; but stay in the city until you have been clothed with power from on high". In the accounting from (Matthew 28; 18-20) it says, "Then the eleven disciples went to Galilee, to the mountain where Jesus told them to go. When they saw, they worshiped Him, but some doubted. Then Jesus came to them and said, "All authority in heaven and on earth has been given to me. Therefore, go and make disciples of all nations, baptizing in the name of the Father and the Son and the Holy Spirit, and teaching them to obey everything I have commanded you. And surely I am with you always, to the very end of the age." (All quotes from St. Joseph's)

In (John 14) Jesus promises to not leave them orphans. Read both chapters 14 and 15 for the promise of the Paraclete, the Holy Spirit.

As Jesus sent them, He is now sending us to deliver the Gospel Message that we each have received through the Power of the Holy Spirit on each of OUR OWN PERSONAL... PENTECOST. It will take the 'Gift of fortitude for us to go out into the world like the Apostles did——but the Holy Spirit will help us when we call upon Him.

On the Feast of the Transfiguration I heard in a homily, "Jesus came, that we each would be Transfigured—PERSONALLY—into

Saints." What we do not realize is that, "Each time we receive the Holy Eucharist, We Begin a TRANSFORMATION, within ourselves." Layer—by—Layer, we put on the "Armor of Christ!" Please Jesus, DRAW me to you with a Humble Heart.... And PLEASE, lead me to the Eucharist frequently. And when I am unable to receive you physically—help me receive you in a spiritual communion. In Jesus name I Pray.

Piety

Piety Is a Gift from God; A Gift of the Holy Spirit

Piety is a word that expresses "devoutness or a pious act." A pious act can be a practice of prayer and of spending time with God (per Webster's). Piety leads us to do good works that reflect God's glory. Pious means having a holy relationship with God. Piety is the result of a great desire to communicate with God. Growth in prayer is a process.

Our personal call to the gift of piety is a call to know God better. We do this by spending time with God in the Word (Scripture) and in prayer. We have to have balance in the different areas of our life to have a healthy relationship between God, my neighbor, and myself. Jesus-Others-You is an acronym for the fruit of joy.

Our call to prayer is a calling from God's heart to our inner spirit; it is a small voice inside of us that we can hear if we listen and answer it with quiet prayer. The length and eloquence of the words do not matter to God. He only desires communication with us. "Oh, God" is a prayer that our Father delights in hearing. It is a call from His child. It's like saying Daddy or Papa; it's music for His heart. Know in your heart that God is waiting for your prayer.

In (John 17), Jesus teaches us to pray to His Father. This was a pious act by Jesus to teach us how to give glory to God. First, He has a conversation with His Father about their relationship. Then He prays to His Father about the disciples and the mission they are being sent on to fulfill the work of spreading the kingdom of God throughout the world and through time. Jesus gave them first hand example of how to manifest the fruit and gifts of the Holy Spirit that were given to them in baptism and how to use their charisms to spread the kingdom of God. Then Jesus prayed to His Father about us.

In (John 17:20–26, St. Joseph's), Jesus says, "I do not pray for them alone, I pray also for those who will believe in me through their word" (that's us!), "that all may be one, as you, Father, are in me, and I in you: I pray that they may be (one)in us, that the world may believe that you sent me. And I have given them the glory that you gave me, that they may be one, as we are one, I living in them, and you living in Me that their unity may be complete. So shall the world know that you sent me, and that you loved them even as you loved me. Father, all those that you gave me, I would have in my company where I am to see this glory of mine which is your Gift to me, because of the love that you gave me before the world began. Just Father, the world also has not known you, but I have known you, and these men know that you have sent me. To them I have revealed your name and will continue to reveal it so that your love for me may live in them, and I may live in them."

It is by Jesus's example that we see that prayer is talking to God about the things that are important in our lives. To understand more fully, read all of (John 17). Jesus taught the disciples to trust themselves to communicate with His Father—our Father—for all our needs.

Piety is about Godliness or reverence for God. "Is not your piety a source of confidence, and your integrity of your life hope?" (Job 4:6, St. Joseph's).

Our call to piety is also a call to love God more and to finding a way to use our charisms in order to "build up the kingdom of God." It is doing something for someone to lead them to God. This surrender to our God, to build up the kingdom of God, becomes an act of piety. Piety is the way we act to give God glory. If we want to live a life of piety as a gift from God, we have to live the fruits and the gifts of the Holy Spirit to become more Christ-like. A lot of piety deals with the way we treat each other, how we live in the world as an adopted child of God.

What St. Teresa of Calcutta did was an act of piety. How she lived was piety. How she prayed was piety. Her steadfastness was piety. Piety enhances our ability to reach out to feed the poor, clothe them, and help them heal. Piety is a reaching out to love them more for the glory of God.

Prayer is one way to come close to God. Prayer can bring us to the place that we will desire to surrender our heart to our God. Each time that we give our heart to God, the Holy Spirit will touch our spirit and fill us with the warmth of God's love. Prayer is all about love, God's great love for us. Our feeble attempts at trying to make a space for God to join Himself to us are a lot like a love letter to God. It is a display of our trying in some small, human way to say, "God, I love you!"

In prayer, we are making the time and the space for God to become alive in our inmost being. It is there in the spot that God created just for Him where the Holy Trinity dwells. But we are responsible for calling Him forward into our life. We make the decision to set aside all that we are for the opportunity to become all that we can be for our Lord Jesus Christ. This process is an act of piety.

Prayer is a sweet caress of God's presence within us. We know not when that caress comes or where it comes from or to where it goes, but when we take the time to pray to be ready to receive God's divine love, God's presence is there. When we cast away all thoughts of our world—our day, anything that draws our mind away from the reception of God in the silence of our heart—He comes. God comes and touches our soul with the warmth of His love. That is a moment of divine union with our God. In this divine union, God tells us that we belong to Him and that He desires this moment alone with us. He desires that we feel His great love and compassion for us. He desires us to be one with Him. That is intimacy with God! The pious act of prayer can bring us to this place of union with God.

This divine union of God's spiritual presence within our spirit is the place where God communicates with us personally in the silence of our hearts. The resulting effects of prayer can be the enhancing of our spiritual growth in the areas of the fruits, the gifts, and the charisms of the Holy Spirit. Our eternity hinges upon our relationship with the Trinity.

We cannot earn God's love. He loves us with an unconditional love that is not paralleled on this earth. Even when we sin, he loves us! Piety asks us to reach out to each other and not be concerned with *me* but learn to be concerned with *thee*. And try to learn how to love like Jesus did when He lived on earth to bring us the opportunity to reach for the kingdom of God.

God calls us to love Him. Jesus calls us to love our neighbor as ourselves. The gifts of the Holy Spirit are showered upon us to enable us to reach beyond our human selves to the place inside of us where God dwells, to help us to be able to choose to grow "in His image and likeness." This place where God dwells is a place that was created by God for God only. Only God can satisfy the longing that He has created deep within us.

When we allow the fruits of the Holy Spirit to infuse into our lives and become a part of us we become a beacon for the light of Christ and reflect to the world the glory of God. Prayer can be as simple as an instantaneous thought that transforms me from where I am in the world of busy actions to the place where God dwells. Life with God is about balance—a balance between prayer, work, and action.

Piety is a practice of prayer. Piety is the action of sharing prayer with another for the glory of God. Piety is a gift of the Holy Spirit that enables us to build a relationship with our God—our Creator, our Savior, our Redeemer, our Comforter, our Teacher, the Lover of our soul. The piety of Moses was the action of building a relationship with God by spending time with Him.

The relationship between Moses and God was one of the most intimate relationships known to mankind. It came to be because Moses recognized the call, and answered it. His continued questions to God built their relationship. His trustful surrender to God helped Moses do what God called him to do.

This kind of intimacy only comes through time spent together. Prayer with and to God is our way to intimacy with God. So intimate was the relationship of Moses and God that when in (Exodus 33:18) Moses said, "Do let me see your Glory!" (19) He answered, "I will make all my beauty pass before you, and in your presence I will pronounce my name, 'Lord' I who show favors to whom I will, I will grant mercy to whom I will. (20) But my face you cannot see, for no man sees me and still lives. (21) Here", continued the Lord" is a place near me where you shall station yourself on the rock, (22) when my glory passes I will set you in a hollow of the rock and I will cover you with my hand until I have passed by. (23) Then I will remove my hand, so that you may see my back, but my face is not to be seen." (St. Joseph's)

A great divine love was shared between God and Moses. This relationship was filled with the fruits and gifts of the Holy Spirit. The charisms of the Holy Spirit came alive in the fulfillment of the mission of freedom for the Israelites. This gift of piety is supported by the fruit of joy, peace, charity, patience, kindness, goodness, generosity, gentleness, faithfulness, self-control, modesty, and chastity. The forty years in the desert are all about the charisms of service, faith, craftsmanship, encouragement, evangelism, leadership, teaching, and probably more, used to build up the kingdom of God for God and neighbor.

The gift of piety is experienced when the fruits of peace and patience, charity, goodness, and kindness are expressed through prayer for another. The fruits of self-control, modesty, and chastity support the gift of piety with the action of chosen surrender of earthly pleasure. Our fruit of faithfulness shows we believe God's loving commands will help us follow Christ to the cross of our redemption.

Building our own personal meeting tent to become intimate with God will be much the same. If we take the time to listen for our God's instructions and follow them explicitly. He will give us the ability to accomplish this goal, just like He gave the Israelites everything that they needed to sustain themselves in the desert for forty years.

Prayer is a process of inviting and allowing the Holy Spirit to fill our being, and as we are filled with the Holy Spirit, a process of emptying begins. Prayer is a process of our "letting go of our thoughts of giving ourselves to God." The more that we invite the Holy Spirit into our life, the more gunk of our life spills out and we are able to hear God say, "Be with me." God comes to us in the closest way possible between God and humans. His spirit touches our spirit, radiating out of us as God's Glory.

Our surrender of the minutes of our day is what God desires. The more of our personal self that we give to God, the more He reaches into our heart to heal our brokenness. This unsheathing of our false self gradually will allow our true self to shine through as the monstrance where Christ dwells. God intended that we humans co-create with him from the beginning of time. He made us to become one with Him. He will not force anything upon us. That is why we are called to come to Him. We are invited personally to create the space within our own life to allow God to become intimate with us. This space becomes our meeting tent with God (like Moses's).

Prayer is communication with God. Prayer is intimacy with our God. What we are saying to God when we make the time to empty ourselves in the letting-go process is we desire to be filled with the Holy Spirit. "Be still and know that I am God." (Psalms 131; 37:7; 46:10, Ignatius).

We humans spend our lifetime trying to fill that void with things of the world (our false self, which is what the world encourages us to be). Nothing but God can fill the hole that was made only for Him within our being. God calls us to Himself constantly. The busyness of our lives (our false self) veils the call of His voice. We each need to quiet ourselves and "be still"—listen to the quiet place inside of you. Jesus chooses to continue to live here on earth within us and within the Eucharist. Jesus exists within each baptized person waiting for us to discover Him and call Him forward into our lives. God does not force anything upon us. His gift to us is our free will. Our gift to Him is our surrender of our false self (things of our flesh) to uncover our true self (things of the Spirit), which is "God within us."

To begin to understand and utilize the gifts of the Holy Spirit within us, we need to recognize that the fruit of the Holy Spirit is the integral key that unlocks the power of God within us. The fruit of the Holy Spirit is the life characteristics of Jesus given as an example lived by Jesus here on earth to guide us to the narrow path (which is Jesus Himself) and through the narrow gate (Matthew 7:13), to the Father. Each of the fruits is ours to keep to help to mold us and shape us into the image of God, our Creator.

Because of His divine love for us, Jesus humbled Himself to become a man like us in all things but sin, to show us the "narrow path to the Father" (Matthew 7:14). This was a great act of piety from Jesus to all mankind. Through the power of the Holy Spirit, we are guided to the Father through Jesus the Christ the Anointed One. Praise God always!

Fear of the Lord

Fear of the Lord: The Gift of the Holy Spirit

God loves us unconditionally, and He has created each of us for a full and happy life in union with Himself, who is Father, Son, and Spirit. We can see evidence of God's love in creation. God's great love and generosity for us was demonstrated in the creation of the world. Just look at the small details. The variations of thousands of creatures and vegetation; look and see the hills, the mountains, and the valleys and the massive oceans to the tiny streams; the forests and the deserts, all created with and by the great love of our Mighty God. He made each thing in the fullness of His glory. He provided for our every need. When we look at nature, we can see a correlation with our lives. We each have mountain top experiences and valleys that we experience throughout our lifetimes. We have fertile and barren times in our lives; it is all a part of our growing and learning and hopefully an opening of our minds, hearts, and souls to the truth that there truly is a God. He created and loved us so much that He provides for our every need, especially providing us the opportunity to say yes to the covenant of our salvation, who is Jesus Christ our Redeemer.

We should each stand in awe and wonder of our Mighty God, whose tenderness for His children is everlasting.

What is awe? "It is a respectful fear inspired by authority." Fear is to have reverent awe of something. Our Father God has authority over all the things that He created! In His great desire to share His great love with another, He created Adam and Eve and said, "Let us make them in our image and likeness." With free will to make choices. There was only one command He gave to Adam: "You are free to eat of any of the trees in the garden except the tree of knowledge of good and bad. From that tree you shall not eat; the moment you eat from it you surely doomed to die" (Genesis 1:26, St. Joseph's).

After their fall to sin, God's plans had to change. God had given them everything, but they wanted more after the subtle seductions of satan. God as a loving Father had to reprimand them, but He did not destroy them. He made His first promise to us, a promise of another to come (Genesis 3:16–19) through another woman the promise of a Savior, His only Son, the Christ, the Anointed One.

Wonder is a feeling aroused by something extraordinary, like a miracle. All life, giving birth to new life, is a miracle from God to us.

Reverent awe and wonder is to respect God's authority over all creation. And that reverence reverses, when at creation God said in (Genesis 1:26, St. Joseph's), "Let us make man in our Image and likeness, Let them have dominion over the fish of the sea, the birds of the air, and the cattle, and over the wild animals and all the creatures that crawl on the ground." Man resembles God primarily because of the dominion that God gives him over the rest of creation.

We were baptized in the name of the Trinity. We must look at what it means to be sustained by the Father's love, to be able to choose the saving presence of Jesus, who is Lord and Christ, and to be immersed in the life of God's Holy Spirit. It is like a fish living in and through water. We are each surrounded by the presence of God's great love, and God's grace surrounds us and is within us when we are living as God intended.

God's divine love for us calls each one of us to a holiness. Holiness is something that we can achieve. Holiness is something that is sacred. God calls us to grow deeper and deeper into our spirituality with, in, and through the Trinity. We can do nothing holy without God!

Community is the place where we share the gift of God's great love with each other. God's love for us was so great that He desired that we humans become a part of their community. We were created with the gift of free will! And after original sin, God gives each of us another free gift: our opportunity to mend the broken relationship that was created by original sin. This gift is Jesus, who is our salvation.

God gave all Eden to Adam and Eve. He created them in His image and likeness, and with that gift, they experienced the presence of God's perfect divine love within their spirits, and within their lives in the garden, God walked with them in the garden, and they knew Him. He gives us that same gift through 'Interior Prayer.'

(Genesis 3:8) says, "When they heard the sound of the Lord God moving about in the Garden at the breezy time of day." In the footnotes it says, "In Palestine a cooling breeze blows from the sea in the evening." God was a part of their lives. In paragraph 373 of the CCC we read, "God gave dominion over the fish of the sea and the birds of the air and over every living thing that moves on the earth." (Genesis 1:27–28). In God's plan man and woman have the vocation of "subduing" the earth as stewards of God. This sovereignty is not to be an arbitrary and destructive domination. God calls man and woman, made in the image of the Creator "who loves everything that exists, to share in His providence toward other creatures; hence—their responsibility for the world God has entrusted to them." WOW…No wonder that one of the "Gifts of the Holy Spirit" is to look at Him with AWE AND WONDER through Fear of the Lord. (St. Joseph's)

With Eve's surrender to the serpent, evil (original sin) came into their hearts, and her desire to be able to see good and bad like God does made her submit to satan's subtle seductions. "Their eyes were opened," and their lack of trust blanketed "the Spirit of God" that God had created within them. They lost communion with God! Now mankind would need to seek God and ask God to come close to them. Our salvation depends on us seeking redemption and reconciling with God through Jesus, – and asking that the fruits and gifts of the Holy Spirit are brought forward in our lives to lead us to communion with God.

In (Job 28:28, St. Joseph's), we read, "Behold, the Fear of the Lord is Wisdom, and avoiding evil is understanding." Wisdom is one of the 'Gifts of the Holy Spirit' that God gives to each one of us in our Baptism and is brought forward in our Confirmation. Wisdom. I always thought that Wisdom was way out of my reach. Webster's also says: 'to have good sense or judgment.' This is something that is not out of my reach.

At the end of that phrase in (Job 28:28), "Behold, the fear of the Lord is wisdom, and avoiding evil is understanding" (St. Joseph's). If we choose to do evil things and disobey the laws set by God, we will fall away from our salvation. Our eternity is a high price to pay for momentary pleasures.

Within the great covenant God gives each human the opportunity to recognize Jesus as our Lord and Savior. When God calls us to Himself and we recognize Jesus as our Savior, and when we call upon Jesus to lead us to the Father, the Holy Spirit, through the gift of counsel, will guide us. When we are baptized with the water of salvation, we are given the fruits and gifts of the Holy Spirit. They are present within us, waiting for us to recognize that we need to ask Jesus to bring them forward in our lives through His Spirit. Activating these will help accomplish God's desire of "Let us make man into our image, and after our likeness" (Genesis 1:26, St. Joseph's).

So great is the love of our God for each one of us that one of the community of God surrendered His life for us! No one *took* His life! Jesus freely laid down upon the cross and stretched out His holy hands and chose the nails, giving each one of us the chance to be able to choose to come to Him on the altar of the cross of our redemption. The choice is ours alone. That is what divine love is! God loves us so much that He gives us a chance and a choice for our salvation; it is a completely free gift. God asks us to accept Jesus as our Lord and Savior! Recognize our sins, face them, and repent! Which means to turn away from sin and change your life. This is called conversion. If we do not stand in complete awe and wonder of God who would sacrifice all for us,—we are blind to all that is good in life.

Fear of the Lord is about knowing in your heart that Jesus Christ is Our Lord and Savior. He paid the greatest price of all for us: His life…for our salvation. I can't even understand that kind of love. Can you? This is why we stand looking at the Trinity in great awe and wonder and reverence to the tabernacle where He lives within our church and within each other and most importantly within our own hearts. We should stand in great awe and wonder that He loves us so much that He would dwell within us.

To dwell within us. Let's reflect upon it. To dwell means to abide or remain, to reside, and to exist. Jesus desires to abide (to live) in each one of us. Abide means to endure. He desires to endure (stay), with each one of us as we go through life. Ask Him into your heart as your Lord and Savior, and wait expectantly for Him, as the virgins waiting for their bridegroom (Matthew 25:1 and 10, St. Joseph's): "While they went off to buy it (oil), the bridegroom came and those who were ready went into the wedding feast with Him." It will be like that on the last day, when God calls us to Himself, we must be ready and waiting with our souls clean, or we will be left behind. Be wise, prepare for the Lord.

Salvation—what does that mean? The important definition for each one of us is this: "Salvation is the saving of a person from sin." (Webster's) Sin is a word that describes the separation of our soul from the community of the Trinity. Sin is a word that describes something, anything, everything that separates us from the love of our God. *Sin* is a word that destroys. Sin is all around us and within us. The word *I* is in the very center of the word *sin*.

But don't worry, God our Father, through the power of the Holy Spirit in union with Mary's permission, created the Incarnate Jesus, who left the community of the Trinity to become the Christ for all mankind. A miracle of divinity and humanity becoming one for our sake. "Christ" means "the Anointed One, the Messiah, the Promised One from the beginning of time when original sin destroyed God's plans for mankind."

Jesus lived, died, and rose from the dead to give us new life. Jesus invites us into a new kingdom, a new way of life, a gift of redemption. We are created in God's image, but fallen and tarnished. We are all affected by original sin. Jesus offers forgiveness and restoration for each of us, and for all who will call Him Lord. God made the world to be a place of peace and justice and happiness—a place in which Jesus would reign.

The world has fallen from its original state of goodness (by war, poverty, and injustice of all kinds). Individuals suffer from a fallen nature as well, through loneliness, isolation, depression, insecurities, meaninglessness, and personal relationships—characterized by fear, anger, and mistrust. Jesus has come to address all these situations. Turn to Jesus to have your burdens lightened, (Matthew 11:28–30, St. Joseph's), "Come to me, all you who are weary and are burdened, and I will refresh you. Take my yoke upon your shoulders and learn from me, for I am gentle and humble of heart. Your souls will find rest, for my yoke is easy, and my burden is light."

Jesus has conquered the power of sin (Romans 3:9, 23) and darkness (Colossians 1:13). We are forgiven, and can start over. Once we are forgiven, Jesus gives us the strength to renounce the devil who now will only have limited power over us (Romans 8:37–39). St. Ambrose said, "When we speak about Wisdom, we are speaking of Christ. When we speak of virtue, we are speaking of Christ. When we speak about justice, we are speaking of Christ. When we speak about Peace, we are speaking about Christ. When we speak about truth and life and redemption, we are speaking of Christ."

We need God and have to make a choice in order to find new life. We must answer the scriptural question Jesus asked Peter: "Who do you say that I am?" (Matthew 16:15). Just like Peter, we must struggle with what this means. At the last Supper, Jesus warned Peter in (Luke 22:31–32)," Simon, Simon, remember that satan has asked for you, to sift all of you like wheat. But, I have prayed for you Simon, that your faith may not fail. And when you have turned back, strengthen your brothers." (St. Joseph's). WOW! Jesus told Peter, "I have prayed for you Simon..."

Jesus was warning Peter that he would deny Him three times, and the Bible goes on to say in (John 21:14–19), "This marked now the third time that Jesus had appeared to them after He was raised from the dead. When they had finished eating, Jesus turned to Peter and said, Simon, son of John, do you truly love me more than these? He said "Yes Lord, you know that I love you."

Jesus said, "Feed my lambs." Jesus said this to Peter three times to signify the three denials by Peter and Jesus's deep commitment to forgiving us when we can see our sin and repent. We are each called to a life of discipleship as a way to live out our response to Jesus's question of "Who do you say that I am?" Every area of our personal and communal lives is meant to echo the truth that Jesus Christ is Lord! In (Proverbs 9:10), it says, "Fear of the Lord is the beginning of Wisdom, and the Knowledge of the Holy One, is Understanding." (All from St. Joseph's.)

Almost all the passages that speak of the fear of the Lord are referring to this: if you follow God's Commandments, you do not need to be afraid of the Lord. Those who choose to live in the ways of the world will not enter the kingdom of God.

(Psalm 103:11, St. Joseph's) says, "For as high as the heavens are above the earth, so great is His love for those who fear Him." It is not God that we should fear; it is ourselves and our inability to put God first.

God has intervened to bring us true peace, justice, and truth: the spiritual realm is not an optional extra. Only in God's kingdom are these things possible. Jesus is Lord, bringing freedom and new life to those who accept Him. Jesus lives in each of us and in His church, which is all of us together, to bring everlasting life to those who are His followers for the sake of the world (Ephesians 2:17–22). This is why in our creed we pray, "We believe in one Lord, Jesus Christ, the only son of God...Through Him all things were made. For us men and for our salvation, He came down from heaven."

When we were baptized, no matter how long ago, vows were made as part of the sacrament. We (or our parents) promised to reject sin, to believe in God—who is Father, Son, and Holy Spirit—and to embrace the church. These vows are also a lifelong commitment, a striving for intimacy with God.

Wisdom, knowledge, and understanding are gifts of the Holy Spirit that are given to us to keep so that we will evaluate events in our lives to help us come to the Lord our God. I think that it is interesting to see how these gifts and fruits are listed separately yet are so interwoven within each other and within fear of the Lord. We also need to remember that it is through continual vigilance that we will stay close to our Lord.

A wise person will look at the Commandments and see blessings that following them will bring us. A wise person will also recognize that not following them will bring our souls to destruction. Fear of the Lord is choosing to live by God's laws that He has given us to follow to help us to make good decisions with our free will. Our life here on earth can bring the fruits and gifts of the Holy Spirit alive in our hearts, souls, mind, and spirit, and that will help us to spend our eternity with God.

In (Psalm 34:8, St. Joseph's), it says, "The Angel of the Lord encamps around those who fear Him, and rescues them." He will protect us from evil when we follow His Commandments." Also (Psalm 147:11, St. Joseph's) says, "The Lord is pleased with those who fear him, in those who hope for His kindness."

In (2 Corinthians 7:1, St. Joseph's), Paul leads off with, "Since we have these promises, dear friends, let us purify ourselves from every defilement of flesh and spirit, and in the fear of the God strive to fulfill our consecration perfectly."

In (Proverbs 3:7 St. Joseph's), it says, "Be not wise in thine own eyes, Fear the Lord, and depart from evil." And in (Psalm 33:18–19, St. Joseph's), it says, "The eyes of the Lord are on those who fear Him, on those whose hope is in His unfailing love, to deliver them from death and keep them alive in famine." So trust in God, and He will take care of you.

In (Psalm 25:14, St. Joseph's), it says," The friendship of the Lord is with them who fear Him, and His covenant, for their instruction." His covenant is Jesus Christ, Our Lord and Savior. Have you met Jesus on the cross, where He sacrificed His body and poured out His blood? It is there on the cross that we are made worthy of the promises of Christ. He is waiting patiently for you to come to Him, He wants to help you understand that it is HIS great desire that you spend your eternity with the Trinity.

"But how narrow is the gate that leads to life, how rough the road, and how few there are who find it" (Matthew 7:13, St. Joseph's). It is with His arms stretched wide that He is reaching for your very own soul. Come to Him; He will hold you gently in His loving arms while He looks at you with great reverence, awe, wonder, and divine love, and then He will take you to His Father. God then becomes our Father. In (Psalm 32:8, St. Joseph's), it says, "I will instruct you and show you the way you should walk; I will counsel and keep my eyes on you." Think of what the Trinity has done and is still doing for us.

In (Jeremiah 29:11), it says, "I know full well the plans I have in mind for you, plans for welfare, not for woe, plans to give you a future full of hope." And in (Psalm 115:13), it says, "He will bless those who fear Him both great and small." You see, nothing matters here on earth except that we love the Lord our God, and our neighbor as ourselves.

We were made in the image and likeness of God (Genesis 1:26) so that we could choose to take on Jesus's life characteristics. In our acceptance of Jesus as our Lord and Savior, we are in fact choosing our second chance at our Christianity. The commandments will help us "stay on the Narrow Path and get through the narrow gate."

(Psalm 128:1): "Happy are you who fear the Lord, who walk in His ways." (Proverbs 19:23) says, "The Fear of the Lord is an aide to life; one who eats and sleeps without misfortune" (St. Joseph's).

Charisms = Grace of the Holy Spirit(CCC 799)

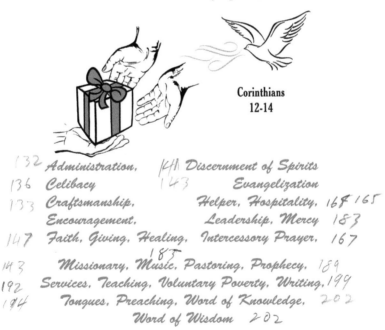

Corinthians
12-14

132 Administration. 141 Discernment of Spirits
136 Celibacy 143 Evangelization
133 Craftsmanship. Helper, Hospitality. 168 165
Encouragement. Leadership, Mercy 183
147 Faith, Giving, Healing, Intercessory Prayer. 167
183
143 Missionary, Music, Pastoring, Prophecy. 189
192 Services, Teaching, Voluntary Poverty, Writing, 199
194 Tongues, Preaching, Word of Knowledge. 202
Word of Wisdom 202

Clairann Nicklin

What are they all about?

127

What Are the Charisms All About?

God desires that all His children come to Him—that is each one of us. I was a mouse in the church pew. I didn't know how to be any different.

God put me into situations where I met people who shared Jesus with me. It has taken over sixty years for me to reach this place where I am today. Each day I am renewing my journey to God. You see, God has touched my heart and has begun peeling the layers of wounds from around my spirit through other people. That is their special spiritual gift to me.

There are some features that are common to all charisms, despite their diversity. All are spiritual gifts. All are a grace from outside ourselves. All are forms of service. All are given to us by the power of the Holy Spirit to be given away to help another and to build up the church. In (1 Corinthians 12:4–7), it states, "There are different kinds of spiritual gifts but the same <u>SPIRIT</u>, there are different forms of service but the same <u>LORD</u>, there are different workings but the same <u>GOD</u> who produces ALL OF THEM IN EVERYONE."

Look at the underlined words in the last sentence: *Spirit, Lord, God.* All three persons of the Trinity take part in bestowing the spiritual gifts to all who are baptized Christians.

We all receive all the gifts. But some of the gifts are stronger in certain individuals than others, because that is what God wants. If we all received all the gifts in the same intensity, we would be clones, and we would not be able to help each other grow and ultimately help our church grow.(Jeremiah 29:11) says, "For I know well the plans I have in mind for you, says the Lord."

I have discovered that small phrase in (Jeremiah 29:11), where God says, "For I know well the plans I have in mind for you. Says the Lord, plans for your welfare, not for woe! Plans to give you a future full of hope! When you call me, when you go to me to pray to me, I will listen to you. When you look for me, you will find me, YES, when YOU SEEK ME with all your heart, you will find me with you, says the Lord, and I will change your lot; I will gather you together from all the nations and bring you back."

That's what we are all here for. God is calling us to grow closer to Him. He has taken the first step and waits patiently for us to respond. What I have discovered is my relationship with God has been changing.

This relationship did not happen overnight. It took baby steps of discovery for me to come to this place. And it was my longing to know and understand my relationship with God that began my search into the fruits, gifts, and charisms of the Holy Spirit. I began to understand that phrase from (Jeremiah 29): that I just shared with you.

God promised our Savior. Our Savior promised another paraclete, who is the Holy Spirit. The Holy Spirit is the giver of all things from God, or the presenter of divine love from the Father.

The charisms are an expression of the Trinity's divine love for each of us. They can begin as a natural gift that is enhanced by the power of the Holy Spirit to help another person through a roadblock in their life, or a sudden empowerment by the Holy Spirit to do something that is normally unlike you to do. The characteristic that makes "just doing something" a charism, is the love of Jesus that you do it with. This love is empowered by the Holy Spirit, and is known as a spiritual gift, also called a charism or a charismatic gift.

The charismatic gifts are listed in (1 Corinthians chapters 12–14). St Paul did not mean for these to be an exhaustive list of spiritual gifts. If we do something for another person and it leads them to God, it is a spiritual gift or charism. Using our spiritual charisms for another is meant to build up the church, and bring another soul to God.

My personal roadblock was an inability to pray like others in eloquent words. I finally discovered and accepted that God doesn't need eloquent words; He only wants my heart to be turned over to Jesus in trustful surrender.

Don't be afraid of the charisms. They are given to us to help us share the love of God that has been given to us with our brother or sister. It does not happen by osmosis. We need to take that one small step into our growth toward God. We need to say yes to the power of the Holy Spirit. That is what each one of us is here for.

We can help build up the kingdom of God within ourselves, which will enable us to build up the kingdom of God within our world.

God only asks us to give what is ours to give. This book was written to help me discover what I could never grab ahold of throughout my whole life. My hope is that it will help you discover your walk with the Lord. It's not a hard road; it has been an adventure for me. The only way we can fail is by not trying. This is about each of our relationships with God.

How the Charisms Come Alive in Each of Us

"Can you be my martyr?" takes on a new meaning for me today. It is not just about physical death. It is about dying to oneself and becoming the monstrance that others will be able to see Christ within this human vessel!

There were eleven of Christ's other disciples gathered together in a small chapel who witnessed the transformation of my life in finding and using the charisms God wanted me to use at that moment. We discovered one evening how to allow our lives to be transformed into the essence of Christ's through the works of charisms in our lives.

I had been on this intense journey to discover the meaning of what the fruits and gifts of the Holy Spirit are supposed to mean for me in my life for ten months, and it has been an exciting journey of discovery. I have hope now. It is my desire to help you to discover how to begin your journey to Christ and ultimately to God our Father.

When we allow ourselves to be used as the vessel that the Holy Spirit works through, we begin to experience life as a part of the community of the Trinity. And when we allow ourselves to be that vessel, the Holy Spirit, brings someone into our lives who needs what we have to share. It is in the sharing of our experiences that the Holy Spirit activates our charisms in a way that the other person will see and feel the divine love of the Trinity! Thus, our charism has become alive, and we, being filled with the love of Christ, become the monstrance from where Christ is living today.

Let's go back to the one book that God wrote, the Bible. Sometimes we need to go to the beginning to understand what thus far has been not understandable. All our lives, we have heard some-one telling us, "God loves you." But it is hard to understand what is not tangible. This is where the eyes of faith become important. The evil one's subtle seductions have created in our world, and each person who ever breathed, a connection to the word *doubt*. When doubt enters into our thoughts, we as weak humans become shaky about the things that we cannot see.

All life began with our Father's divine love. The community of the Trinity shared their divine love with each other: Father, Son, and Holy Spirit, also known as the Triune Godhead, three persons in one God. It is a hard concept for us to understand. But this is where the virtue of faith comes to our aide.

I think most of us understand the importance that water plays in our lives. Our bodies are about 70 percent water. Water exists in three forms: liquid, ice, and vapor (mist or fog). The Trinity exists in three forms: Father, Son, Holy Spirit. It is just that simple! Don't try to look beyond for anything more.

Thus, the charisms come alive in us as we go through our day doing what we do best. When our efforts reach beyond our own life into the life of another and help ourselves or them to become more like Christ, it is then that we are helping to build up the kingdom of God. Primarily the charisms are for the other, but occasionally, some of the grace remains with us.

Charisms Described

Charisms are the action that reaches out to another in their time of need. Charisms are the spiritual gifts that are dispensed by the Holy Spirit as He wills. They are listed throughout (1 Corinthians chapters 12, 13, and 14). They come alive when we discover and use our Isaiah gifts. When we use our Isaiah gifts, our fruits pour forth from within us and the "other" can see or feel the presence of Christ. The fruits and gifts are ours to keep to develop our Christ-like personality. The charisms are given to us to be given away to another to help them either find Christ or deepen their relationship with Him.

We find the spiritual gifts in (Isaiah 11:22–23). They are wisdom, understanding, knowledge, counsel, fortitude, piety and fear of the Lord. It is through the power of the Holy Spirit that we are given these gifts, and when we ask the Holy Spirit to help us to bring them forward in our lives, we begin to develop our relationship with God.

When we use our spiritual gifts that were given to us in our baptism and enhanced in our confirmation, it enables the fruits to come alive and be present within us. These spiritual gifts are what molds and shapes us into the image and likeness of God. The fruits of the Holy Spirit are brought forward in us in a special way that makes us more like Jesus when He lived here on earth to teach us how to come to the Father (Galatians 5:22–23).

Charism of Administration

Charism of Administration, Also Called Organization

We hear the story about Joseph being sold by his brothers to a traveling caravan, and he was raised in Egypt. He was given the charism of administration, and the king noticed that everything he touched turned to good. (Genesis 39:2–6) tells us, "The Lord God was with Joseph and he became a successful man and administrator. The pharaoh king of Egypt said to Joseph, 'Behold, I have set you over all the land of Egypt." And in verse 52, it says, "Moreover, all the Earth came to Egypt, to Joseph to buy grain, because the famine was severe over all the earth."

In (Acts 6:3), it says, "Therefore brethren, pick out from among you seven (7) men of good repute, full of the Spirit of wisdom, whom we may appoint to this duty" (dispersing the goods as necessary).

In (1 Corinthians 12:28), it says, "And God has appointed in the church first Apostles, second prophets, third teachers, then workers of miracles, then healers, helpers, administers, speakers in various kinds of tongues." The Holy Spirit dispenses the gifts as He wills so that we can work together to build up the kingdom of God.

Administrators are able to plan and coordinate what needs to be done for good things to happen. Administrators get us there by delegating work to others to share the workload. Administrators are good problem solvers.

"Lay Christians are entrusted by God with the apostolate by virtue of their Baptism and Confirmation, they have the right and duty, individually or grouped in associations, to work so that the divine message of salvation may be known and accepted by all men throughout the earth. This duty is more pressing when it is only through them that men can hear the Gospel and know Christ. Their activity in ecclesial communities is necessary so that, for the most part the apostolate of the pastors cannot be fully effective without it" (CCC, p. 900).

"The laity can also feel called, or be in fact called, to cooperate with their pastors in the service of their ecclesial community, for the sake of its growth and life. This can be done through the exercise of different kinds of ministries according to the grace and charisms which the Lord has been pleased to bestow on them" (CCC, p. 910). My charism of Administration came alive when Our church needed to pay for a new roof on a portion of the church building. I organized and ran a garage sale for a small portion of the fee. we raised $3,000 to help offset the cost.

Patron saints for the charism of administration:

- St. Margaret of Scotland (1045–1093). Married the king of Scotland and had eight children.
- St. Dominic (1170–1221). Founded the Dominican Order.
- St. Pulcheria (399–454). Coruler of the Byzantine Empire with her brother at age fifteen.

Charism of Artistic Creativity

Charism of Artistic Creativity and Craftsmanship Charism

"The Lord said to Moses, "See, I have called by name Bezald…I have filled him with the ability and intelligence, with Knowledge and all the craftsmanship to devise artistic designs, to work in gold, silver, and bronze, in cutting stones for setting, and in carving wood, for work in every craft... I have appointed with him Oholiab…I have given to all able bodied men ability, that you may make all that I have commanded you: the tent of meeting, and the Arc of the covenant, and the mercy seat … furnishings … table and its utensils. Pure lamp-stand and utensils, and the altar of incense, altar of burnt offering with its utensils…lavor and its base, and the finely worked garments, the holy garments for Aaron…his sons … anointing oil and fragrant incense for the holy place. According to all I have commanded you, they shall do" (Exodus 31:1–1, Ignatius).

The ephod was the vestment created by the artisans from the gifts that the people brought "as their heart directed them" and per the instructions given to Moses by the Lord God. In (Exodus 39: 24–26 St. Joseph's) it gives specific directions on how to place the "Bells of Gold and the Pomegranates all around the Hem of the Robe; first a bell, then a pomegranate, and thus alternating all around the hem of the robe which was to be worn in performing the ministry—all this, just as the Lord had commanded Moses."

This ephod was the special vestment to be worn so that while the priest moved around in the sacred place, the golden bells (according to Jewish tradition, gold was a symbol of the Holy Spirit) could be heard making clear sounds (a tinkling, while He moved about in the holy place). Pomegranates were placed in between the bells to protect the bells from clanging together and making unpleasing sounds. They were placed on the vestment around the hem of the garment as God commanded. Pomegranates, according to Jewish tradition, were a symbol of "life, righteousness, fruitfulness, knowledge, learning and wisdom." While contemplating this symbolism when I began this journey, it came to me that the 'Gold Bells' were the gift's of the Holy Spirit, and the 'pomegranates' represent the fruit's of the Holy Spirit. How consistent our God is. The interblending of the fruits and gifts of the Holy Spirit while 'the priest moved around in the sacred place (the priest's work)' gives us an example of how they are created by God to work together—nothing stands alone with God.

In (2 Samuel 6:12–16, Ignatius) it says, "David danced before the Lord with all his might. …with shouting and the sound of the horn. King David, leaping for Joy."

(1 Kings 7:14, Ignatius): "A worker in bronze, he was full of wisdom, understanding and skill, for making anything in Bronze."

In (2 Chronicles 34:10, St Joseph's): "And these in turn used it to pay the workman in the Lord's house who were restoring and repairing the Lord's house."

(Exodus 25–28); These chapters give explicit instructions for the people of Israel to make an offering to God of their material possessions and their artistic creativity and craftsmanship abilities to make and construct the tent of meeting and Arc of the Covenant for worship of God.

(Acts 18:3 St. Joseph's): "By trade, they were all tentmakers."

CCC (p. 338) says, "Nothing exists that does not owe its existence to God the Creator."

CCC (p. 349), the eighth day. "But for us a new day has dawned: the day of Christs Resurrection. The seventh day completes the first Creation. The eighth day begins the new creation. Thus the work of creation culminates in the greater work of redemption. The first creation, finds its summit in the new creation in Christ, the splendor of which surpasses that of the first creation." Do we understand what that says to us? All that was created at the beginning of time and after, just built up to the Incarnation of Christ the Redeemer. Nothing that was ever created, will ever surpass the Life of Christ.

CCC (p. 2415): "Man's dominion of inanimate and other living beings granted by the Creator is not absolute; it is limited by concern for the quality of life of his neighbor, including generations to come, it requires a religious respect for the integrity of creation."

CCC (p. 2427): "Human work proceeds directly from persons created in the image of God and called to prolong the work of creation by subduing the earth, both with and for one another. Hence work is a duty: "If one will not work, let him not eat." Work honors the creator's gifts and the talents received from Him. It can also be redemptive."

Through the power of the Holy Spirit, God teaches us how to beautify our physical world. This includes sewing, gardening, cooking, writing, dancing, painting, embroidery, like on the ephod for the high priest, contained in the list is anything we create. It does not have to be something spiritual if it beautifies our world.

My Artistic Creativity came alive when I was challenged to 'write a paper on each fruit and gift of the Holy Spirit.' The power of prayer came alive as I asked the Holy Spirit to direct my understanding so I could complete this task. The Charism of writing is given to help the person who is given the Isaiah gifts of Knowledge, Understanding, and Wisdom the ability to share this new found information from, or about God to others. It cannot be kept to themselves or it will not be a charism. I was also given the desire to share my love of the "Peace Prayer Chaplet" with others. So the Holy Spirit led me in the development and construction of the Peace Prayer Chaplet Bracelets, to invite others to prayer more.

Patron saints:

St. Joseph the Carpenter. Mary's husband and foster father of Jesus. Patron of workers and a great favorite of St. Teresa of Avila, and St. Lawrence of Brindisti, also a Dr of the Church, believed that St Joseph was… "an indispensable instrument in the work of redemption." (lives of the saints, catholicism.org).

Charism of Celibacy

This is a quote from St. Teresa of Calcutta: "Priestly celibacy is not just not getting married, not to have a family. It is undivided love of Christ in Chastity. Nothing and nobody will separate me from the love of Christ. It is not simply a list of DON'T'S, it is love. We need Freedom to love, and to be all things, for all people. We need freedom and poverty and simplicity of life. Jesus could have had everything but He chose to have nothing. We to must choose to not have or to use certain luxuries, For the less we have for ourselves, the more we can then give Christ, and the more we have for ourselves, the less of Jesus we can give. As Priest, you must all be able to experience the Joy of that freedom, having nothing, having no one, you can then love Christ with undivided love in chastity. That is why a priest who is completely free to love Christ, the work that He does in obedience is, his love for Christ in Action. The precious blood is in his hand, the living Bread he can break and give to all who are hungry for God."

St. Theresa continues, "Let those who are called to follow Jesus in priestly Celibacy and to share in His Priesthood, pray and ask for courage to give." To give till it hurts. "This giving is true love in action and we can do it only when we are one with Jesus, for in Him, with Him, and through Him only, Jesus will be able to do great things" (through us) "even greater things than He Himself did."

The call to celibacy is a gift from God. Jesus displayed what a chaste life was. Chaste means being virtuous or pure, celibate, pure in thought or modest. Celibate means abstention from genital sexuality. The call to celibacy at times in our lives is to help us come to the fire of purification. The call to celibacy is a call to womanhood and manhood, with the love of our God at the very center of our being. This center, is the place that God created especially for Him. A place that only God can fill. This spot is called our inmost being. It is located at the very center of us. I think that it is beyond our soul in a sacred place called the tabernacle of God. The CCC states in paragraph 358, "God created everything for man, but man in turn was created to serve and love God and to offer all creation back to God."

Our individual call to celibacy is a call to discover the personality of Jesus within our own. Once we have accepted Jesus as our personal savior, it begins. We change "into the image and likeness of God." (Genesis 1:26). But first, we must encounter Jesus.

Now we need to try to understand the word *celibacy*. Celibacy is a vow made to God to live your life restraining from any genital sexual expressions. God could have created each one of us the same way that he did Adam and Eve, but He desired that we humans co-create with Him. He wanted us to understand the Joy that He feels when He looks at His child (us). He desired that we experience the complete self-giving love of man and woman in the emotional, physical, mental, and spiritual ways of sharing God's divine love with another. Genital sexual expression is intended for a man and a woman who devote their lives to making the other one complete. It is a gift from God to allow us humans to co-create with Him in the miracle of life! Celibacy is choosing to give that creative love to God in service to another through, with, and in Jesus Christ!

The sacrament of marriage is designed after this philosophy of a shared union in creating life with the Creator, who is our Father God. Our Father God knows our bodily desires. He created them for a beautiful expression of His divine love within the boundaries of His marriage covenant. To use the desires of our genital sexuality for pleasure only (self-gratification) is to put distance in our relationship with God. Each time that we submit to this self-gratification, we step farther and farther away from our relationship with our Father God. It is our free will choice that we are making.

The charism of celibacy comes to life when the celibate person (priest, religious, or laity) uses their gifts to share God's love with another, such as drawing from the gift of counsel or understanding or wisdom; the celibate person's fruits of; joy, patience, or generosity (the list goes on depending on what is needed) come forward and can help the other person heal a wound or make a choice, or whatever their needs were. The gift of celibacy to God creates a space in the celibate person's life that helps them to be available for another person's needs. And using their fruits and gifts to build up the kingdom of God draws the celibate person closer to God.

Using our fruits, gifts, and charisms draws each one of us into the circle of God's divine love.

"In the consecrated life, Christ's faithful, moved by the Holy Spirit, propose to follow Christ more nearly, to give themselves to God who is loved above all and, pursuing the perfection of charity in the service of the Kingdom, to signify and proclaim in the Church the glory of the world to come" (CCC, p. 916).

Patron saints of celibacy are the following:

- St. Isabells of France, born 1225–1270. Led a life of prayer and service to the poor and sick.
- St. Phillip Neri (1515–1595). He befriended young men of Rome, founding a hospital and caring for the poor.
- St. Kateri Tekakwitha (1656–1680). Kateri lived as a consecrated lay woman till death at twenty-four.

Charism of Deliverance

Charism of Deliverance from Spirits

(Mark 16:14) says, "Afterward He appeared to the Eleven themselves as they sat at table and He upbraided them for their hardness of heart, because they had not believed those who saw Him after He had risen. And He said to them, "Go out into all the world and preach the gospel to the whole of creation. He who believes and is baptized will be saved; but he who does not believe will not be saved. And these sign will accompany those who believe: in my name they will cast out demons; they will speak in new tongues; they will pick up serpents, and if they drink any deadly thing it will not hurt them; they will lay their hands on the sick, and they will recover."

(Matthew 10:1) says, "And He called to Him His twelve disciples and gave them authority over unclean spirits, to cast them out, and to heal every disease and every infirmity." This is a gift that is given to few. Jesus gave it to His disciples. It will take the intertwining of all the fruits and gifts of the Holy Spirit to be able to have the fortitude to step forward in this role. God equips those He desires to do this great service for those who need it.

The coming of God's kingdom means the defeat of satan's. (Matthew 12:28) says, "If it is by the Spirit of God that I cast out demons, then the Kingdom of God has come upon you." Jesus's *exorcisms* free some individuals from the domination of demons. They anticipate Jesus's great victory over the ruler of this world (satan). The kingdom of God will be definitively established through Christ's cross: "God reigned from the wood" (LH, CCC 550).

Deliverance also comes in the confessional. The priest has been given the Power to forgive and release us from the sin in our lives that keep us from God. With the expression of our deepest sorrow, the Holy Spirit showers us with the grace to choose to overcome that sin.

Read also (Matthew 12:43–45, Mark 5:1–20, Mark 9:28–29, Mark 16: 17–20, Luke 10:17–20, Acts 8:5–8, Acts 16:16–18, and Acts 19:13–16).

Sometimes when I am going to 'Prayer,' I can feel troubled. Any feeling of fear or anxiety is not of God, therefore I pray a 'Cleansing

Prayer' to chase away any spirits that might be gathering near me to catch me off guard and be able to tempt me away from my special time with God. My prayer is this. 'Any spirits that are not of the Holy Spirit, I COMMAND in the name of Jesus Christ my Lord and Savior, to leave my presence, leave my husband's presence, my children's presence (by name) my grandchildren's presence (by name), leave my neighborhood, my church, our workplaces, our places where we play, our Government, and our leaders of the world, and be BOUND TOGETHER and cast to the foot of the Cross of Jesus Christ and remain there until He decides what to do with you. I further ask that you Holy Spirit, come and fill all those empty spaces with your presence and the presence of your angels and saints, to guide, protect, direct and correct me as you see fit. Amen."

I also use this same prayer after we have our Prayer meetings where we pray for other's needs, and healings, sometimes spirts are involved that are not the Holy Spirit. This prayer is a protection from those spirits trying to cling to someone else. They do not enter into us unless we invite them in, but they can cling to us. When I pray for the 'Group,' I simply leave out 'Me and say, "Everyone here present and their families and their homes . . ."

My friend Mary, who receives visions and words during prayer, saw something move swiftly upward out of our circle of prayer. This is deliverance of unwanted spirits, and the infilling of good ones that we can trust to lead us to Jesus.

I have a priest friend from Africa, who told us the story about being awakened to give the last rites to a lady who had been ill for some time. He went prepared to administer the last rites with, Holy Oil, Holy Water and Holy Eucharist! When he arrived, the lady was semi-conscious with her family surrounding her in prayer. He did the Anointing of the Sick for the lady, which includes, anointing with The Holy Oil, Prayers of Absolution, blessing with Holy Water, and giving her The Holy Eucharist. A little while after he was finished, she awakened and looked at Fr. and said, "What are you doing here?" he answered, "You were sick, and I was called to give you the last rites." She looked at all the people and asked, "What are you doing here?" They said, "Praying for you." She has been well since that anointing.

Through the Anointing of the sick, she was cured, and the sickness has left her. (James 5: 14–15) states; "Is any among you sick? Let him call for the elders of the church, and let them pray over him, anointing with oil in the name of the Lord, and the prayer of faith will save the sick man, and the Lord will raise him up; and if he has committed sins, he will be forgiven". (Matthew 8:17) states, "He took our infirmities and bore our diseases." These graces flow from the atoning death of Jesus Christ, for "this was to fulfill what was spoken by the prophet Isaiah." Jesus sent out the Apostles and Disciples to do as He did! Believe it! Your Faith in what is spoken in the Bible will save you.

Patron saints of deliverance:

- St. Michael the Archangel
- St Raphael (for healing and protection and peace).

We have been commissioned by the virtue of our baptism to be free of evil spirits and to help others to be free also.

Charism of Discernment of Spirits

Discernment of Spirits

"Scripture speaks of a sin of these angels. This 'fall' consists in the free choice of these created spirits, who radically and irrevocably *rejected* God and His reign. We find a reflection of the rebellion in the tempter's words to our first parents: 'You will be like God.' The devil has sinned from the beginning he is a liar and the father of lies" (CCC 392; Genesis 3:5; and 1 John 3:8; John 8:44).

The fall of the angels was an irrevocable sin. Evil came into being when angels that God created good chose to turn away from the Creator. His word to Eve reflects the lie and has been interwoven into all of mankind's lives since the beginning of time, as you can see.

"It is the irrevocable Character of their choice, and not a defect in the infinite divine Mercy that makes the angels' sin unforgivable. 'There is no repentance for the angels after their fall, just as there is no repentance for men after death.' (CCC 393, St. John Damascene, *de Fide orth*).

"Satan may act in the world out of hatred for God and His kingdom in Jesus Christ, and though his actions may cause grave injuries—of a spiritual nature and indirectly, even of a physical nature—to each man and to society, the action is permitted by divine providence which with strength and gentleness guides human and cosmic history. It is a mystery that providence should permit diabolical activity, but, 'we know that in everything God works for good with those who love Him'" (CCC 275, Romans 8:28).

These two passages in (Acts 5:1–20) tell us how satan can twist our thoughts in little ways that we don't understand (and) then God sees deception in our hearts and death can come physically but surely spiritually. In (Acts 8:20–24), Peter can see that the man thinks he needs to *buy* his relationship with God by giving, but Peter teaches him that through repentance, he can get his heart right with God. We are to give *freely*, but for no other reason than we *want to give* out of the fruit of charity.

Discernment of spirits is the ability to see into another person's heart and help them to come to conversion. We each need to reach that point in our lives, or no matter how we think we are living a Christian life, we cannot. Christianity is based on the fact that "the church on earth is endowed already with a sanctity that is real, though imperfect" (LG). "In her members perfect holiness is something yet to be acquired: 'Strengthened by so many and such a great means of salvation, all the faithful, whatever their condition or state—though each in his own way—we are called by the Lord to that perfection of sanctity by which the Father himself is perfect'" (LG, CCC 825).

Discernment of spirits is endowed to the Lord's shepherds by means of their ordination. It is *released* as pastoral discernment, and is deeply enhanced by the fruit of charity that is in the heart of the Shepherd. "Charity is the soul of holiness to which all are called: it 'governs, shapes, and perfects all the means of sanctification'" (LG 42, CCC 826). God has given other people than priests the ability to discern spirits. They are a part of Jesus's prayer warriors.

This is also a gift of listening to our guardian angels: "From infancy to death human life is surrounded by their watchful care and intercession (Matthew 18:10; Luke 16:22; Psalm 34:7; Psalm

91:10–13; Job 33:23–24; Zechariah 1:12; Tobias 12:12). Beside each believer stands an angel as protector and shepherd leading him to life. Already here on earth the Christian life shares by faith in the blessed company of the angels and men united in God" (CCC 336). We each have this little voice inside us that we have heard when danger approaches. Whether we listen to it or not is up to us (God's free will gift to us). So you see, the gift of discernment of spirits is within us all to use as we choose.

Other passages to read are (Matthew 16:22–23; Acts 13:6–12; Acts 16–22; 1 Corinthians 12:10; 1 Thessalonians 5:19–22; 1 John 4:1–6).

Patron saints of discernment of spirits: Peter the apostle, Padre Pio, St. John of the Cross, St. Anthony of Padua, St. John Bosco. St. Philip Neri, St. Francis of Paola, St. Paul of the Cross, St. Joseph of Cypetero, St. Catherine of Sienna, St. Hedwig, St. John Vianney (the Cure of Ars), to name a few.

Charisms of Evangelism, Missionary, and Apostle

Some teachings of evangelism, missionary, and apostle are very narrow in their descriptions. They all describe sharing your faith with another. Each of these three charisms describe going to faraway countries. Some go to different cultures. All just simply go out into the world to share the love of God with another person. Some people simply stay within the Christian community and share what they have discovered in their life about Jesus. I want to just talk simply about the basics of being an evangelist, apostle, or missionary.

From Russell Shaw on a Catholic Internet site while searching for the meaning of *apostolate*, he explains how Vatican Counsel II's constitution works: "It's a special vocation, making faith present and fruitful." He explains simply, "Lay Ministry happens on Sunday at Church, Lay Apostolate happens in the big, wide secular world, and what Catholics should be doing every day of the week."

An evangelist/apostle/missionary is a person who moves about in the world sharing the love of Jesus and His mission in the world. This charism brings people to Christ by sharing His message of love. His message of love is the message of our salvation. We can give a person a piece of bread to eat for his daily bread, or we can teach him how to make the bread so he can eat daily.

Our charism of evangelism can bring a new beginning to someone who has never heard of Jesus, or it can be a second chance at Christianity for someone who has fallen away from the path that Jesus walks. Or it can be an awakening for the Christian who is stagnant in their spirituality. Or it can call a Christian to a deeper relationship with our Lord. The possibilities are endless. The Holy Spirit has given me the Gift of Evangelism. It is expressed through my charism of Writing (this book, prayer cards, teachings in our bulletin). It's about sharing my faith within and beyond the church. My charism of craftsmanship came alive in the Peace Prayer Chaplets, making a conscious effort to invite people to pray more through a simple bracelet.

Apostleship is another one of my stronger gifts. Recognition of this gift is being able to perceive and accept God's call to lead others in their spirituality, and to help others to recognize grace in their lives and share the grace in my own life. I have been blessed with several gifts used in healing prayer, and I help people to not be afraid of it … and become a part of it.

My personal Evangelism and apostleship Charisms are mainly used within the Catholic Church, in the pews.

(Romans 10:14–17) says, "But how shall they call on Him in whom they have not believed? And how can they believe unless they have heard of Him? And how can they hear unless there is someone to preach? And how can men preach unless they are sent? Scripture says, "How beautiful are the feet of those who announce good news!" But not all have believed the gospel. Isaiah asks, "Lord, who has believed what he has heard from us?" Faith, then, comes through hearing, and what is heard is the word of Christ."

(Ephesians 4:7–13) says, "Each of us has received God's favor in the measure in which Christ bestows it. Thus you find Scripture saying: "When He ascended on high, He took a host of captives and gave gifts to men." "He ascended" what does that mean but that He first descended into the lower regions of the earth? He who descended is the very one who ascended high above the heavens, that

He might fill all man with His gifts. "It is He who gave apostles, prophets, evangelists, pastors, and teachers in rolls of service for the faithful to build up the body of Christ, till we become one in faith and in knowledge of God's Son, and form—that perfect man who is Christ come to full stature."

(Ephesians 3:6–8) says, "It is no less than this: in Christ Jesus the Gentiles are now co-heirs with the Jews, members of the same body and sharers of the same promise through the preaching of the gospel."

In (Galatians 1:15–17), Paul teaches, "But the time came when He who had set me apart before I was born and called me by His favor chose to reveal His Son to me, that I might spread among the Gentiles the good tidings concerning Him. Immediately, without seeking human advisers or even going to Jerusalem to see those who were apostles before me, I went off to Arabia; later I returned to Damascus."

In (Galatians 2:7–10), Paul also states, "On the contrary, recognizing that I had been entrusted with the gospel for the uncircumcised, just as Peter was for the circumcised (for He who worked through Peter as His apostle among the Jews had been at work in me for the Gentiles), and recognizing too, the favor bestowed on me, those who were the acknowledged pillars, James, Cephas, and John, gave Barnabas and me the handclasp of friendship, signifying that we should go to the Gentiles as they should go to the Jews. The only stipulation was that we should be mindful of the poor—the one thing that I was making every effort to do."

(Galatians 1:1) says, "Paul, an apostle sent, not by men or by man, but by Jesus Christ and God His Father who raised Him from the dead."

In (1 Corinthians 12:12), it says, "Indeed, I have performed among you with great patience the signs that show the apostle, signs and wonders and deeds of power."

What is an apostle? "One who initiates or advocates a great reform." What is an evangelist? "A writer or a preacher of the Gospel." What is a missionary? "One who is sent out to a foreign country to preach the Gospel."

Suggested further study to understand: (Matthew 10:2–15; Matthew 28:16–20; John 13:12–17; Acts 5:27–32, 42; Acts 8:4–5, 26–29; Acts 9:13–17; Acts 10:25–28; Acts 11:20–21; Acts 14:21–28; Acts 8:5–6; Acts 8:26–40; Acts 14:13–21; Acts17:19–31; 1 Corinthians 9:19–23; 1 Thessalonians 1: 4–6; 2:13; and 2 Timothy 5:1–5).

(All quotes from St. Joseph's.)

CCC 863: "The whole Church is apostolic, in that she remains, through the successors of St. Peter and the other apostles, in communion of faith and life with her origin: and in that she is "sent out" into the whole world. All members of the Church share in this mission, though in various ways. "The Christian vocation is of its nature, a vocation to the apostolate as well." Indeed, we call an apostolate "every activity of the Mystical Body" that aims "to spread the Kingdom of Christ over all the earth."

CCC 864: "Christ sent by the Father, is the source of the Church's whole apostolate" thus the fruitfulness of apostolate for ordained ministers as well as for lay people clearly depends on their vital union with Christ. (John 15: 5) In keeping with their vocations, the demands of the times and the various gifts of the Holy Spirit, the apostolate assumes the most varied forms. But charity, drawn from the Eucharist above all, is always "as it were, the soul of the whole apostolate."

Read in the CCC about the lay faithful, paragraphs 897–907.

Patron Saints of missionaries, etc.: St. Francis Xavier, Blessed Raymond Luil (1232–1316)

(from CCC 763–768; 774–782; 836–856; 931; 1256–1261; 1275–1284).

Charism of Faith

The Charism of Faith

Faith is a charism we give away to help build up the kingdom of God.

"The Best and most beautiful things in the world cannot be seen or even touched. They must be felt with the heart" (Helen Keller).

CCC 166 says, "Faith is a personal act, the free response of the human person to the initiative of God who reveals Himself. But faith is not an isolated act. No one can believe alone, just as no one can live alone. You have not given yourself faith as you have not given yourself life. The believer has received faith from others and should hand it on to others. Our love for Jesus and our neighbor impels us to speak to others about our faith. Each believer is thus a link in the great chain of believers. I cannot believe without being carried by the faith of others, and by my faith I help support others in the faith."

In (John 20:19–22 St. Joseph's), it says, "On the evening of that first day of the week, even though the disciples had locked the doors of the place where they were for fear of the Jews, Jesus came and stood before them. "Peace be with you," He said. When He said this, He showed them His hands and His side. At the sight of Him the disciples rejoiced. "Peace be with you, He said again. "As the Father has sent me, so I send you." Then He breathed on them and said: "Receive the Holy Spirit. If you forgive men's sins, they are forgiven them: If you hold them bound, they are held bound."

In (John 20:30 St. Joseph's), it says, "Jesus preformed many other signs as well signs not recorded here in the presence of His disciples that are not written. But these have been recorded so that you might believe that Jesus is the Messiah, the Son of God, and that through this faith you may have life in His name."

In (Luke 24: 44–49 St. Joseph's), it says, "Then He said to them, "Recall those words that I spoke to you while I was still with you, that everything written about me in the law of Moses and in the Prophets and Psalms must be fulfilled. Then He opened their minds to the understanding of the Scriptures. He said to them, "Thus it is written that the Messiah would suffer and rise from the dead on the third day and that repentance, for the forgiveness of their sins, would be preached in His name to all the nations, beginning from Jerusalem. You are witnesses of these things. See, I send down upon you the promise of my Father. Remain here in the city until you are clothed with the power from on high."

In (John 20:29 St. Joseph's), it says, "You became a believer because you saw me. Blest are they that have not seen, and have believed."

It has been two thousand years since Jesus walked on this earth and we have received and believed the message that He is our redeemer. Now we have to go further than just believing. We need to act on that belief by sharing our faith with others. To have faith in God means to have complete trust in God.

In (Acts 2:3–4 St. Joseph's), after Jesus died and was resurrected, it says, "When the day of Pentecost came it found them gathered together in one place. Suddenly from up in the Sky there came a noise like a driving wind which was heard all through the house where they were seated. Tongues as of fire appeared, which parted and came to rest on each one of them. All of them were filled with the Holy Spirit. They began to express themselves in foreign tongues and make bold proclamations as the Spirit prompted them." Through the years we have heard this Passage MANY, MANY times. But do we really understand what it is telling us? Every principle of our CHRISTIAN FAITH IS BUILT UPON THIS TRUTH! Trust in God is 'Faith in God!"

Jesus promised in (Luke 24:49), "I WILL SEND ANOTHER, The Paraclete" (Rheims New Testament and the Jerusalem Bible. Also translated as "Advocate" in the NAB, and NRSV, also the "Counselor" listed in the RSV).

The paraclete is the Holy Spirit, the third person in the Trinity. The Trinity is composed of three persons: our Father, Jesus the Son, and the Holy Spirit. They together are the Triune God. Three persons individually and together one God.

The Apostle's Creed is one of the foundations of our faith. CCC 167, "I Believe" (Apostle's Creed), is the faith of the church professed personally by each believer, principally during baptism. "We Believe" (Nicene Creed) is the faith of the church confessed by the bishops assembled in council or more generally by the liturgical assembly of believers (Holy Mass). "I Believe" is also the church, our mother, responding to God by faith as she teaches us to say both "I Believe" and "We Believe."

I have been guilty of just saying the words. It was honestly very hard for me to memorize as a child. So much of our Catholic theology passed me by because of my dyslexia. At sixty-three years old, I just began to understand this journey into my soul, and I love it. I am a cradle Catholic, but much of my faith was just assumed and kind of passed through my consciousness. I practiced my Catholic faith very well, but I didn't necessarily know how to live it. I did not know what a gift I had until recently.

Depending on our family life, some cradle Catholics are like the people born into a family with the proverbial silver spoon in their mouths. Some cradle Catholics do not know what a gift we have been given. The richness, graces, and blessings of our Catholicism pass us by until the grace of God touches our hearts with the Trinity's great love for us in a way we cannot miss!

In Philemon, Paul wrote this in a letter (Philemon verse 6, Ignatius): "And I pray that the sharing of your faith may promote the knowledge of all the good that is ours in Christ." In our baptism, we receive the fruits and gifts of the Holy Spirit, and when we live them to the fullest, we will be sharing our faith with others. We will be evangelizing, just like when Jesus sent the disciples out to spread the good news to all the nations. That is our charisms in action.

In (Ephesians 2:8 St. Joseph's), it says, "I repeat, it is owing to His favor that salvation is yours through faith. This is not your own doing, it is God's gift!" There's those words again: *gift* of God. God desires us so much that He has gone to great lengths to entice us to Him, but He will not force us. God woos us to Himself like a lover to his beloved. He woos us with an everlasting love. He wants us for Himself. He wants to spend eternity with each one of us. That was His desire from the beginning of time. Remember, the choice is ours alone.

In (Hebrews 10:22), it says, "Let us draw near to God with a sincere heart in full assurance of faith, having our hearts sprinkled to cleanse us from a guilty conscious and having our bodies washed with pure water." This speaks to us of surrender of our hearts to Jesus. Believe that He came to earth for you. From His cross He reaches for your soul, with His arms stretched wide. Believe it! Assurance of faith means a pledge of faith to God, or the security of faith in God. In Paul's letter to the (Ephesians 3:17), it says, "I pray that Christ will live in your hearts by faith." Faith is the only way we can believe that Jesus is the redeemer of the world.

Faith, hope, and love are some of the greatest virtues that we are given to help us to understand God's great love for us. In (Hebrews

11:1), it, says "Faith is confident assurance about what we hope for, and conviction about things we do not see. Because of faith the men of old were approved by God. Through faith we perceive that the worlds were created by the Word of God, and that what is visible came into being through the invisible." I think that what this means is that we hope there is more than this life here on earth. I think the biggest percentage of humans are not really happy with our life here on earth. We keep trying to fill the space that God created just for Himself with human pleasures, but only God can fill that space.

The lasting virtues are "faith, hope, and divine love. And the greatest of these is love." (1 Corinthians 13:13) St. Joseph's. God loves us more than we can possibly know or understand. His love began when He dreamed a dream of us spending our eternity together. It is not my desire to disappoint my Heavenly Father, so I need to follow the path I believe that Holy Spirit is leading me to. I need to begin by surrendering my fear of the unknown to Jesus, the one who sacrificed everything for me. I will try to sacrifice a little for Him.

Self-surrender is a key word in enjoying your life in Christ. Layer by layer I can begin the process of removing my old self and become a new person in Christ. We each can teach ourselves by just taking one small step at a time. Surround yourself with other Christians who want to and are willing to walk this journey with you. And do not be afraid, because Jesus has walked this path before us. We just need to look for His footprints and ask Him to carry us until we can walk in His strength.

God's love for man is shown in this passage in (Romans 9:28): "We know that God makes all things work together for those who have been called according to His decree. Those whom He foreknew He predestined to share the image of His Son, that the Son might be the first-born of many brothers. Those He predestined He likewise called; those He called He also justified; and those He justified He in turn glorified. What shall we say after that? If God is for us, who can be against us? Is it possible that He who did not spare His own Son but handed Him over for the sake of us all will not grant us all things besides?"

Faith is believing in something you cannot see. My search for Jesus has given me a new joy in my life, a peace that cannot be measured. I have felt the presence of God's divine love for me and in me. Divine love is known in the sacrificial salvation recognized by all Christians by the sign of the cross. We have been given the greatest of all gifts in the world: a chance to choose our eternity! And we have been given all the tools that we will need to reach that heavenly destination.

God's promise to us was a Redeemer, His Son, our Savior. The Trinity, together as the Triune God, has given us the fruits and the gifts of the Holy Spirit to be bestowed upon each one of us as individuals, at our baptism in Jesus Christ as our Lord and Savior. These same fruits and gifts are enhanced in our lives when we each make the conscious decision to call upon the Holy Spirit to fill us with the grace to live the life of Jesus. It will not be easy, but the reward will be our eternity with God our Father.

Faith is a surrender of your Spirit to our Lord Jesus Christ. Faith is believing in the unseen; faith is a knowing that there is more than we can possibly imagine.

Since my open-heart surgery, my desire to know more about God and His Gifts to us has been enhanced. In my recovery, Jesus helped me write this section about the Charisms, to be able to validate them from Scripture and the Catechism of the Catholic Church, to help people to 'not be afraid" of what seems to be the unknown. "I Believe," in what Jesus said, "If you ask anything in my name," As I stated above in CCC 166, "Faith is a personal act—the *free* response of the human person to the initiative of God who reveals Himself. But faith is not an isolated act." We need each other, to help each other to believe. That is why we need our community of believers to be there for us in our times of doubt and troubles as well as our moments of Joy and Peace.

The Charism of Faith is a deep conviction that God exists, and *that* faith, cannot be shaken. My belief that The Triune Godhead, comes to me in prayer, is my Gift of Faith. When I first began to go to Interior prayer, it was my blind faith, that God can do anything that He wants to with me when I surrender my heart to Jesus.

My Faith, has opened me to the Mystical world of our God. Through Prayer, I experience direct communion with God through Spiritual Experiences. When I first began interior prayer, it was diffi-

151

cult to quiet my mind. My spiritual director told me to learn how to 'BE' with God!' I had no idea what that meant ... so I went to God in prayer and said, "God, if you want me to do this ... then you will have to teach me!" I prayed in my 'Gift of Tongues" Prayer language, so that I would not jumble my prayer up with empty words in English. In tongue prayer, I can *surrender my whole self* to God. When I felt finished, I went back in the first pew in the church where I had written almost all of the 'fruits and gifts' directly in front of the Tabernacle where Jesus is present. I sat there, in the presence of God ... in quietness, because my whole spirit was quiet from my tongue prayer. I did not have thoughts. I sat in the quiet and felt my mind dropping backwards into an even quieter space of my consciousness. I sat there awhile ... there is 'no time' in God's space ... and It felt warm, and peaceful, a wonderful place to be. Then something came into my view ... inside the darkness of my mind's eye, I saw a box, and within it was – IS 18 -, that was all, and it faded away. I continued to sit in the quiet with God until I felt He was finished. I sat there just a little while thanking God for the time with Him. I didn't think any more about that prayer until I was driving home, when it occurred to me that it might mean that I needed to read (Isaiah 18). When I arrived home, I just got busy with my day. I thought about–IS 18–later that afternoon. So, I took my bible out and read it. I couldn't make head nor tails of what that verse had to do with me. I remember hearing that 'when your read scripture you should read it three times, slower each time.' So, I read it through two more times, and I was still confused. I just closed the bible to look at it later.

Later came the next morning after my morning prayer. I remembered how my father taught me to make decisions with a 'pro and a con list.' I took that idea, and adapted it for my need of understanding this bible verse. IS 18, "Ah, land of buzzing insects, beyond the rivers of Ethiopia, sending ambassadors by sea, in papyrus boats on the waters! Go, swift messengers, to a nation tall and bronzed, to a people dreaded near and far, a nation strong and conquering, whose land is washed by rivers. All you who inhabit the world, who dwell on earth, when the signal is raised on the mountain, look! When the trumpet blows, listen! For thus says the Lord to me: I will quietly look on from where I dwell, like the glowing heat of sunshine, like a cloud of dew at harvest time. Before the vintage, when the flowering has ended, and the blooms are succeeded by ripening grapes, then comes the cutting of the branches with pruning hooks and the discarding of lopped off shoots. They shall all be left to the mountain birds of prey, and to the beasts of the land: The birds of prey shall summer on them and on them all the beasts of the earth shall winter. Then will Gifts be brought to the Lord of hosts, from a people tall and bronzed, from a people near and far, a nation strong and conquering, whose land is washed by rivers—to Mount Zion where dwells the name of the Lord of hosts." I wondered why God had given me that passage ...

I dissected the sentences, looking at one line at a time, I found the word that touched my heart, and in the other column I wrote what that meant today in my life. What I discovered in this passage that I believe that the Holy Spirit wanted me to understand was; I was full of busyness, concerned about so many things, that I could not make a difference about. I will send my Spirit to help you, and the blossoming will begin. Being pruned at the proper time is a good thing, it produces more growth. And the pruned branches are not waste, but can be used for whatever God desires. God wanted me to focus my attention on Growth towards Him. "Look to the mountain," the Eucharist. "Come when I call." Be ready! "I am watching from the quiet place where I dwell," that, is within me. He has a mission for me to accomplish for Him, and I must continue, and I know by my strong Faith that God will always be there to guide me. I have not been afraid of the unknown since then. The Charism of Faith comes alive when I trust God to lead me in the ways of Jesus. The 'ways of Jesus,' are about loving our brother as our self, that means taking care of those who are wounded and have less than they need. Sharing my spirituality with others is important to the Trinity. That is why I have these pictures to share with you, to help you know that God in three persons does exist.

These two Holy Spirit pictures were given to me to be shared with other's as a sign of God's presence in our world. Each were shown to me after my routine of prayer: 1) interior prayer, 2) morning office (scripture, both that I do alone), 3) Rosary, 4) Holy Mass, 5) Divine Mercy Chaplet, which we do in community, then personal prayer after all the others have left the church. I love to just sit and look at Jesus on the Cross and in the Tabernacle, contemplating what He did for me. Many days I will go to the Altar steps and kneel there for a while. Sometimes in the silence of Adoration, sometimes in praise and thanksgiving, sometimes in petition. Most always I do not know what to say to Him…I am overwhelmed with God's Divine Love. It is then that I turn to my Spiritual Gift of Tongue Prayer and allow the Holy Spirit to use my voice in lifted prayer. This is also the Spiritual Gift of Faith. It takes great faith to surrender to the Power of the Holy Spirit and allow yourself to be the vessel of Our Lord Jesus Christ.

On February 22, 2017 after Kneeling on the Altar steps and praying a while… I seemed finished. I got up and turned around and went to gather my things in the pew. I turned to look at Jesus one more time, and I saw the most incredible thing. The whole area around the Sanctuary candle was all aglow in bright red (something that I had never seen before in all the times that I had been in this same situation). There was a 'light form' above the candle which was moving. It looked like a bird flying, the wings were moving up and down…in rhythmical motion. I stood there in amazement for a little while, and then decided to try to take a picture of it. To my delight the picture appeared in my camera. I took several more, closer each time. I tried to take a video of it but all that I got was the red flicker of the candle flame without the glow around the candle. That made me smile and thank God for the Supernatural picture that He allowed me to preserve in my camera. Supernatural gifts like this need to be shared to build up the faith and belief of the Body of Christ.

Six weeks later, I had the same experience, only this time the light form was more distinctly a Bird (Dove, in my eyes the Holy Spirit). I obviously took this picture to. When I show these pictures to others they are just as amazed as I was. Many people see Christ on the Cross in the picture, I can see Christ Resurrected, many see the Holy Spirit, some see God the Father in the darkness above the light form. My heart tells me that each person who ponders these pictures, will see what they need to see to increase their faith. Thank you, God, for allowing me to be a part of this Miracle of light.

Further reading: CCC 163–165, 168, 171–173, 176–177, 179, 181–183, 183–184, 222–227, 1814–1816.

(Luke 7:1–10; 17:5–6; Acts 27:21–25; Romans 6:18–21; 1 Corinthians 12:9; 2 Corinthians 4:13–14; 16–18; 5:7; and Hebrews 10).

Patron saints of faith: all those who listen and trusted the call from God and followed His instructions… all the apostles who followed Jesus and all those who were martyred for their faith from Jesus's death until now, and those who will be till the end of time.

Charism of Giving or Almsgiving

Charism of Giving Is Also Almsgiving

(Luke 3:11) says, "He who has two coats, let him share one with one who has none, and he who has food, let him do likewise."

(Luke 21:1–4) says, "This poor widow has put in more than all of them, for they all contribute out of their abundance, but she out of her poverty put in all the living she had."

(John 12:3–8) says, "Mary anointed Jesus' feet with costly oil."

(Acts 4:32–37) says, "The believers share their possessions."

(Acts 20:35) says, "It says, "In all things I have shown you that by so toiling one must help the weak, remembering the words of the Lord Jesus, how He said, "It is more Blessed to give than to receive." Ignatius Bible.

(Romans 12:8) says, "Contribute in liberality."

In (2 Corinthians 8:2–5) it says, "They gave according to their own free will...but first they gave themselves to the Lord and to us by the will of God."

(Malachi 3:10) says, "Bring the full tithes into the storehouse, that there may be food in my house; and thereby put me to the test, says the Lord of host, if I will not open the windows of heaven for you and pour down abundant blessing."

CCC (p. 1438) says, "Lent and Fridays, in memory of Christs death for us are appropriate for spiritual exercises, penitential liturgies, pilgrimages as a sign of penance, voluntary self-denial such as fasting and almsgiving, and fraternal sharing charitable and missionary works."

There are countless ways that we can give to our brothers and sisters. God just wants us to take care of each other with the love Jesus shared when He was on earth. His commandment spawned a song of "Love one another, love one another as I have loved you, and care for each other, care for each other and bring each other home."

Patron saints of giving or almsgiving (fraternal sharing):

- St Katherine Drexel (1858–1955). She started schools for natives and African Americans.
- Blessed Bartolo (1841–1925). He was a vigorous advocate of the rosary, cared for orphans, and supported forty-five seminarians.

Time, Talent and Treasure...Are all gifts of the charism of Giving.

TIME—help is needed everywhere. The charisms of Helps and Service come to life when you help your neighbor, your church, groups like St. Vincent De Paul- with their many aspects of service. Funeral meals, comfort to the sick and elderly, being a Eucharistic Minister to the Altar, or the Homebound, and even to the Nursing Home. The prospects are endless.

TALENT—The skills that you have with your job are great to share with the poor who cannot afford your knowledge—nurses and Pyhsicians at a free clinic once a month, lawyer help, taxes help, bookkeeping help, help to the elderly with cleaning in their house and outside and repairs, etcetera.

TREASURE—The greatest Treasure we have to give to anyone is OURSELVES, and our Spiritual Gifts to help build up the Kingdom of God to give His love to all the world. But by Our Lord's own words, we are to give of what we have: (Luke 3:11), "…he who has…give," and, (Luke 21: 1–4), "…they contribute out of their abundance, but she out of her poverty, put in all the living she had." We are to give as our heart leads us.

Charisms of Healing and Miracles

The Charism of Healing and Miracles

Padre Pio said, "I didn't do the Miracle, I only prayed for you. The Lord healed you."

In (Exodus 14:21–31), Moses listens to God and raises his arms and God parts the sea for the passage of the Israelites to pass to freedom.

(Exodus 15:26) says, "I am the Lord, who heals you."

In (1 Corinthians 12:9–10), Paul says, "To another faith by the same Spirit, to another gifts of healing by the one Spirit, to another the workings of Miracles." In (1 Corinthians 12:28–30), it says, "And God has appointed in the church first apostles, second prophets, third teachers, then workers of miracles, then healers."

Scripture tells us of many healings and miracles by Jesus and His disciples, such as in (Mark 16:15–18): "After Jesus' Resurrection,

He appeared to the Eleven, and said to them. "Go into all the world and preach the gospel to the whole of creation. He who believes and is baptized will be saved; but he who does not believe will be condemned. And these signs will accompany those who believe in my name and they will cast out demons; they will speak in new tongues."

In (John 14:12), Jesus tells His apostles, "Truly, truly, I say to you, he who believes in me will also do the works that I do, and greater works than these will he do, because I go to the Father. Whatever you ask in my name, I will do it that the Father may be glorified in the Son, if you ask anything in my name, I will do it."

Whoever believes in Jesus receives the commission to continue His healing work.

Patron saints of healing: St. Agatha; St. Perigrine Laziosi, St. Francis Xavier, St. Phillip Neri, St. Anna Maria Taigi, Padre Pio, the apostles, and unknown more.

We all have wounds. It is difficult to measure *pain*, and it cannot be compared to anyone else's pain. Each one's pain is uniquely their own. The Gospels and Epistles have so many stories of Healings of all kinds, even of bringing a dead person back to life. Jesus sent His 'Followers' out to do what He did, to build up the Kingdom of God. They did what Jesus asked of them through the power of the Holy Spirit, in all aspects of ministry. Today, that includes us! And Jesus said to the Apostles as He sent them into the world, "Be not afraid, and He breathed on them and gave them His Spirit." He gives us that same Spirit in our Confirmation, and we are sent forth, only most of us do not understand what that means. Padre Pio understood very clearly, because he said to a person who was healed, "I did not heal you, I only prayed for that end." That is what all people that are part of a healing prayer team do also, we pray for that end … but God does the healing.

There are many *KINDS OF HEALINGS: Emotional, physical, mental, spiritual, and ultimate (which is bodily death, into Spiritual life).* When we pray for each other as we are told to do by Jesus, we are to simply pray to God for His Mercy upon the person, God does as He desires for them.

I personally know of many prayer healings. Miracles happen suddenly, without any MEDICAL intervention! Healings can happen now, or over time. It just depends on what God wants. The first one that I want to share with you is with my friend Karen. After a spiritual retreat weekend, we decided to share our spiritual Journey with each other. We began by sharing a meal together and then we shared our 'stories.' After a couple of weeks, our sharing went to a *deep level.* I noticed some physical pain due to an illness, and emotional pain from her history. I asked her if I could pray with her. She said "Yes" and we began our Journey into prayer.

At that time, I only had 'one' tongue prayer word, it was 'Shanaya.' As I prayed that word in surrender to the Holy Spirit, it came out in different tones and rhythms. I prayed awhile ... I don't know how long. I was within the time Realm of God, and God does not have a time clock. When I am there in His presence, I am only aware of my mind, heart and hands.

Having surrendered myself to Jesus ... to be His hands and voice in sharing His love with Karen, the Holy Spirit moved my hands to different spots on her back and legs and stomach. I had no idea why but I allowed my hands to *'go wherever I felt directed.'* I could feel heat coming from my hands and they were tingling, both are manifestations of the Power of the Holy Spirit working through you. I always 'hover,' not touch. Somehow, the Holy Spirit lets me know that He is finished, and the Spiritual space fades ... and my worldly space returns. I have gone to this same 'space' while in my 'Interior Prayer' with God. And what a beautiful place it is, free of pain, worries, anxiety of any kind, I have 360-degree vision with a gray veil over my eyes ... and I can *FEEL* the presence of God.

When the prayer was finished, she turned to me with tears pouring down her face and asked, "How did you know where to put your hand? I could feel the heat coming out of your hand onto my back! And the pain that I had before is less." I said, I don't know, I just let my hands go where I feel they are directed. She said, "I feel as though I have been washed clean! I will take spiritual healing any day over physical healing!" We embraced for a while, knowing that we just had experienced God's deep abiding love.

It is such an honor and a privilege to be an instrument of God, but it will take your willingness to let go of your control of self… and give it to Jesus in 'Trustful surrender to the Power of God, before He can work through you. There can be no pride in your work, because it is not you that does it. It…is GOD! And it is what God does *through* me that builds up the Kingdom of God. Karen said to me, "You can't possibly know what that word means in God's language! Through you, God was saying to me, "I LOVE YOU! I LOVE YOU! I LOVE YOU!" And the different rhythms and tone inflections that you used, enhanced God's expression of His love for me. It was so beautiful!" Karen has the Spiritual gift of Interpretation of tongues, and has said that she does not know that people are not speaking in English until later when others talk about the tongues.

Then one evening after our healing mass, I was praying with Ashley over my husband Nick for his back pain. This was also when I had only one tongue word. I began praying shanaya, and moving my hands over his back. I could feel that I was in 'God's Space' like when I had my 'out of body experienced'… aware of my surroundings, but *in the presence of God!* Aware of my mind, my words, and my hands as they moved about in prayer. Once again, I could see all around me. In this *presence,* I could feel the hand of God moving me, new tongue words were coming out of my mouth, and I just let them come, and prayed with my husband. His back pain was relieved some when we stopped praying.

Another friend called me one day to ask for prayers. I said yes, and began calling other people who I knew were off work and asked them the pray the "Blessed Mother Teresa Novena" for Judy. It is nine Memorares in a row, prayed for urgent needs. Our Prayer group was meeting that evening and at prayer time, Judy shared with us, "I could feel your prayers! And lots of them." I invited her to come up to seal the prayer. She came up, and we prayed with her. Afterwards she said, "I could smell incense that was not being burned, and the power of God during your prayer "Prayer rise like incense" (Psalms 141:2). But, as Clairann was praying her tongue prayer, it was not Clairann's voice anymore. Clairann was gone! Blessed Mother Teresa was standing right in front of Clairann. Anyone who has heard

Blessed Mother Teresa speak, knows that distinct voice and it was She who was praying for me." None of us really understood what happened, but we all knew that it was the workings of the Holy Spirit, and we were simply the conduit He flowed through to reach a hurting soul who loved Jesus very much.

Most of the time I prayed with my sister Bonnie as my partner. I was the *voice* that the Holy Spirit spoke through, but she was always the Power behind me. Like Aaron was for Moses. After another healing Mass, we had the praying teams gathered, and we had been praying for a little while. We were praying for our friend Bob who had multiple Surgeries and sever pain from them. While we were praying I could feel the power coming out of me, and I could feel the strength of my sister Bonnie, we prayed awhile and when we were finished, Bob went back to the pew., and another person came forward for prayer. The next morning, I was in the church writing for this book, and my friend Chris came through the church and stopped to talk to me about last night. She said, "I needed prayer, but the Power of the Holy Spirit was coming through Bob so Powerfully that I did not need to come up for Prayer. I received all that I needed. I couldn't see you or Bonnie but I could feel your prayers. I cried many tears."

When we allow the Holy Spirit to use us as the conduit that God's Divine Love pours through, we *are* His hands, feet and lips to a world that needs God so badly. Thank you, God for giving us the Spiritual Gifts that enable us to help you to build up your Kingdom.

My Friend Peggy had done a lot of yard work, and messed up her hip. She suffered with it for quite a while, went to a chiropractor without relief. Several months later, my prayer partner's Dave and Carol and I asked her if we could pray with her. She didn't know what this was all about, but was willing to let us pray with her. One morning after Mass, I took her to the altar and had her sit down in the server's chair, Dave, Carol and I gathered around her. I looked her in the eyes and told her to "Go to the quiet place where you talk to God." She closed her eyes in trust of us and God. And we called upon the Holy Spirit to intercede for us and Peggy, and we each prayed in our own tongue prayer language, in unison it is beautiful, "Prayer is Incense being raised to God." Tongue Prayer is God's language. When we were finished, Peggy opened her eyes and said while motioning with her hands, "While you were praying, I felt myself being lifted off this seat, I floated there for a while, and then was slowly lowered back down, not dropped! It was beautiful. We all smiled, because God is so beautiful and tender with all His creatures. Dave told her that "Your job is to pray every day in thanksgiving for the healing. Healing usually happens over time." Peggy told me a few days later, that after three days of thanksgiving prayer on her part, the pain was totally gone! Praise God!" She told me yesterday that, "I pray every day thanking God for the Healing!" She is like the "One leper who came back to thank Jesus," unlike the 9 who just went on with their lives. That healing prayer was about a year ago.

Twenty-four years ago, my friend and Prayer partner Carol thought she had a hernia and was being examined by her Dr., who said, "Honey, you have a much bigger problem! She had numerous 'lumps' down the middle of her body down the Aorta, from mid chest to lower abdomen, with the one down low being about the size of a Grapefruit. After she went home someone called her and told her it was Cancer.

She called all her sisters because her husband was not home. Obviously, she was very upset

But they were a prayerful family and went to a Charismatic Prayer service that her brother Deacon Bill leads. The group prayed over her, Bill's wife Ann, could 'see' the tumors. And while they were praying, one of the women in the group told Deacon Bill, "She needs the Eucharist NOW! He said, "Go get Jesus." She did. From the moment, the woman got in Carol's presence—-the Host was 'Hard for her to hold on to. It was like a *magnet being drawn toward Carol.* So, Carol received Jesus in the Holy Eucharist.

After Prayer, she saw the Dr. and the Dr. could not feel them anymore. All the tumors were gone but the large one in the lower abdomen, it was smaller but still present. The Dr. wanted her to do Stem Cell transplant and Chemo and Radiation. They went to the prayer group again. Carol felt that God would heal her completely (Carol's strongest Charism is Faith). But the consensus of the whole group was that she should go through with the harvest of her own stem cells and do the radiation and chemo to be healed completely.

Her brother-in -law Fr. Gabriel called a prayer time with both sides of the family (a lot of people) they gathered in Carol and Dave's basement and though foreign to most of them...at Fr. Gabriel's request they all laid their hands-on Carol... and prayed with her. Fr. Gabriel also brought a 'RELIC OF THE TRUE CROSS' with him to bless her with.

The next morning over fifty people were gathered at their church for the Celebration of the Holy Mass with them before they left for the Hospital. She said both she and her husband Dave were not afraid. They could feel the peace and love of God, and all fear was gone. They felt that they were in God's hands and everything was going to be," Ok."

Carol went through the stem cell transplant and the Radiation and Chemo while in Isolation at the hospital for one month. She listened to 'Praise music all the time. Her sister Eileen came every day to be with her. She arraigned Carol's cards on the wall in the shape of a heart to express the love from everyone. (The Charism of Artistic Creativity) Twenty- four years later, Carol is still spreading the love of Christ which is proof that she was healed through Prayer. In my opinion, this was not only a Healing, but also a Miracle because of the disappearance of most of the tumors before the treatment took place. Praise God!

I believe that we don't see Miracles in our lives, because we don't look for them. And maybe we don't believe in them...but Miracles happen every day! A Miracle for me that I will never forget happened on September 17, 2016. After watching my thirteen-year-old grandson David pitch a great game, my husband took me home to start dinner. He went to the store to get milk. My grandson David came over to, 'get a drink.' His mom said, "We have drinks here!" He said, "I want what Nana has." So, he came over and found me able to walk, but not with it mentally. He helped me with what I was trying to do, then went into the pantry to call his mother. He told her, "You had better come over here, Nana is not right." She came over quickly, and looked me over well, and asked me where her father was. I remember thinking for a while, and saying, "I don't know!" He came in shortly and decided to take me to the Hospital. The next morning, I was diagnosed with *big* heart issues, and after a gamut of tests, I had OPEN HEART SURGERY with a double by-pass done 3 days later. Eight months later I found out from my new Dr. that I was extremely lucky! I had the 'Widow maker' heart attack. I also had strokes, both before my surgery. In my opinion, my grandson David, saved my life by his following the lead of the Holy Spirit to come to my house for a drink … and his astuteness in assessing my actions. I feel that was pretty good for a thirteen-year-old. God has plans for me that I hope that I can fulfill.

Charisms of Helps and Service

The charism of helps is intended to the benefit of an individual. The charism of service is intended for the benefit of a group.

(Numbers 11:16–17) says, "Then the Lord said to Moses, "Assemble for me seventy of the elders of Israel, men you know for true elders and authorities among the people, and bring them to the meeting tent. When they are in place beside you, I will come down and speak with you there. I will also take some of the spirit that is on you and will bestow it on them, that they may share the burden of the people with you. You will not have to bear it by yourself." This is the charism of helps.

The charism of service: in (Luke 22:24–27), it says, "A dispute arose among them about who should be regarded as the greatest. He said: "Earthly kings lord it over their people. Those who exercise authority over them are called their benefactors. Yet it cannot be that way with you. Let the greater among you be as the junior; the leader as the servant. Who, in fact, is the greater, he who reclines at table or he who serves the meal? Is it not the one who reclines at table? Yet I am in your midst as the one who serves you. You are the ones who have stood loyally by me in my temptations. I for my part assign to you the dominion my Father has assigned to me. In my Kingdom you will eat and drink at my table, and you will sit on thrones judging the twelve tribes of Israel."

CCC 786 says, "Finally, the People of God share in the royal office of Christ. He exercises His kingship by drawing all men to Himself through His death and resurrection. Christ, King, and Lord of the universe, made Himself the servant of all, for He came "not to be served but to serve and to give His life as a ransom for many. For the Christian, "to reign is to serve Him," particularly when serving "the poor and the suffering, in whom the church recognizes the image of her poor and suffering founder. The people of God fulfills its royal dignity by a life in keeping with its vocation to serve with Christ."

CCC 1936 says, "On coming into the world, man is not equipped with everything he needs for developing his bodily and spiritual life. He needs others. Differences appear tied to age, physical abilities, intellectual or moral aptitudes, the benefits derived from social commerce, and the distribution of wealth. The 'talents' are not distributed equally."

CCC 1937 says, "These differences belong to God's plan, who wills that each receive what he needs from others, and that those endowed with particular "talents" share the benefits with those who need them. These differences encourage and often oblige persons to practice generosity, kindness, and sharing of goods; they foster the mutual enrichment of cultures: ... I have willed that one should need another and that all should be my ministers in distributing the graces and gifts they have received from me."

Patron saints of the charisms of helps and service: St. John Burke, St. Catherine Jarrige, St. Macrina, St. Paula, Brother Leo, St. Anne Lynn.

Charism of Hospitality

(Matthew 25:35) says, "For I was hungry and you gave me food, I was thirsty and you gave me drink, I was a stranger and you welcomed me."

(Genesis 18:1–8) says, "Abraham showed hospitality to three strangers in the desert ... they gave him a prophecy of a son to come."

(Hebrews 13:1–2) says, "Let Brotherly love continue. Do not neglect to show hospitality to strangers, for thereby some have entertained Angels unawares."

(Luke 10:38–42) says, "A woman named Martha received Him into her house. And she had a sister named Mary, who sat at the Lord's feet and listened to His teaching. But Martha was distracted with much serving and she went to Him and said, "Lord, do you not care that my sister has left me to serve alone? Tell her to help me." But the Lord answered her, "Martha, Martha, you are anxious and troubled about many things, one thing is needful. Mary has chosen the better part, which shall not be taken from her."

In (1 Peter 4:9–10), it says, "Practice hospitality ungrudgingly to one another. As each has received a gift, employ it for one another, as good stewards of God's varied grace."

In (3 John 5:100), it says, "It is a loyal thing you do when you render any service to the brethren, especially to strangers, who have testified to your love before the church. So we ought to support such men that we may be fellow workers in the truth."

(Deuteronomy 15:11) says, "You shall open wide your hand to your brother, to the needy and to the poor in the land."

CCC 2449 says, "Jesus makes these words His own: 'The poor you will always have with you, but you do not always have me.'"... "He invites us to recognize His own presence in the poor who are His brothers."

CCC 2447 says, "The works of Mercy are charitable actions by which we come to the aid of our neighbor in his spiritual and bodily necessities (Isaiah 58:6–7). Instructing, advising, consoling, comforting are spiritual works of mercy, as are forgiving and bearing wrongs patiently. The corporal works of mercy consist especially in feeding the hungry, sheltering the homeless, clothing the naked, visiting the sick and imprisoned, and burying the dead. (Matthew 25:31–46) "Among all of these, giving alms to the poor is one of the chief witnesses to fraternal charity; it is also a work of justice pleasing to God."

Other readings (John 12:8; Matthew 25:34–45; Acts 16:14–15; Galatians 4:14; 2 Kings 4:8–17; Luke 17:19–31 and 17:28–31; Romans 12:13; Hebrews 13:1–2).

CCC 2463 says, "How can we not recognize Lazarus, the hungry beggar in the parable (Luke 17:19–31) in the multitude of human beings without bread, a roof or a place to stay? How can we fail to hear Jesus: "As you did it to one of the least of these, you did it to me" (Matthew 25:45)."

Patron saints of hospitality: St. Teresa of Calcutta, St. Vincent de Paul, St. Benedict, St. Margaret Clitherow, Dorothy Day.

Charism of Prayer and Intercessory Prayer

CCC 2697 states, "Prayer is the life of the new heart. It ought to animate us at every moment, but we tend to forget Him who is our life and our all. Prayer is a remembrance of God often awakened by the memory of God in the heart: "We must remember God more often than we draw breath." But we cannot pray 'at all times" if we do not pray at specific times, consciously willing it."

There are many kinds of prayer. One of them is intercessory prayer. That is a prayer or petition in favor of another.

Jesus taught His apostles in (Mark 11:25), "Everything that you ask and pray for, believe you have it already and it will be yours." It takes faith in the promises of God to believe He can and will answer prayer. In (Galatians 3:26), it says, "You are all sons of God through faith in Christ Jesus." And in (1 Corinthians 2:5), it says, "Your Faith should not be in the wisdom of men but in the Power of God." Also in (Ephesians 3:12), it says, "Because of Christ and our faith in Him, we can now come boldly and confidently into God's presence." In (John 20:29), it says, "Blessed are they that have not seen, and yet have believed."

CCC 2752 says, "Prayer presupposes an effort, a fight against ourselves and the wiles of the Tempter. The battle of prayer is inseparable from the necessary "spiritual battle to act habitually according to the Spirit of Christ: we pray as we live, because as we live, we pray."

CCC 2753 says, "In the Battle of prayer we must confront erroneous conceptions of prayer; various currents of thought; and our own experience of failure. We must respond with humility, trust and perseverance to these temptations which cast doubt on the usefulness or even the possibility of prayer."

CCC 2754 says, "The remedy lies in faith, conversion and vigilance of heart."

CCC 2756 says, "Filial trust is put to the test when we feel that our prayer is not always heard. The Gospel invites us to ask ourselves about the conformity of our prayer to the desire of the Spirit."

CCC 2757 says, "Pray constantly" (1 Thess. 5: 17). It is always possible to pray. It is even a vital necessity. Prayer and Christian life are inseparable."

CCC 2761 says, "The Lord's Prayer "is truly the summary of the whole gospel." "Since the Lord ... after handing over the practice of prayer said elsewhere. 'Ask and you will receive,' and since everyone has petitions which are peculiar to his circumstances, the regular and appropriate prayer (The Lord's Prayer) is said first, as the foundation of further desires."

(Luke 11:1–4) says, "One day He was praying in a certain place. When He had finished one of His disciples asked Him, "Lord, teach us to pray, as John taught his disciples. He said to them, "When you pray, say; "Father, hallowed be your name, your kingdom come. Give us your daily bread. Forgive us our sins for we too forgive all who do us wrong; and subject us not to the trial."

(Luke 11:9) says, "So I say to you. "Ask and you shall receive; seek and you shall find; knock and the door shall be opened to you."

(James 5:13–15) says, "If anyone among you is suffering hardship, he must pray. If a person is in good spirits, he should sing a hymn of praise. Is there anyone sick among you? He should ask for the presbyters of the church. They in turn are to pray over him, anointing him with oil in the Name (of the Lord.) This prayer uttered in faith will reclaim the one who is ill, and the Lord will restore him to health. If he has committed any sins, forgiveness will be his. Hence, declare your sins to one another, and pray for one another, that you may find healing."

This is the reason the Catholic Church has the sacrament of the anointing the sick. The priests (presbyters) are ordained to "do what Jesus did." (John 14:12) says, "I solemnly say to you, the man who has faith in me will do the works I do, and greater things far than these. Why? Because I go to the Father, and whatever you ask in my name I will do, so as to glorify the Father in the Son. Anything you ask me in my name I will do. If you love me and obey the commands I give you." (Ignatius)

The one body of Christ comes alive when we each do what the Holy Spirit has given us to do. In (1 Corinthians 12:27–31), it says, "You then are the Body of Christ. Every one of you is a member of it. Furthermore, God has set up in the church first apostles, second prophets, third teachers, then miracle workers, healers, assistants, administrators, and those who speak in tongues." (St. Josephs). God intends for each one of us to do our part in the salvation of the world.

An intercessor is a person who is a mediator or someone who prays for another person. Jesus prayed many times for others. Every person who experienced healing by Jesus was healed by a prayer to God His Father. Jesus taught His apostles in (Mark 11:24), "I give you my word, if you are ready to believe that you will receive whatever you ask for in prayer, it shall be done for you," (St. Joseph's).

It takes faith in the promises of God to believe He can and will answer prayer. In (Galatians 3:26), it says, "Each one of you is a son of God because of your faith in Jesus Christ." And in (1 Corinthians 2:5), it says, "Your faith rests not on the wisdom of men but on the power of God." Also in (Ephesians 3:12), it says, "In Christ and through faith in Him we can speak freely to God, drawing near Him with confidence." In (John 20:29), it says, "Blessed are they that have not seen, and yet have believed." All quotes are from St's Joseph's.

Being healed of our sins is all about surrender. Surrender your sins to Jesus at the foot of His cross and receive forgiveness. Forgiveness of your sins brings your false self to the surface and allows you to see your sin and ask forgiveness. As you invite Jesus into your heart as your Lord and Savior, He fills you with His Holy Spirit. Through your continual healing from the sins and burdens that hold you captive within yourself, the Holy Spirit peels layers of your old self off, layer by layer, and fills you with the Trinity's divine love. This divine love that is the gift of charity is what radiates out of you to others. As

God's divine love touches other people through your charisms, it is fulfilling the great mission that Jesus sent us out to do.

Over two thousand years have separated us from when Jesus was living His example of charisms in action here on earth. It has been more than years that have separated us from Jesus. The subtle seductions of satan have gradually taken us down the road of human pleasure, and blinded not only our visual perception to the truth but also our spiritual vision. The truth is that Jesus came to heal us of our sins and burdens and wounds of any kind—spiritual, mental, physical, and emotional. Jesus heals our wounds through the power of the Holy Spirit. It is through the human earthen vessels that are Jesus's living hands, feet, and lips here on earth that the living water of Jesus's healing pours through. Human death comes to us all. The reality of human death is that it is the ultimate healing if our eternity will be spent with the Trinity.

Each person who has been baptized in the name of Jesus Christ as Lord and Savior has the power to do all that Jesus did. In (John 14:12–21), it says "I solemnly assure you, the man who has Faith in me will do the works that I do, and greater works far than these. Why? Because I go to the Father, and whatever you ask in my name I will do. If you love me and obey the commands I give you. I will ask the Father and He will give you another Paraclete to be with you always [a heavenly intercessor] the Spirit of truth, whom the world cannot accept, since it neither sees Him nor recognizes Him; but you can recognize Him because He remains with you and will be within you. I will not leave you orphaned [without family to protect you and teach you]; I will come back to you. A little while now and the world will see me no more; but you will see me as one who has life, and you will have life. On that day you will know that I am in the Father and you in me, and I in you. He who obeys the commandments that he has from me is the man who loves me; and he who loves me will be loved by my Father, I too will love him and reveal myself to Him." (St. Joseph's)

In (John 14:26–27 St. Joseph), it says, "The Paraclete, the Holy Spirit whom the Father will send in My name, will instruct you in everything, and remind you of all that I told you. "Peace is my farewell to you, my Peace is my Gift to you; I do not give it to you as the world gives peace, do not be distressed or fearful."

In (Romans 8: 26–27 St Joseph), it says, "The Spirit too helps us in our weakness, for we do not know how to Pray as we ought; but the Spirit Himself makes INTERCESSION FOR US WITH GROANING THAT CANNOT BE EXPRESSED TO SPEECH. HE WHO SEARCHES HEARTS KNOWS WHAT THE SPIRIT MEANS, FOR THE SPIRIT INTERCEDES FOR THE SAINTS AS GOD HIMSELF WILLS."

It is all about trust. God the Father trusted His son Jesus to redeem the world of its sin, Jesus fulfilled His mission. Jesus entrusted the spreading of the message of the kingdom of God being here to the apostles, the disciples, and the evangelists who wrote the Gospels, and they accomplished their mission because two thousand years later we know about our salvation. Now it is our turn to step up to the plate and, as Jesus said, "do greater things than I do." (John 14:12).

As a human, we cannot do anything without the power of the Trinity. In (Acts 1:8), it says, "You will receive Power when the Holy Spirit comes on you." The Holy Spirit came upon each one of us when we were baptized and confirmed. Now that we truly know that the Holy Spirit dwells within us already, we need to become an active participant and ask the Holy Spirit to awaken in our hearts. In (John 16:13), it says, "When the spirit of truth comes, He will guide you into all the truth." And in (John 20:21–22), it says, "Peace be with you; as the Father has sent Me, I also send you." And when He had said this, He breathed on them and said to them, "Receive the Holy Spirit." All quotes from St. Joseph's bible.

Our God is an awesome God! Now He is asking you and me to trust Him to fill us with His Holy Spirit, and as the Holy Spirit guides us in using our charisms to spread the kingdom of God, we will be doing what Jesus has asked us to. Intercessory prayer isn't anything fancy; it is something that you are probably already doing. Every time you pray for someone, you are acting as a mediator between that person and God. It's just that simple.

Healing prayer is also just that simple. Healing prayer is just Intercessory prayer. It is asking God to help someone through a trying time. It could be prayer for healing, help for a job, healing of body, mind, soul or emotions, or divine intervention for whatever has hurt their heart. What that means to us is that we need to be there for others and support them and their needs. When praying for others, we are sharing our charisms with them, to bring them to the kingdom of God in their heart. This is something that we can do.

Begin with a prayer in your heart to hear what God is asking you to do. Then listen. Learn to wait upon the Lord. He will send His Holy Spirit into your heart to direct you. It can be a thought, or a feeling, or a knowing. Your part in this is to wait, listen, and discern the message. Now you need to act on that message. If you are called to prayer, then go pray. Trust the Holy Spirit to direct your path. He will even direct your prayer. Believe that God desires to answer your Prayer more than you are unsure how to ask for it. He is our loving Father.

Answered prayer will build up the church. We the people are the church. We are the only hands that Jesus has to work with on this earth today. Our priest said in his homily the other day, that the phrase "Be not afraid" is in the Bible 365 times. That is one "Be not afraid" for each day of the year! I think that God is telling us, to trust Him completely. From that same priest, "Always remember that the love of God will never take you where the grace of God cannot protect you."

My husband has taught me that "it is not what God can do for me, it is not what I can do for God, but it is what God can do *through* me that counts." Ponder those words. Weave them into your personality, and you will be accepting the personality of Jesus Christ into your soul. Pray to become the empty earthen vessel that the power of the Holy Spirit can work through.

Just about a week ago, while I was in prayer, I heard, "You are my minister of peace. Believe in yourself. I believe in you." With that message from God, how can I not step out in faith and be His intercessor for prayer?

"To intercede is to go between" (CCC 2634). Jesus, Mary, and the Holy Spirit are the greatest go-betweens between us and God.

But through the Holy Spirit, God has given us go-betweens that are touchable: humans with the charism of intercessory prayer.

We are all called to pray for each other. But some people are given a great drive to pray for someone and may not even know who it is. They simply know they *have* to pray, and they do it until they are released from that call.

CCC 2626–2649; 2863–2864; 2683; 2690; 2827; 2850–2865; 2892–2894.

Scripture: (Luke 11:10–13; Acts 12:5–11; 2 Corinthians 1:10–11; 1 Timothy 2:1–8).

Patron saints of intercessory prayer: St. Dominio, the martyrs of Compiegne (sixteen Carmelite nuns who were beheaded for their faith), St. Theresa of Liseaux, Padre Pio.

In the last several years I was hearing a lot about '*Intimacy with God,*' and had absolutely no idea what that meant ... nor how to reach it! I asked people what that meant to them, and mostly the answer was "I don't know." Or "Spending time in Prayer." God touched me with a desire to grow closer to Him (He made the first move by giving me the desire to know Him better). Therefore, I *was driven* to discover what this meant, especially for me in my life. After all I am not getting any younger. I asked my first Spiritual Director about Centering Prayer ... it was something that I had heard him talk about. He said, "Before I teach you, I want you to read the book by Fr. Thomas Keating called, *Open Mind, Open Heart.*" I read the book, took notes on it, and asked questions, and we began our journey into Prayer.

It was all very vague and confusing to me. Definitions of unknown words, with words that are not in the regular dictionary made it hard for me to understand. Above in CCC 2752, "Prayer presupposes an effort, a fight against ourselves and the wiles of the tempter." What this means is, 'born in the world...we become of the world!' The tempter is the evil one, and has very subtle ways of tempting us to placing our sensual natures first. That, can be as simple as eating too much (gluttony), because it tastes good...to a different one of the Seven Deadly Sins. Sin separates us from God. So, it is very difficult to invite God into our heart if we have sin covering it. God does not live where sin is!

My '*Intimacy with God*' began when I discovered what Interior Prayer is. One of the meanings of interior is, 'inside or inner.' So, Interior Prayer is, Prayer that takes place inside of you, verses Vocal Prayer, which is Prayers said out loud. Interior prayer begins with the *desire* to allow God to help me, a mere human, to give myself to Him. We have all heard many clichés about "let go and let God," or "Put God in the driver's seat." Whatever the clichés, it all means the same thing…we need to give our heart to God, so that He can give His heart to us. That giving of our heart to God is called *surrender*. To be able to come to the place within us of interior prayer, we need to surrender the moments of our day (the grocery list, that disagreement with someone, the laundry, whatever it is that occupies our mind at this moment, let it float away to wherever thoughts go…and just look at God.

When we "Look at God," we see Him through the 'eyes of our soul," not our human eyes. Therefore, everyone *can* see God in their heart, it simply takes desire, time, practice, a willingness to surrender the thoughts that distract you, and the belief that God will come when you call Him for you to be able to come to *Interion Prayer.* … Prayer and Christian life are inseparable. CCC 2752, "…The battle of prayer is inseparable from the necessary "spiritual battle" to act habitually according to the Spirit of Christ: we pray as we live, because we live as we pray." So, if we do not make time for prayer in our life, we will not learn how to pray.

When you go into the interior place of prayer…don't expect anything to happen. If you have those few moments where thoughts do not come…consider the time spent with God, a total success! God does all the work. All we are supposed to do is give Him our time, be faithful to that time, never let temptation disturbed the time you have chosen for God alone. God will touch you with His Divine Love in Some way. Over time in prayer you or others will notice a change in you. That is how we are to measure 'Success in Interior Prayer."

The Charism of Prayer comes to those who desire to discover God! As a Charism, it must be shared. It cannot be kept to themselves or it is not a Charism. That is just the rules set by God Himself. The Charism of prayer changes us 'into the image and likeness of God,' not because of what we do ... but because of what God does in us as we spend "*TIME*"with Him. So, the moments that we spend with God in Interior Prayer, are the blessings of our lives.

When we use our charism of prayer in intercessory prayer we are praying for another person's needs. While we are praying, the Isaiah Gifts come forward by giving us the power of the Holy Spirit to allow the Fruits to manifest themselves in us through love, peace, patience, gentleness, goodness, and kindness. These fruits will poor forth into the one being prayed for, and they will most likely feel the love, or peace of God.

Interior Prayer is for my Growth towards God, which will change me, and change the way others see me, therefore, I *share* my charism of prayer by allowing God to 'make me into His image and likeness,' so that the love of Jesus will shine out of me into the world. There is no pride in this because 'I' can't do anything to make it happen. The more that I spend *time* with God ... the more He allows the Isaiah gifts to come forward for me to be able to share some knowledge, or give an understanding hug which shares the fruit of the love or peace of Christ.

Bishop Barron says in his CD on "My Beloved Son, "The fruit of Prayer always leads to action." In November 2009, I was blessed to experience The Peace Prayer Chaplet after a Mass at St. Sharbel's Church. The chaplet is a group of prayers that Our Lady has asked us to pray for Peace in our world. It starts with the Creed, then seven groups of three prayers, beginning with Our Father, Hail Mary, and Glory Be. That is 22 prayers dedicated to whatever Peace you need in your Life. Such as, Peace in your heart, in your family, your neighborhoods, in your workplace, your church place, your schools, places where you play, Peace in our government, our state, Washington D.C, our Nation, and our World! The prayer is YOUR'S ... you cannot pray it wrong! MAKE IT YOUR OWN!

I needed peace in my life very badly at that time, and this prayer brought me 'inner peace.' After a month, I felt the need to share this prayer with my family and friends. So, I was on a quest to make these prayer beads that looked like a 'tiny Rosary.' They could not be bought here in America. I learned how to make a Rosary, and adapted it to make this 'Peace Prayer Chaplet,' and my WORK for Our Blessed Mother began.

My Friend Karen, who had invited me to the Mass where I experienced the Peace Prayer Chaplet, said one day, "We should get together with a bunch of women and make these Chaplets, and pray the Rosary while making them." Each one took one and one-half hours to make, and was hurting my right arm which had to do all the twisting and shaping the wires. The group of women never got together, but I did begin to pray the Rosary while making them. While I was making the tenth one, and praying the Rosary, I received a very distinct message in my soul. *"You have to work a little faster! You have to make them for the masses!"* I never doubted the message. (I would never have thought that up on my own!) I told my husband and he never doubted it either. So, I replied in my mind, 'Well, OK, but I will have to find another way to make them!" So, my Charism of Craftsmanship came alive as I designed "Peace Prayer Chaplet Bracelets." And My Charisms of Faith, and Giving came alive also, and my Trust in God poured forth. You see, I had hurt my knee on the job and when I was released to 'regular duty' with limitations... they decided to reduce my hours from forty a week to sixteen a week, which devastated us financially. So, the Mission of making Chaplets for the masses for *free*, was a test in my Faith and trust in God to provide all that I needed to do His work! He has been providing for the past seven years. It always makes me smile and say a prayer when I receive money or beads just when I need them.

It was funny to me how the Holy Spirit works. Our Family was going to the July 3, 2010 Fireworks. Nick and I went early to get seats on the flat ground and brought the food. With my mission from our Blessed Mother, I didn't have a moment to waste, so I brought my bead makings, plus the Hundred that were already made and blessed, just in case that someone wanted one. I had written a paper telling about this prayer and how to do it. There was a family that had staked out a place for their family not far from us. After a while the Father of the family asked me "What are you doing?" I was surprised, and thought a second and said to myself, "Ok Holy Spirit! I will tell them!" I put my things aside and grabbed a few bracelets and the paper that I had written, and went to the man and his family. I told them the story, and said, "I can tell that you are Christian, but not Catholic. Here is the story and Instructions. If you think that you would like to do this prayer, I will be right down here with the bracelets. About 15 minutes later a girl about Seventeen, came to me with the paper and said, "They think that I need this prayer for the Holy Spirit." I smiled and said, "You can pray either the Peace or Holy Spirit prayer on this same bracelet. Do you think anyone else is interested?" She said' "Yes." I took my newly Blessed bracelets to them and each member there took one. I was amazed at how the Holy Spirit Works in me and other people. This story doesn't end here. Through the evening, as family kept coming for both them and us, his family would come and timidly ask if they could have a bracelet too because they would do it with their family also. My daughter finally asked me, "How did all this get started?" I told her and she just smiled. And I smiled and gave God Thanks for using me as His instrument.

That was the beginning of a Prayer Ministry for me. The Charisms of Craftsmanship, Encouragement, Evangelization, Faith, Giving, Healing, Leadership, Intercessory Prayer, Shepherding, Teaching and Writing came alive in me through the Power of the Holy Spirit. Because God *CHOSE TO WORK THROUGH ME* in this way… the Spiritual Gifts listed in (Isaiah 11:2-3), were pulled forward in me. I shared the Knowledge that I had just discovered about how increasing prayer in your life can be so simple and how it changed my life. The gift of Understanding gave me the courage to follow the lead of the Holy Spirit and invite all that He sends to me to pray this simple prayer. It was wonderful to see that no one was 'offended' with the Hail Mary no matter what their Religion. This prayer reached beyond Religious barriers because it was the desire of God. The gift of Piety came alive in me, because my prayer life had increased greatly… and God desired that I share this simple prayer with others. Fear of the Lord shown through as I stood in Awe and Wonder that God could work through 'little Clairann' in such a mighty way.

It is in the sharing of the Isaiah Gifts that the fruits *pour forth from us to God's other children.* First, Peace flowed through me or others would not have been drawn to me and this prayer. Charity (love), Kindness, Generosity, Faithfulness were some of the *'fruits'* that I shared with the making and distribution of these peace prayer Chaplet Bracelets. They have always been given away FREE. Donations came to me of beads and money, exactly when I need more supplies. Thank you, God, His hand has been in this small prayer ministry since Nov 2009, and continues today in the different Novenas and other prayer chaplets that I have been led to create.

After two and one-half years I stopped counting. I had made and given away over 12,000 bracelets to Cursillos, TEC's, Watch's, Army battalions going to IRAC, Hatti, and Africa and China. Plus, unknown more. When I gave them away, I gave the directions of how to make them, and where the cheapest places to find the parts. It reached across religion's. The 'WALK TO EMMAUS' program (Methodist) made them and gave them wherever they held an EMMAUS. A Priest that I noticed was wearing one, told me, "I got mine in Hong Kong from the Emmaus Team that I was on." I was in utter amazement at the thought of 'How did this happen!" It was then that I could track it back to the Cursillo, and someone from the Walk to Emmaus was touched by this prayer, and began making the Chaplets to hand out themselves. God works wonders for those who work for Him!

How wondrous is our God! A small prayer chaplet shared with me… came alive in me as a charism without my knowledge, without any help from me other than I heard the words that came to me through the power of the Holy Spirit, and followed His and Mary's instructions to, "make them for the masses!"

Charism of Knowledge

The charism of knowledge empowers a person to be a channel of God's truth through study. Empowered by the strong drive to learn about God and how we can draw ourselves close to Him, this person is compelled to find a way to share this new found truth with the church and beyond to the world.

What a person with the charism of knowledge uncovers is not for them alone; it is given to them so that they can share it, and it must be shared to help our neighbor and the world grow in the knowledge of God. The charism of knowledge requires sustained intellectual work that awakens this Christian person to ideas that are critical to our walk with Christ. That truth will help our fellow Christians on their journey to Jesus. Christians with this gift are usually given other gifts that will help them find a way to share the new knowledge, such as writing or teaching, encouragement, leadership, or prophecy.

What makes this identifiable as a charism is that the person did not have the ability or the desire to study before. They didn't have prior experience or knowledge of the material that they are now sharing with others. And they did not have the ability to share it. They experienced an identifiable change.

Paul's letter to the (Romans 5:14 St. Joseph's) verifies this: "I myself am satisfied about you, my brethren, that you yourselves are full of Goodness, filled with all knowledge, and able to instruct one another." And Paul teaches us that humility is very important. In (2 Corinthians 12:70 St. Joseph's), Paul says, "And to keep me from being too elated by the abundance of revelations, a thorn was given me in the flesh, a messenger of satan to harass me, to keep me from being too elated."

The reason that this knowledge is imparted to the most unlikely person is so that it is believable! (Ephesians 3:14–19) shares this: "For this reason I bow my knees before the Father, from whom every family in heaven and on earth is named, that according to the riches of His glory He may grant you to be strengthened [fortitude] with might through His Spirit in the inner man [baptism and confirmation, Holy Eucharist and reconciliation], and that Christ may dwell in your hearts through faith [your beliefs with the help of the Sacraments]; that you, being rooted and grounded in love [charity], may have the power to comprehend [understand] with all the saints what is the breadth and length and height and depth, and to know the love of Christ which surpasses knowledge, that you may be filled with all the fullness of God." (all in parentheses are my thoughts).

The fruits and gifts and virtues all intertwine here in this passage to help us understand that nothing stands alone—not even the Trinity. That is why we say "Triune Godhead"—the community of the Trinity of Father, Son, and Holy Spirit.

The CCC paragraph 94 states, "What Christ has entrusted to the apostles. They in turn handed on by their preaching and writing, under the inspiration of the Holy Spirit, to all generations, until Christ returns in glory."

This charism of knowledge comes alive when I allow the Holy Spirit to expand my heart to receive the goodness of God in these fruits and gifts of the Holy Spirit, and then they will pour forth out of me as the charism that God has designed for me to share.

Patron saints of knowledge:

- St. Thomas Aquinas (1225–1274). Was one of the greatest scholars of his day, and was a universal doctor of the church.
- St. Thomas More (1478–1535). Beheaded for his faith.
- Venerable John Henry Newman (1801–1890). His ideas permeated the Second Vatican Council, which has been called the Council of Newman.
- Blessed Edith Stein (1891–1942). Jewish born, very intellectual, read St. Teresa of Avila, entered the Carmelite Monastery, was sent to Auschwitz with her sister Rosa, where they died in the gas chamber.

The Charism of knowledge is given, to be given away. The words that Jesus said from the cross, "I THIRST", are the words that I have been saying for the last five years, I have been hungry for more of Jesus…in scripture, in the Mass, in the Eucharist, in understanding the Catholic Churches teachings, and I still can't get enough! The fulfillment of my charism of knowledge is expressed through my writings, sharing in bible classes, teachings in our church bulletin and Creating Holy cards with prayers, novenas, and mystical pictures.

Charism of Leadership

CCC 763 states, "It was the Son's task to accomplish the Father's plan of salvation in the fullness of time. Its accomplishment was the reason for His being sent." The Lord Jesus inaugurated His church by preaching the Good News—that is, the coming of the reign of God, promised over the ages in the scriptures. To fulfill the Father's will, Christ ushered in the kingdom of heaven on earth. The church "is the Reign of Christ already present in mystery."

CCC 764 states, "This Kingdom shines out before all men in the WORD, in the WORKS and in the PRESENCE of Christ." The seed and the beginning of the kingdom are the little flock of those whom Jesus came to gather around Him, the flock whose shepherd He is (Luke 12:32; Matthew 10:16, 26:31; John 10:1–21). They (the flock) form Jesus's true family (Matthew 12:49). To those whom He thus gathered around Him, He taught a new "way of acting" and a prayer of their own (Matthew 5–6).

The beatific way of life is a life filled with the love of the Trinity shared with another through the spiritual gifts of the Holy Spirit. By living the Beatitudes, we will be molded into the image and likeness of God. Which will lead us to someday see God in His fullness.

The leader of all leaders is Jesus Christ Himself.

CCC 765 states, "The Lord Jesus endowed His community with a structure that will remain until the Kingdom is fully achieved. Before all else there is a choice of the Twelve with Peter as their head (Mark 3:14–15). Representing the twelve tribes of Israel, they are the foundation stones of the New Jerusalem (Matthew 19:28; Luke 22:30; Revelations 21:12–14). The twelve and the other disciples share in Christ's mission and His power, and also in His lot (Matthew 10:25; Luke 10:1–2; Mark 6:7; John 15:20). By all His actions, Christ prepares and builds His Church."

CCC 766 states, "The Church is born primarily of Christ's self-giving for our salvation, anticipated in the institution of the Eucharist and fulfilled on the cross. "The origin and growth of the Church are symbolized by the blood and water which flowed from the open side of the crucified Jesus. (John 19:34). "For it was from the side of Christ as He slept the sleep of death upon the cross that there came forth the 'wondrous sacrament of the whole Church.' As Eve was formed from the sleeping Adam's side, so the Church was born from the pierced heart of Christ hanging dead upon the cross." We, the followers and believers of Jesus Christ as Lord, Savior and Redeemer of mankind are the Church.

CCC 767 states, "When the work the Father gave the Son to do on earth was accomplished, the Holy Spirit was sent on the day of Pentecost in order the He might continually sanctify the Church. Then the Church was openly displayed to the crowds and the spread of the Gospel among the nations, through preaching, was begun." As the "convocation (calling together)" of all men for salvation, the Church in her very nature is missionary, sent by Christ to all the nations to make disciples of them (Matthew 28:19–20)."

CCC 768 states, "So that she (The Church) can fulfill her mission, the Holy Spirit "bestows upon (the Church) varied hierarchic and charismatic gifts, and in this way directs her." "Henceforward the Church, endowed with the gifts of her founder (Jesus) and faithfully observing His precepts of charity, humility, and self-denial, receives the mission of proclaiming and establishing among all the peoples the Kingdom of Christ and of God, and she (The Church) is on earth the seed and the beginning of that kingdom."

(Exodus 18:13–27) states Moses led the Israelites from bondage and out of Egypt. In 1 (Timothy 3:1–7), it speaks of how someone who wants to be a bishop, needs to be a good manager of his own household and his own children before he should take care of the church. He needs to "be well thought of by those outside of the church, to be sure that he does not fall into disgrace and the devils traps."

A leader is a person who shares a strong goal and finds a way to get to the destination, and others want to help them to get to the goal. The main thing noted about the person who leads is that people are following. A leader, when they turn around, people are following. A leader will guide others to a road that makes a difference in their lives and in the lives of others . A Leader will get us there.

Scripture about leaders: (Romans 12:8; 1 Thessalonians 5:12–13; 1 Timothy 3:1–7; 1 Timothy 5:17–22; 1 Samuel 10:1; Nehemiah 2:17–18; Mark 9:33–41; Romans 12:8; Acts 1:5–26; Acts 6:1–6; Hebrews 13:7).

More CCC passages: 769–771; 874–896; 897–900; 903; 907–913; 1878–1885; 1897–1948; 2442.

Patron saints of leadership: Jesus Christ Himself and all the apostles and disciples throughout these two thousand years, St. Ignatius of Loyola, St. Teresa of Avila, St. John of the Cross, all the saints great and small, etc.

(CCC punctuation and capitals are mine.)

Charism of Mercy

The Charism of Mercy

(Luke 10:33–35) speaks to us of the Good Samaritan, and what he did for the man beaten and left for dead by his attackers and the Levite and priest who passed by him and left him alone in his pain. The Samaritan alone came to his rescue by cleaning and covering his wounds, putting his own cloak on the man, and placing him on his animal to take him to town to care for him better. Then when leaving for his own business, he paid for the man's care, with the promise to pay more if it was needed on his return trip. He was Jesus in a Samaritan's skin for the wounded man's needs.

(Matthew 25:40) says, "Truly, I say to you, as you did it to one of the least of my brethren, you did it to me. (Ignatius Bible)."

(James 2:14–17) says, "What does it profit, my brothers, if a man says he has faith but does not have works? Can his faith save him? If a brother or sister is poorly clothed and in lack of food, and one of you says to them, "Go in peace, be warmed and filled, without giving them the things needed for the body, what does it profit? So, faith by itself, if it has no works, is dead."

Mercy is compassion shown to an offender. The look of mercy that Jesus gave Peter after he denied Jesus for the third time (Mark 14:66–72) was what drove Peter to deep sorrow and repentance, and Peter received the forgiveness of Jesus. In (Luke 23:41), it says, "For this man has done nothing wrong. And the repentant thief said, "Jesus, remember me when you come into your kingly power." And Jesus said to him, "Truly, I say to you, today you will be with me in Paradise."

The New Testament is filled with stories of Jesus's mercy. And He calls us to "do what I have done." That includes mercy. We are the visible face, of the invisible God who showers His mercy upon us when we ask. We each are called by God Himself, through the words of Jesus in the Gospels, to have mercy on all our brothers and sisters.

Mercy is a fruit of charity, along with peace and joy. "Love (charity) is the fulfillment of all our works (CCC 1829)." My eight-year-old grandson said to me when we were talking about this book and what the fruits and gifts were, he jumped up and said, "Nana, I don't draw very well but I have an idea!" He got a piece of typing paper and drew the picture on the inside cover of this book. Two years later, I asked him if he remember the picture? He said, "Yes, I drew it for your book!" I asked him what he was thinking about when he drew it. He said, "That's God, trying to help us get to heaven!" It seems to me that my eight-year-old grandson has a better handle on all of this than most adults.

Fr. Dave Whitside told me when he saw the picture that, "Throughout the whole bible, clouds have always represented the Holy Spirit. He was Prophetic and didn't even know it." Neither did I!

So, it was through a 'child's spirit' that the Holy Spirit placed this in Landen's mind. This is why God tells us, 'I assure you, unless you change and become as little children you will not enter the Kingdom of God." (Matthew 18:3). It is the Holy Spirit that gives us the Gifts necessary to be able to reach God. And God's hand is always there for us, waiting for us to come to Him. The Holy Spirit lifts us up, and holds us there if we desire, until we can reach God. And we do this by allowing the fruits and gifts and charisms to become alive in our lives. "Works of mercy are charitable actions by which we come to the aid of our neighbor in his spiritual and bodily necessities. Instructing, advising, consoling, comforting are spiritual works of mercy, as are forgiving and bearing wrongs patiently. The corporal works of mercy consist especially in feeding the hungry, sheltering the homeless, clothing the naked, visiting the sick and imprisoned, and burying the dead. Among all these, giving alms to the poor is one of the chief witnesses to fraternal charity; it is also a work of justice pleasing to God." (CCC 2447).

Patron saints of mercy:

- Pope John Paul II
- St. Theresa of Calcutta
- St Faustina Kowalska, a Polish nun to whom Jesus gave the Message of Divine Mercy
- And many, many more

Charism of Music

The charism of music is expressed by the performing of music with singing or playing an instrument to the delight and nourishment of others and the ultimate praise of God. Music as a charism does not have to be religious in nature. Anything that beautifies our world musically is a charism of music.

Some people are given a talent to play an instrument that brings beauty to our world with melodious notes and harmonies. Some are given the ability to match those notes with their voices and therefore glorify God through music. When we come together with voices and instruments lifted in song to God in thanksgiving for His goodness and kindness to us, we are giving Him the praise that is due to Him for creating such a beautiful world and what is in it.

A person who is able to write words that flow together to tell a beautiful story and put a melody to it is using their spiritual gift of artistic creativity, and expressing thoughts and feelings that work together for the glory of God. When a person is using their charism of music to touch the life of another, they experience a closeness to God in a very personal way. It is the presence of the Holy Spirit within your being that brings the depth of your charism alive.

When I use my charism of healing prayer, I feel heat and tingling in my hands as I hover over the person that I am praying with. I also feel it within my whole being. My friend Jennifer says that she feels that same heat and tingling in her chest when she is singing for the glory of God. Another friend Eileen says that when she is playing her instrument, it can put her in a meditative place spiritually. Another friend, Marilyn, says, "Singing for the glory of God brings me great joy. And I feel very blessed to be able to sing and be able to draw people closer to God through the music and the words of songs. I find myself saying a prayer for the composer of those wonderful words and music. What a gift from God!"

CCC 2502 says, "Genuine Sacred Art draws man to adoration, to prayer, and to the love of God, Creator and Savior, the Holy One and Sanctifier."

This deep communion with God draws the person closer and closer to Jesus and magnifies the moment that is shared with another. Music has the ability to draw all of us closer and closer to God.

CCC 1140 says, "Liturgical services are not private functions but are celebrations of the Church which is the 'Sacrament of Unity,' namely, the holy people united and organized under the authority of the bishops. Therefore, liturgical services pertain to the whole Body of the Church."

CCC 1156 says, "The musical tradition of the universal Church is a treasure of inestimable value, greater even than that of any other art. The main reason for this pre-eminence is that as a combination of sacred music and words, it forms a necessary or integral part of solemn liturgy."

The composition and singing of inspired psalms, often accompanied by musical instruments, were already closely linked to the liturgical celebrations of the Old Covenant. The church continues and develops this tradition: "Address... one another in psalms and hymns and spiritual songs, singing and making melody to the Lord with all your heart" (Ephesians 5:19). "He who sings prays twice" (St. Augustine).

St. Hildegard of Bingen (1098–1179) wrote sacred music, which beautified our Liturgy.

CCC 1157 says, "Song and music fulfill their function as signs in a manner all the more significant when they are "more closely connected...with the liturgical action, according to three principal criteria: beauty expressive in prayer, the unanimous participation of the assembly at the designated moments, and the solemn character of the celebration. In this way they participate in the purpose of the liturgical words and actions: the glory of God and the sanctification of the faithful."

Charism of Pastoring and Shepherding

Shepherding or pastoring is a spiritual gift that is given to someone to help lead others to Christ, and not only lead them to Christ but also help them stay on the narrow path by nurturing the relationships within a group. The Holy Spirit gives the charism of pastoring or shepherding to the laity and clergy, men and women, to be able to serve all people.

CCC 910 says, "The laity can also feel called, or be in fact called, to cooperate with their pastors in the service of the ecclesial community for the sake of its growth and life. This can be done through the exercise of different kinds of ministries according to the Grace and Charisms which the Lord has been pleased to bestow on them."

In (1 Peter 5:1–3), it says, "To the elders among you I, a fellow elder, a witness of Christ's sufferings and sharer in the glory that is to be revealed, make this appeal. God's flock is in your midst give it a shepherd's care. Watch over it willingly as God would have you do, not under constraint: and not for shameful profit either; but generously. Be examples to the flock, not lording it over those assigned to you, so that when the chief Shepherd appears you will win for yourselves the unfading crown of glory."

(Ephesians 4:11–13) says, "It is He who gave apostles, prophets, evangelist, pastors and teachers in roles of service for the faithful to build up the Body of Christ—till we become one in faith and in the knowledge of God's Son, and form the perfect man who is Christ come to full stature." (Punctuation is mine.)

CCC 1545: "The redemptive sacrifice of Christ is unique, accomplished once for all; yet it is made present in the Eucharistic sacrifice of the Church. The same is true of the one priesthood of Christ; it is made present through the ministerial priesthood without diminishing the uniqueness of Christ's priesthood: "Only Christ is the true priest, the others being only his ministers.""

CCC 1547: "The ministerial or hierarchical priesthood of bishops and priests, and the common priesthood of all the faithful participate, "each in its own proper way, in the one priesthood of Christ." While being "ordered one to another," they differ essentially.[22] In what sense? While the common priesthood of the faithful is exercised by the unfolding of baptismal grace a life of faith, hope, and charity, a life according to the Spirit—the ministerial priesthood is at the service of the common priesthood. It is directed at the unfolding of the baptismal grace of all Christians. The ministerial priesthood is a *means* by which Christ unceasingly builds up and leads his Church. For this reason, it is transmitted by its own sacrament, the sacrament of Holy Orders."

(Acts 20:28–31) says, "Keep watch over yourselves, and over the whole flock the Holy Spirit has given you to guard. Shepherd the Church of God, which He has acquired at the price of His own blood. I know that when I am gone, savage wolves will come among you who will not spare the flock. From your own number, men will present themselves distorting the truth and leading astray any who will follow them. Do not forget that for three years, night and day, I never ceased warning you individually even to the point of tears. I commend you now to the Lord, and to that gracious WORD of His which can enlarge you, and give you a share among all who are consecrated to Him. Never did I set my heart on anyone's silver or gold or envy the way he dressed. You yourselves know that these hands of mine have served both my needs and those of my companions. I have always pointed out to you that it is by such hard work that you must help the weak. You need to recall the words of the Lord Jesus Himself, who said, "There is more happiness in giving than receiving."

In (1 Timothy 4:11–16), it says, "Such are the things you must urge and teach. Let no one look down on you because of your youth, but be a continuing example of love, faith, and purity to believers. Until I arrive, devote yourselves to the reading of Scriptures, to preaching and teaching. Do not neglect the gift you have received when, as a result of prophecy, the presbyters laid hands on you. Attend to your duties; let them absorb you, so that everyone may see your progress. Watch yourself and watch your teaching. Persevere at both tasks. By doing so you will bring salvation to yourself and all who hear you."

(John 10:14–18) says, "I am the good shepherd. I know My sheep and My sheep know Me in the same way that the Father knows Me and I know My Father; for these sheep I will give My life. I have other sheep (the Gentiles) that do not belong to this fold. I must lead them, too, and they shall be one flock then, one shepherd. The Father loves Me for this: that I lay down My life to take it up again. No one takes it from Me; I lay it down freely. I have power to take it up again. This command I received from My Father."

Charism of Prophecy

A person to whom God has given the spiritual gift of prophecy has already built a relationship with God and has learned to trust God and the grace that God bestows upon him. Grace is a free unmerited gift from God to help us make good decisions and be able to turn away from sin (things of this world that separate us from God) and turn towards a virtuous life. Those who have learned to be with God first learned to listen to the depths of their hearts and discern what it is they hear.

Prophecy is "an inspired utterance of a prophet."

CCC 218 says, "Thanks to the Prophets, Israel understood that it was again out of love that God never stopped saving them and pardoning their unfaithfulness and sins."

CCC 64 says, "Through the prophets, God forms His people in the hope of salvation, in the expectation of a new and everlasting Covenant intended for all, to be written on their hearts (Isaiah 2:2–4; Jeremiah 31:31–43; Hebrews 10:16). The prophets proclaim a radical redemption of the people of God, purification from all their infidelities, a salvation which will include all the nations. Above all the poor and humble of the Lord will bear this hope. Such holy women as Sarah, Rebecca, Rachel, Miriam, Deborah, Hannah, Judith, and Esther kept alive the hope of Israel's salvation. The purest figure among them is Mary."

(Genesis 3:15) is a promise of Jesus, our Redeemer, through Mary.

God loved Adam and Eve. He created them in His own image. The image of love itself. (Genesis 1:26) says, "God created man in His own image; in the divine image He created him; male and female He created them." To share all that was good and kind and loving with one another.

We were given this life freely from God in the beginning. But sin entered in, and truth was covered by our own desires.

In (1 John 4: 1-6 St. Josephs), it says, "Beloved, do not trust every spirit, but put the spirits to a test to see if they belong to God, because many false prophets have appeared in the world. This is how you can recognize God's Spirit: every spirit that acknowledges Jesus Christ come in the flesh belongs to God, while every spirit that fails to acknowledge Him does not belong to God. Such is the spirit of the antichrist which, as you have heard, is to come; in fact, it is in the world already. You are of God, you little ones, and thus you have conquered the false prophets. For there is One greater IN you than there is in the World. Those others belong to the world: that is why theirs is the language of the world, and why the world listens to them. We belong to God and anyone who has knowledge of God gives us hearing, while anyone who is not of God refuses to hear us. Thus do we distinguish the spirit of truth from the spirit of deception."

It is not simple to discern God's spirit from satan's because satan is so subtle. Remember Eve? But if we listen to Scripture (God's Word made flesh in Jesus) and draw it into our hearts, our eyes will be opened to the light of the world and of heaven.

CCC 79 says, "The Father's self-communication made through His Word in the Holy Spirit, remains present and active in the Church: "God, who spoke in the past, continues to converse with the Spouse of His beloved Son. And the Holy Spirit, through whom the living voice of the Gospel rings out in the Church, and through her in the world, leads believers to the full truth, and makes the Word of Christ dwell in them in all its richness" (Colossians 3:16).

We listen to the voice of God through the Scriptures. Our pastors help us understand the messages through their teachings, and explanations are found in our catechism of the Catholic Church.

CCC 711 says, "Behold, I am doing a new thing." (Isaiah 43:19) Two prophetic lines were to develop, one leading to the expectation of a Messiah, the other pointing to the announcement of a new Spirit. They converge in the small Remnant, the people of the poor, who await in hope the "consolation of Israel" and "the redemption of Jerusalem."

In (Luke 4:18–19), Christ makes His own this passage of (Isaiah 61:1–2): "The Spirit of the Lord is upon me, because the LORD has anointed me to bring good tidings to the afflicted; He has sent me to bind up the broken hearted, to proclaim liberty to the captives, and the opening of the prison to those who are bound; to proclaim the year of the Lord's favor." Isaiah's prophecy in chapter 61 is fulfilled in Jesus Christ our Savior written in Luke 4.

In (2 Peter 1:20–21), it says, "First you must understand this: there is no prophecy contained in Scripture which is a personal interpretation. Prophecy has never been put forward by man's willing it. It is rather that men impelled by the Holy Spirit have spoken under God's influence."

In (1 Corinthians 14:29), it says, "Let no more than two or three prophets speak, and let the rest judge the worth of what they say."

"Those with this Charism must communicate the message that they have been given and then leave the results to God and the discernment of the Christian Community. This Charism requires a great deal of on-going pastoral discernment and nurture if the community is going to benefit from this gift of God" (Catherine of Siena, Spiritual Gifts Inventory).

More Scripture: (Deuteronomy 13:1–5; Deuteronomy 18:18–22; 1 Samuel 3:1–21; Matthew 7:15–20; Matthew 24:11 and 23–24; Acts 15:32; 1 Corinthians 12:28–29; 1 Corinthians 14:3 and 22–40;

1 John 4:1–6; Revelation 1:1–3; Luke 3:1–18; Acts 11:27–30, 15:30–35, and 21:9–14; Romans 12:6; 1 Corinthians 12:10 and 28; Ephesians 4:11–16).

CCC 61; 436; 712–715; 783, 785, 2447.

Uses: prayer groups, long-term planning, evangelistic events, prayer teams, prayer chains.

Patron saints of prophecy: the apostles, the writers of Scriptures, Phillip Neri, Arbogast (first century), Blessed Anna Maria Taigi (1769–1857), who was consulted by popes, religious and civic leaders.

Under this heading of prophecy, we also have "word of wisdom and word of knowledge." They are spiritual gifts given to individuals to share with either an individual or a group that God wants led in a certain way. This is usually manifested within prayer groups.

Charism of Teaching

When a person with the charism of teaching shares knowledge, others learn. The charism of teaching brings with it a great desire on the part of the teacher to make sure that the listener learns the message. In other words, they care if the listener understands the message.

(James 3:1) says, "Not many of you should become teachers, my brothers; you should realize that those of you who do so will be called to a stricter account. All of us fall short in many respects."

(Matthew 28:18–20), the commission of the apostles after Jesus's resurrection, says, "Jesus came forward and addressed them in these words: "Full authority has been given to me both in heaven and on earth; go, therefore, and make disciples of all the nations. Baptize them in the name of the Father, and the Son, and the Holy Spirit. Teach them to carry out everything I have commanded you. And know that I am with you always, until the end of the world!"

In the footnotes of the St. Joseph's Bible, it says, "The apostles are to teach the world not merely the doctrine of the Resurrection but the historical teaching of Jesus. This the evangelist Matthew obviously considers to be contained in the gospel he has written. 'I am with you always': The Power of the Risen Christ will ever sustain those whom He has commissioned to preach the 'good news' of salvation to the world."

(Acts 20:20–27) says, "Never did I shrink from telling you what was for your own good, or from teaching you in public or in private. With Jews and Greeks alike I insisted solemnly on repentance before God and on faith in our Lord Jesus. But now, as you see, I am on my way to Jerusalem, compelled by the Holy Spirit and not knowing what will happen to me there except that the Holy Spirit has been warning me from city to city that chains and hardships await me. I put no value on my life if only I can finish my race and complete the service to which I have been assigned by the Lord Jesus, bearing witness to the gospel of God's grace. I know as I speak these words that none of you will ever see my face again. Therefore, I solemnly declare this day that I take the blame for no man's conscience, for I have never shrunk from announcing to you God's design in its entirety."

Wow! How straightforward is that? Paul gave everything he had to the spreading of the Gospel of Jesus. Paul gave the people what Jesus Himself gave him (Acts 22:18, Acts 23:11).

(Acts 26:6-23) says, "But today I stand trial because of my hope in the promise made by God to our fathers. The twelve tribes of our people fervently worship God day and night in the hope that they will see that promise fulfilled … Let me ask why you, above all, who are Jews, should find it hard to believe that God raises dead men to life."

"For my part, I once thought it my duty to oppose the name of Jesus the Nazorean in every way possible…With the authority I received from the chief priest, I sent many of God's holy people to prison. When they were to be put to death I cast my vote against them."

"On one such occasion I was traveling toward Damascus armed with the authority and commission of the priests. On this journey, Your Majesty, I saw a light more brilliant than the sun shining at midday. It surrounded me and those who were traveling with me. All of us heard a voice saying to me in Hebrew, "Saul, Saul, why do you persecute me? It is hard for you to kick against a goad." I said, at that, "Who are you, sir? And the Lord answered: I am that Jesus whom you are persecuting. Get up now and stand on your feet. I have appeared to you to designate you as my servant and as a witness to what you have seen of me and what you will see of me. I have delivered you from this people and from the nations, to open the eyes of those to whom I am sending you, to turn them from darkness to light and from the dominion of satan to God; that through their faith in me they may obtain the forgiveness of their sins and a portion among God's people."

"King Agrippa, I could not disobey that heavenly vision. I preached a message of reform and of conversion to God, first to the people of Damascus, then to the people of Jerusalem and all the country of Judea: yes. Even to the Gentiles. I urged them to act in conformity with their change of heart. That is why the Jews seized me in the temple court and tried to murder me. But I have had God's help to this very day, and so I stand here to testify to great and small alike. Nothing that I say differs from what the prophets and Moses foretold: namely, that the Messiah must suffer and that, as the first to rise from the dead, He will proclaim light to our people and the Gentiles."

Not all of us will receive a mission like St. Paul did. But we each, through our given charism, will receive a mission of our own to be completed in God's time. Pray that we will be able to understand what God is telling us to do for Him.

Scripture: (Acts 18:24–28; Romans 12:6–7; 1 Corinthians 12:28–31; Ephesians 4:11–14).

CCC 425–429; 767–768; 785; 849; 888–892; 900; 903–904; 906; 2447.

Patron saints of the charism of teaching: St. Theresa of Avila, St. John of the Cross, St. Theresa of the Trinity, St. John Baptist de la Salle (1651–1719), Nano Nagle (1718–1784, Ireland), Blessed Mary Mac Kippop (1842–1909, Australia), and countless more.

Charism of Tongues and Interpretation of Tongues

This charism is a spiritual gift given to help a person be a channel of God's love in giving a message to either a person or a group of people.

Included in this gift is the following.

The Descent of the Holy Spirit

(Acts 2:1–13) says, "When the day of Pentecost came it found them gathered in one place. Suddenly from up in the sky there came a noise like a strong, driving wind which was heard all through the house where they were seated. Tongues as of fire appeared, which parted and came to rest on each of them, all were filled with the Holy Spirit. They began to express themselves in foreign tongues: and make bold proclamation as the Spirit prompted them." ("Ecstatic prayer in praise of God" is written in the footnotes of the St. Joseph's edition.)

(Acts 10:44–46) says, "Peter had not finished these words when the Holy Spirit descended upon all who were listening to Peter's message. The circumcised believers who had accompanied Peter were surprised that the gift of the Holy Spirit should have been poured out on the gentiles also, whom they could hear speaking in tongues and glorifying God."

Acts 19:6 says, "As Paul laid his hands on them, the Holy Spirit came down on them and they began to speak in tongues and to utter prophecies."

(Romans 8:26–27) says, "The Spirit too helps us in our weakness, for we do not know how to pray as we ought; but the Spirit Himself makes intercession for us with groanings that cannot be expressed in speech. He who searches hearts knows what the Spirit means, for the Spirit intercedes for the saints as God Himself wills."

In (1 Corinthians 12:10), it says, "One receives the gift of tongues, another that of interpreting the tongues." As in (Acts 2:5–8): "Staying in Jerusalem at the time were devout Jews of every nation under the heaven. These heard the sound, and assembled in a large crowd, They asked in utter amazement. "Are not all of these men who are speaking Galileans? How is it that each of us hears them in his native tongue? ... Yet each of us hears them speaking in his own tongue about the marvels God has accomplished."

(Acts 2:9–1)1 says, "Not just Greek, but over twelve languages were heard"

(Colossians 1:23) says, "But you must hold fast to the faith, unshaken in the hope promised you by the gospel you have heard. It is the gospel that has been announced to every creature under heaven, and I, Paul, am its servant."

All this is given as a gift from God for the purpose of growing His church. This type of "tongue language" is referred to as public tongues. Otherwise, how could the apostles "go into all the world and proclaim the good news to all creation" if they could only speak their native language? (Mark 16:15 St. Joseph's).

In my opinion only, this is a reversal of the tower of Babel (Genesis 11:9): "That is why it is called Babel, because there, the Lord confused the speech of all the world." And in the days of the apostles, God chose to send down His Holy Spirit to join the people together in the language of the Spirit of God so they could be of "one mind and one heart" (Acts 2:42–46).

(Mark 16:17) says, "Signs like these will accompany those who have professed their faith: they will use my name to expel demons, they will speak entirely new languages."

CCC 2003 says, "There are furthermore special graces called Charisms after the Greek term used by St. Paul and meaning "favor," "gratuitous gift," "benefit." Whatever their character sometimes it is extraordinary, such as the gift of miracles or of tongues. Charisms are oriented toward sanctifying grace and are intended for the common good of the Church. They are at the service of charity which builds up the Church" (1 Corinthians 12)."

Speaking in tongues with interpretation of tongues is the same as prophecy. They work together to draw people to God. And it is given to upbuild the church.

More Scripture: (1 Corinthians 14:13–19).

CCC 799–801; 951; 2003–2005.

Interpretation of tongues is present in all those who were listening to the apostles. In today's world, there is less need of this type of preaching, or teaching. Interpretation of tongues is necessary today if someone has spoken in tongues in a group setting (*spoken* means preached or given a message from God).

Private prayer language, as in (1 Corinthians 14:4): "A man who speaks in a tongue is talking not to men but to God. No one understands him, because he utters mysteries in the Spirit. The prophet, on the other hand, speaks to men for their upbuilding, their encouragement, their consolation. He who speaks in a tongue builds up himself, but he who prophesies builds up the church. I should like it if all of you spoke in tongues, but I much prefer that you Prophesy. The Prophet is greater than the one who speaks in tongues, unless the speaker can also interpret for the upbuilding of the church."

I feel that private prayer language was given to me, to develop my trust in God, and help me not only understand how to surrender my being to the Holy Spirit but also experience that total self-giving love of Our Lord. In my tongue prayer, Jesus, through the power of the Holy Spirit, connects me to the Father in praise, worship, and grace. Gift given, gift received.

My private tongue prayer has opened up a whole new way of communication with God for me. I do not understand what I am saying. I don't need to understand, God does because it is His language. All that I am doing is surrendering my heart to Jesus by allowing my lips to move with "the groanings of the Holy Spirit" (Romans 8:26).

CCC 688 says, "Prayer, wherein He intercedes for us." What I have discovered is that my charisms of writing and healing prayer have become effortless since my tongue prayer began. I can feel the presence of the Holy Spirit within me whenever I am using my charisms for the good of the church (God's people).

My faith has deepened since I was given my first tongue word, *shanaya* interpreted as "I love you." In God's language, that means so much more than our language. It speaks of the breadth, length, depth, and height of what God is willing to do for us. (Ephesians 3:18) says, "Thus you will be able to grasp fully, with all the holy ones, the breadth and length and height and depth of Christ's love, and experience this love which surpasses all knowledge, so that you may attain to the fullness of God Himself."

Wow! What the grace of God can do for us—if only we realize it and not only allow the Spirit to work inside of us but also ask for the Holy Spirit to do with us as God wills. For me, the key to all this was learning to surrender my spirit to the Spirit of God. Thank you, God, for giving me the grace to discover how to do this.

Patron saints of tongues: all the apostles and disciples who were obedient to Jesus and "went out into all of the world" with only their faith in God that He would lead them and give them the ability to do what He asked of them. And this has been fulfilled throughout these two thousand years, including us.

One evening four years ago, my husband and I were watching our three grandsons. Their great-grandfather lived across the street with his son. The ambulance came with flashing lights and we had our faces at the window. He had not been well, but we saw that he came out on the stretcher with his head uncovered, so I told the three boys that we needed to pray. We gathered in a circle, and I began with, "Lord God, we ask that you have the paramedics and the emergency room doctors take care of grandpa Ray the way that you want him taken care of." I didn't know what else to say, so I began to pray in tongues. After lifting my voice in prayer for a little while, I began to hear more 'tongue prayer!' I opened my eyes and looked towards my oldest grandson David who was nine years old. He was looking at me with eyes big and shining brightly! His mouth was in a wide-open smile as the words were spewing out of his mouth. I just smiled at him and turned toward Landen who was seven years old. He had his head tipped toward me, and he had a little flat smile on his face as the tongue words were coming out of his mouth. And I smiled at him too. Then I looked at little Owen, and His lips were pressed together and *sealed shut*. He was four and a half years old, had a speech impediment, and we had trouble understanding him some-times, but he knew what he was saying, but now he had no idea what he was saying, and wouldn't let it come out. *THAT* was the power of the Holy Spirit coming alive in a prayer circle! Owen still takes my hands, closes his eyes, and prays, he says, "I am praying in my head."

When I have a great need, I ask for one of them to pray with me, or for me, they come to me and take my hands and their prayer language emerges, as beautiful as anything that I have ever heard, because it is God's Divine Love that flows out of them like living water. I Praise you God for the revelation that prayer tongues, is a wonderful, healing gift given by your very own 'Spirit of love.' And most importantly, none of us should 'be afraid.'

My own private Tongue Prayer can take me to a place of seren-ity…Where I am in communion with God. It is most beautiful. Allowing my mouth to be an instrument of the Holy Spirit is a wonderful experience of self-surrender to God. I call it, Trustful-Surrender, that comes from Spiritual- Humility. Spiritual-Humility is Poverty of spirit.

Charism of Voluntary Poverty

The voluntary poverty of the life of Jesus Christ Our Lord, Savior, Redeemer, King, Brother is the same story as the "greatest story ever told." It's all about divine love.

We all know the story of Jesus's birth into poverty. It was a huge part of God's divine plan to set the example for mankind to believe that God will provide. When a choice was not humanly able to be made about Jesus's birthplace, God provided a warm, clean place for His Son, Jesus, to be born in a lowly stable and laid in a manger. Ironic that a manger was a serving place for food of the lowly crea-tures that God had created.

God provided the choir of angels to give "honor and glory to the newborn king," and God chose to have the poor and humble shepherds be the first to hear the message of the long-awaited Savior's birth. They went to where the light shown down from the heavens, and they found a tiny baby wrapped in swaddling clothes, nothing more than rags.

Not many knew of His birth, but both rich kings and poor shepherds came to give homage to Christ, the Messiah, as God the Father had planned. Very symbolic of this was the distant travel of the Three Kings of the Orient, who traveled "far to honor a newborn King" and brought gifts that ultimately sustained the Holy Family in their exile. God's plan was to have the poor shepherds and rich kings of mankind that were not threatened by this King's birth to be the ones to give Jesus honor and glory that was due the "King of heaven and earth." Jesus—born in a lowly stable, laid in a manger for His bed—became our Shepherd and our King, and ultimately "our food for eternal life."

Poverty is "lack of money or material possessions. *Voluntary* is to make a free choice. *Voluntary poverty* is "willingly choosing to live your life without comfort."

Jesus chose to leave the glory of heaven to be born into poverty, to live a simple childhood, to learn a simple way of life from His earthly parents, to be human, and to walk with us on this road. He faced temptation and conquered satan. He did this *freely* to show us that we too can conquer satan. In (2 Corinthians 8:9), it says, "For your sake He made Himself poor though He was rich, so that you might become rich by His poverty." WOW! How deeply complicated that is! We become Rich (Spiritually) by Jesus's self-sacrificing Himself into worldly poverty.

Jesus gave us the example of how to come to God through self-giving love. It is not impossible for us to follow Him. Jesus taught us how through His beatific way of life, and He left us a path to follow "in the Beatitudes" (Matthew 5:3). *Poor in spirit* means to be reduced to a beggar. To be able to see our sins, and then beg Jesus to forgive us, this is the reason Jesus came into our world, to bring us to eternal life, through forgiveness of our sins.

Spiritual poverty is complete dependence on God. We empty ourselves of self so that God can fill us with His Spirit, which leads us to life and love. Christ is the perfect example of spiritual poverty. We all have the choice to be born into spiritual poverty. It will be through God's grace that we will learn how to strive for holiness in our lives. (Psalm 37:4) says, "Take delight in the Lord, and He will grant you your hearts requests."

In (1 Timothy 6:6–10), it says, "There is of course, great gain in religion provided one is contented with a sufficiency (sufficient quantity to meet one's needs). We brought nothing into this world, nor have we the power to take anything out. If we have food and clothing we have all that we need. Those who want to be rich are falling into temptation and a trap. They are letting themselves be captured by foolish and harmful desires which drag men down to ruin and destruction. The love of money is the root of all evil. Some men in their passion for it have strayed from the faith, and have come to grief amid great pain." (St. Josephs).

(Philippians 2:5–8) says, "Your attitude must be that of Christ: Though He was in the form of God, He did not deem equality with God something to be grasped at. Rather, He EMPTIED Himself and took the form of a slave, being born in the likeness of men. He was known to be of human estate, AND IT WAS THUS THAT HE HUMBLED HIMSELF obediently accepting death on a cross."

Jesus came into this world naked, in a lowly, borrowed stable, in humility. And because of the Roman's cruelty, Jesus most likely left this world on the cross, naked, without anything to call His own, just to humiliate Him further. Jesus lived in the world for our sake, but He was not of the world, that is the example we are to follow.

CCC 2053 states, "The law has NOT been abolished, but rather man is invited to REDISCOVER IT IN THE PERSON OF HIS MASTER who is its perfect fulfillment. In the three synoptic Gospels, Jesus's call to the rich young man to follow Him, in the obedience of a disciple and in the observance of the Commandments, is joined to the call to poverty and chastity. The evangelical counsels are inseparable from the Commandments."

These three—poverty, chastity, and obedience—are the three evangelical counsels that we are given to follow Jesus to the Father. Jesus, in His humanness, lived the evangelical counsels of poverty, chastity, and obedience perfectly.

Some people are given this charism of voluntary poverty to be able to discover the fruit of the Holy Spirit within them that is waiting to be shared with another. Material poverty can be a means to deepen our commitment to the poor whom Jesus loved so much. Spiritual poverty is trusting God, and frees us from the anxiety about tomorrow.

St. Theresa of Calcutta's work was to bring Jesus's love to the most vulnerable of God's children. St. Theresa of Avila's work was to bring those who would listen to a closer union with God through interior prayer and the simplicity of life in both material and spiritual poverty. St. John Paul II's work was to shepherd mankind toward God the Father, through the recognition of God's divine mercy that was enlightened through Jesus's teachings to St. Faustina of Poland. St. Margaret of Scotland married the king and had eight children, but had a special love of the poor, and helped them. Throughout history we have many examples of those who followed Christ by using the charism that they were given by God, through the Holy Spirit, to build the body of Christ, the church, right here on earth.

Jesus said to the scribe in response to his statement of "Teacher, wherever you go I will come after you, "The foxes have their lairs, the birds in the air have their nests, but the Son of Man has nowhere to lay His head" (Luke 9:58).

CCC to review: 915; 928–929; 1973–1974; 1986; 2443–2463; 2544–2557.

Scripture: (Acts 2:44–45; Acts 4:32–37; 1 Corinthians 13:3; 2 Corinthians 6; 10; Philippians 4:11–13; Matthew 5:3; Matthew 6:19–33; Luke 9:57–58).

Patron saints of voluntary poverty: the apostles and disciples; St. Francis of Assissi, St. Clare, St. Theresa of Calcutta, St. Teresa of Avila, and many, many more.

Charism of Wisdom

Listed in (Isaiah 11: 2–3), the spiritual gift is given to everyone who is baptized in the name of Jesus Christ the Son of God! Whether we use it or not is our choice. The charism of wisdom is given to those whom the Holy Spirit has endowed with a special gift of grace to share God's message with another. It is the responsibility of those with this gift to find the way to share it with the world.

CCC 215 says, "The sum of your word is truth; and every one of your righteous ordinances endures forever." (Psalm 119:160) "And now O LORD God, you are God, and your words are true," (2 Samuel 7:28), this is why God's promises always come true." (Deuteronomy 7:9). "God is truth itself, whose words cannot deceive. This is why one can abandon oneself in full trust to the truth and faithfulness of His word in all things. The beginning of sin and of man's fall was due to a lie of the tempter who induced doubt of God's word, kindness, and faithfulness."

CCC 216 says, "God's truth is His wisdom, which commands the whole created order and governs the world." (Wisdom 3:1–9),

"God who made heaven and earth, can alone impart true knowledge of every created thing in relation to Himself" (Psalm 115:15; Wisdom 7:17–21).

CCC 217 says, "God is also truthful when He reveals Himself, the teaching that comes from God is "true instruction." (Malachi 2:6) "When He sends His Son into the world it will be to bear witness to the truth." (John 18: 37) "We know that the Son of God has come and has given us understanding, to know Him who is true" (1 John 5:20; John 17:3).

"The reason I was born, the reason that I came into this world is to testify to the truth" (John 3:7). Jesus, in His death and resurrection, bore witness to God's great love for mankind. How do we humans dare doubt anything in scripture? Eve listened to the tempter, and we know how that turned out for all mankind.

CCC 1831 says, "The seven Gifts of the Holy Spirit are wisdom, understanding, counsel, fortitude, knowledge, piety, and fear of the Lord. They belong in their fullness to Christ, Son of David. (Isaiah 11:1–2) They complete and perfect the virtues of those who receive them. They make the faithful docile in readily obeying divine inspirations." "Let your good Spirit lead me on a level path" (Psalm 143:17). By praying this prayer, we are asking God to help us walk the path with Jesus.

(Revelations 1:4) opens with John saying to the seven churches that are in Asia, "Grace to you and peace from Him who is, and who was and who is to come, and from the seven spirits who are before His throne."

The "seven spirits" stand for God's power and omniscience (having infinite awareness, understanding, and insight) and intervention in the events of history. In (Zechariah 4:10), divine power is symbolized by the seven "eyes of the Lord, which range the whole earth." In (Revelations 5:6), John tells us that the seven spirits of God sent out into all the earth are the seven eyes of the Lamb, that is Christ.

This symbolism (also found in Isaiah 11:2) is used to show that God the Father acts through His Spirit and that this Spirit has been communicated to Christ, and by Him to mankind. So when John wishes grace and peace from the seven spirits of God, it is the same as saying "from the Holy Spirit," who is sent to the church after the death and resurrection of Christ. Patristic (relating to the church fathers and their writings) tradition has in fact interpreted the seven spirits as meaning the septiform Spirit (divided, each gift stands alone and yet together) with His seven gifts as in (Isaiah 11:1–2) (St. Jerome's translation, the Vulgate Bible. (Revelation, The Navarre Bible)

So the charism of wisdom is given through the power of the Holy Spirit to individuals to help them transform their life and be a channel of God's kindness, mercy, and love, and helps them to discover solutions to problems.

Scripture: (1 Kings 3:5–28; 1 Corinthians 12:7–8; James 3:13–18; Wisdom chapters 7–10; Acts 6:3–10; 1 Corinthians 2:1–16; James 1:5–6; 2 Peter 3:15).

CCC 1749–1756; 1776–1802; 1805–1806; 1831; 1835; 1845.

Patron saints: St. John Joseph of the Cross (1654–1734) St. Nicholas of Flue (1417–1487).

The word of knowledge and the word of wisdom are different from the charisms and the Isaiah gifts. These two are special gifts that are given to a person who also is able to hear or know a word or a message that another person needs to hear; it is meant for an individual or group, or someone involved in counseling.

From the Catholic Charismatic movement and from Paul's letter to the Romans: "I affirm that … the gentile peoples are to praise God because of His great mercy." And the CCR goes on to say, "The word of Wisdom and Knowledge are the gifts that takes us beyond our own natural resources into the power of the Spirit. It helps us counsel, minister and bring healing to people who are looking for and need more than mere worldly ideas and wisdom. God's people are encouraged to seek the Holy Spirit to provide words of knowledge and wisdom and to ask God to confirm those words in some tangible way. Sometimes by simply moving forward and doing what we think God is saying, we will find out whether or not it was God's word spoken to us. We don't need to be afraid of making mistakes if we approach these gifts with discernment and humility.'"

Charism of Writing and Exhortation

The charism of writing is a written form of exhortation. Something that can be studied over and over again, not just listened to one time.

The charism of writing is given to bring beauty and truth into the world, but it does not have to be about God. It can be about the beauty of our earth. Beautiful love relationships. It can be lyrics for music, poetry, prose, etc. It will never be used to write anything evil. A charism is always about sharing God's love with another. I was working on the research for the charism part of this book and had most of it completed when I had the stroke and memory loss. My daughter Megan has told me recently that it took several months for me to get a lot of my memory back. I know how near death I was again … and I remember thinking that I needed to get this book done before I died. I knew in my heart that God wanted this book finished, so in my recovery, I sat on the couch with my research information, my Catechism, my bible, and my computer, and 'one line at a time' I began the process of 'discerning' what God wanted where, for each charism.

God choses the most unlikely persons to do a task. Remember, I am dyslexic. I type with two fingers…one on each hand so that I can see what I am typing. So, this Book…is a miracle that it is finished in five years. I did not know how to find anything in the bible, I had never used the catechism or owned one. In other words, I had no idea of where to begin or how to go about this task of mine. But I let my prayer and the thoughts that followed just happen. This is the charism of writing being brought to life by the guidance and power of the Holy Spirit. I hope and pray that this book will help all the readers to unlock the mysteries of the Fruits, Gifts and the Charisms of the Holy Spirit. God Bless you all!

(Psalm 45:1) says, "My heart overflows with a goodly theme; as I sing my ode to the king, my tongue is nimble as the pen of a skillful scribe."

(Philippians 3:1) says, "For the rest, my brothers, rejoice in the Lord. I find writing you these things no burden, and for you it is a safeguard."

The charism of writing is a safeguard for the memory, something that is to help us stay on the path with Jesus.

In (1 Timothy 4:14–16), it says, "Although I hope to visit you soon, I am writing you about these matters so that if I should be delayed you will know what kind of conduct befits a member of God's household, the church of the living God, the pillar and bulwark of truth. Wonderful, indeed, is the mystery of our faith, as we say in professing it: "He was manifested in the flesh, vindicated in the spirit; Seen by angels; preached among the Gentiles, Believed in throughout the world, taken up in glory."

Patron saints of the charism of writing: all the prophets and biblical writers, the fathers of the church. Other saints down through the ages: St. Theresa of Avila, St. John of the Cross, St. Teresa the Little Flower.

Writers from modern times, like G. K. Chesterton, Scott Hahn, Father Gaitly, Fr. Mark Toups, Matthew Kelly, Jeff Cavins, Max Lucado, and many, many more.

List down your own favorites who have touched your heart and changed your life. The charism of writing awakens our heart and soul to the presence of God within us for both the writer and the reader.

Fruits

36 *Joy*
40 *Peace*
45 *Patience*
51 *Charity*
54 *Kindness*
57 *Goodness*
61 *Generosity*
65 *Gentleness*
70 *Faithfulness*
73 *Self-Control*
77 *Modesty*
82 *Chastity*

Gal 5:22-23

Gifts

88 *Wisdom*
92 *Understanding*
99 *Knowledge*
104 *Counsel*
106 *Fortitude*
113 *Piety*
114 *Fear of the Lord*

Isaiah
11:2-3

Charisms = Grace of the Holy Spirit(CCC 799)

Corinthians
12-14

132 *Administration.*   *Discernment of Spirits* 141
136 *Celibacy*   *Evangelization* 143
133 *Craftsmanship.*
Encouragement.   *Helper. Hospitality.*
147 *Faith. Giving. Healing.*   *Leadership. Mercy*
Intercessory Prayer.
143 *Missionary. Music. Pastoring. Prophecy.* 189
142 *Services. Teaching. Voluntary Poverty. Writing.* 199
194 *Tongues. Preaching. Word of Knowledge.* 202
Word of Wisdom

Clairann Nicklin

ABOUT THE AUTHOR

Clairann Nicklin is married to Jack "Nick" and they have one daughter Megan, who is married to David. Their sons are David Jr., Landen, and Owen who brighten life greatly. This book began as an assignment from her Spiritual Director to help her discover through study what the "Fruits and Gifts" were supposed to mean in our lives.

Not having any idea of where to begin, she began with prayer. This became a spiritual journey into the bible, opening a whole new world of *relationship with God* that has grown into the development of an *intimate prayer life with God* and has led her to seek more of Jesus than Sunday Mass obligation. A deep daily prayer life resulted in seeking to discover what the secular Carmelites are all about, and if she was being called to this *lifestyle of prayer*. Carmelite spirituality is a way of life that follows Jesus in walking the path of the gospels. She has been given an intense thirst to know God and to experience Him. Carmelite spirituality focuses on prayer and a loving relationship with God which can result in a gift of grace from God, that is contemplation, also called *union with God.*

Carmelite spirituality calls us to transform our lives and then witness God's great love for all mankind. This is what God's plan is for humanity! *All* are called to the heavenly reward, but few choose to respond to the beatitude way of life that is centered on *others.* Choosing to live our lives *for,* and *with,* and *in* Christ is not a sacrifice, it brings great *joy* into our lives. The "fruit of joy of the Lord" transforms our lives into the "life of Christ," well worth whatever small things of the world that we choose to give up. It has been an incredible journey into the meaning of divine love.

God calls each of us into *service* to share his love with all we meet. We are his hands, feet, and lips in this world today. I have heard that the words "Do not be afraid" is in the bible 365 times—one for every day of the year!

    Christ in Our Midst was birthed in moments of prayer and the journaling of thoughts during prayer. We are each called to share the love of Jesus with another. This came to me in prayer the other day, "What an honor it is to rest in my Presence…and let me speak to your heart. Jesus." Find your way to "interior prayer," and let go, and let God be in the driver's seat.

    God bless you.

Bishop Edward O'Rourke wrote
His book Gift of Gifts

Page 45   ST Josephs translation

Page 47   ST Joseph in Parenthas?

      49   Pictur of Glaucoma

CPSIA information can be obtained
at www.ICGtesting.com
Printed in the USA
LVHW01s1740110418
573008LV00002B/2/P